SUE SHEPARD

MY SHADOW BELOW ME

My Shadow Below Me

JAMES HEARST

THE IOWA STATE UNIVERSITY PRESS / *Ames, Iowa*

Composed and printed by The Iowa State University Press

First edition, 1981

Library of Congress Cataloging in Publication Data

Hearst, James, 1900–
  My shadow below me.

   1. Hearst, James, 1900–   —Biography. 2. Poets, American—20th century—Biography. 3. Physically handicapped—United States—Biography. 4. Farm life—Iowa. I. Title.
PS3515.E146Z47   811′.52   81–14265
ISBN 0–8138–1136–8   AACR2

*This book is humbly dedicated
to those who in the service of love
give without asking.*

Ah, what avails the classic bent
    And what the sculptured word,
Against the undoctored incident
    That actually occurred.

—KIPLING

CONTENTS

PREFACE

I would not talk so much about myself if there were anybody else whom I knew as well.

• • • •

I require of every writer a simple and sincere account of his own life.

—Henry David Thoreau in WALDEN

THIS IS AN ACCOUNT of a journey into the country of myself to see if the landmarks, boundary lines, fields, the hills and the valleys are important enough to be mapped. It is the way I have come and begins in my nineteenth year where footsteps end. I do not examine the virtues of the simple life but inquire with an investigator's caution into the meaning, if there is one, of what happens. No voluntary excursion, rather a fated one and I do not refuse the summons. My search, not to count the number of angels that can stand on the head of a pin, was to discover if any paths at all led out of the dark woods. Shadows and sunlight gave no final answers but I found a path where wounds are healed, bonds broken, and the voice of the spirit argues for hope against despair. The masked face of fear may be exposed by the clear and steady eyes of love's promise. I believe this is so.

Truth

How the devil do I know
if there are rocks in your field,
plow it and find out.
If the plow strikes something
harder than earth, the point
shatters at a sudden blow
and the tractor jerks sidewise
and dumps you off the seat—
because the spring hitch
isn't set to trip quickly enough
and it never is—probably
you hit a rock. That means
the glacier emptied his pocket
in your field as well as mine,
but the connection with a thing
is the only truth that I know of,
so plow it.

The Accident

THIS IS HOW IT BEGAN. I sprang off the dock in a high jackknife dive. At the top of the dive, when the body poises an instant before turning down, I pulled my legs and arms together, parallel to each other, head between my arms, my rump the high point. Then as I started down I straightened my legs until, like an arrow, I entered the water with scarcely a splash. Each motion was executed skillfully as I sprang from the dock three feet above the river's surface. It pleased me to be able to perform with such ease and grace. I did not know that the water below me was only two and a half feet deep.

I had slept late that morning. It was a warm, bright Memorial Day morning at the end of the school year. When I woke up I dressed, shaved, folded up a big red blanket that belonged to my aunt, and clattered downstairs. I stopped to say goodbye to Mrs. Parker, our landlady, and to thank her for making our bed on the mornings when Carroll Cole, my roommate, and I forgot or were late for class. Mrs. Parker, a thin, nervous widow unaccustomed to young men, said she would miss me.

I'll bet she will too, I thought. The house will seem quiet without us tiptoeing upstairs at one in the morning and then having the bed crash down as we piled into it. I would miss the room where Carroll and I had slept, studied, smoked, argued, and played poker with our friends. Carroll and I had decorated the window sill with alternate tins of Tuxedo (blue) and Prince Albert (red), which held the smoking tobacco for our pipes. All of my clothes and books I had taken home, out to the farm.

My athletic equipment, baseball shoes, glove, and jockstrap, I had stored in a locker in the gym. I was light of foot and fancy-free this morning. Carroll had gone home the day before and taken all of his belongings.

I had looked forward to this day, the end of the school year. My fraternity always rented a cottage up the river for a week to celebrate. Several sororities had cottages nearby. Some of the guys had "steadies" among the girls. I had taken out one girl all spring. I had not pinned her yet but I probably would now. I liked Norine a lot and she seemed to respond with affection.

3

I felt shy around girls. I had not lived down or outgrown a sense of inferiority, of being not "quite as good as my peers," a need to wait on their opinions and decisions. I had grown up on a farm four miles from town, a farm that my grandfather had settled in 1859, that my father now farmed. My brothers and sister and I grew up on the farm, attended country school, and did our share of the unending chores. The Sunday ride to church (Congregational at Sixth and Clay streets, the church with the beautiful stained-glass windows) furnished my only contact with town boys my age. The horseplay of the town boys in my Sunday school class shocked me. I had been brought up by the book, which said that young folk shall be mannerly, polite, and respectful, especially in church, especially to elderly people.

I remembered a scolding I once received from my grandfather for an answer I gave to one of the church stalwarts.

Every Sunday after the sermon, as we made ready to go home, this elderly man captured my small hand in both of his and asked, in a rather pompous voice, "You are afraid of me, little man, aren't you?" He went through the same performance with my sister and she dreaded his approach. Perhaps the effort to protect her—for I loved my sister—gave me the desperate courage to say, "No, you old fool, I'm not." Grandfather Hearst found no humor in that answer but Father hid a smile when he heard of it. I did not know how to answer such an absurd question.

The country school I attended, District Number 7, called the Hearst School, had squeezed enough knowledge into my grubby little mind to enable me to keep up easily with my high school class. I studied Latin for three years to please my mother and learned more about the structure of language than I had known before.

In high school I also learned that boys did not aspire to high grades. One month my grade in my English class rose to ninety-eight. The pointed remarks from the other boys forced me to bring it down in a hurry. My next month's grade was seventy-four; and then I heard from my mother.

I still felt like an outsider who did not belong in a city high school. It helped me when I saw some of the other country boys win athletic honors. They were big strong young men with hands like hams and the shoulders of wrestlers. Every coach wants men like them. But I was slim, weighed about 130 pounds, and had no prospects for the football team. I played basketball in my senior year and ran a respectable mile on the track team. I trained for track by running home from school each afternoon.

Much to my astonishment I finished high school in three and a half years. I enrolled in two college classes the last half year because I had only one high school class to attend. My teacher was in one of my college classes. We kept it a secret. When the United States entered World War I, I joined my classmates in throwing our German books out the window. I felt guilty about it. Books cost money, and it seemed so senseless. But I did not want to be thought *different.*

Some of my diffidence and self-consciousness wore off in college. I was asked to join one of the best fraternities. But still, as if excusing myself, I told my mother that all the other members were athletes, and the fraternity needed someone who could write to keep the minutes of the meetings.

I played basketball in college but never on the first team. I lacked aggressiveness—that determination to win that makes a good player. But I enjoyed the game. I also pitched on the baseball team, but I enjoyed the fun more than winning. One afternoon I had just struck out the batter and was pleased with my curve ball. But the coach rushed to the third base line and called out in a harsh voice, "Quit your grinning and get to work."

Under an assumed name I pitched some semipro ball in a few small towns in northeast Iowa, five dollars if I lost, ten if I won. It helped me pay my tuition. I think that using a different name gave me a strange confidence I did not have under my true identity.

But I would never be a first-class athlete. I enjoyed the game too much. Once, in a game against another college, I pitched a slow curve for a third strike. The batter reached for it, missed, looked foolish. I was pleased with myself.

My eighteenth birthday came on August 8, 1918. I enlisted in the army and was called September 1. The war ended in November and I was discharged for Christmas. I did not feel especially patriotic. I enlisted because I thought it was one of the things I should do.

But I learned something in the army about being a man and it helped me grow up. I learned that I could, given the opportunity, drill a company of men with precision and authority. I learned I was one of the best sharpshooters in the company. I could outwalk most of the men on a ten-mile hike. On a hike, a private, Robert Corning, said that if the captain would give him permission he would run all the way back to the barracks. The captain turned to me and said, "Private Hearst, follow him and see that he does it."

Once, in the locker room after baseball practice, I told a rather gamey joke. One of the faculty men taking a shower rushed out and exclaimed, "I ought to throw you out of here." I looked him in the eye, grinned, and answered, "You and who else?" A few months in the army had toughened me in more ways than one.

I came from a family who worked; worked hard; worked until the work was finished. Always the farm demanded more work than we had time. This trait belonged to the Hearst side of the family. My mother protested against the attrition of body and spirit caused by too much hard work. But her gentle Bavarian upbringing was no match for the steel in the Scotch-Irish Hearsts. It resulted in my feeling bitter about the farm. While still a boy I once accused my father, "You make hired men out of us kids. All you want us for is to work."

I wanted more play time. I envied the boys in town who had no chores to do, who rode their bikes, who went swimming whenever they wanted to. I hated the strict regimen of the farm, with the everlasting chores. When I played, I played with abandon and took chances. A coach once scolded me, "You don't use good sense. Learn to control yourself."

But as the twig is bent. . . . The baseball team was scheduled to play at Dubuque one Saturday and it was my turn to pitch. The previous Friday night Father had phoned and said, "I wish you'd come home tomorrow and plant corn. I have to be gone. I'm afraid this good weather won't hold and it's time the corn was in."

I phoned the coach. "I can't go tomorrow. I'm needed at home."

I could hear the line sizzle. "Jesus Christ, Jim, why don't you wait until the last minute! You know that little old letter you might not get."

I regretted later that I didn't tell him where he could stick that little old letter. But I just said, "Sorry, I have to help my father."

"Work always comes first at our house," I said to my mother. I planted corn all day. I enjoyed handling my father's special team of half-Morgan mares, long-legged, high-steppers. I tried to make the straight rows for which my father was famous. I pulled and set the check wire, kept the planter boxes full, and watched that no dirt clogged the shoe where the seed dropped into the ground. I had been taught that if you are going to do a job you do it well.

At the dinner table my mother said, "I'm sorry you had to come home. But your father can't get good help these days. Since the war, farm help is hard to find."

"It's all right, Mother," I said. "I can always play ball." But the familiar rebellion seethed in me like an echo of the way I had felt as a boy. My two younger brothers, Robert and Charles, pitched in and did their share of the work. So did my sister Louise. We will all be old men and women ahead of our time, I thought.

My head struck the bottom of the river like an explosion. I must have had my arms out in front too, for my wrists were all swollen from the shock. I felt far away from myself. I opened my eyes in the murky water and drifted with the current, unable to move. "This is the last of me," I said to myself. "This is the last of me." No pain, no motion, just black aimless drifting. I was upside-down in a dark cell of water. I had no feeling, could make no resistance. A submerged body with a dull message, "This is the end of me." Then I was aware of lying on stiff grass on the bank. Two of my friends bent over me. Bill Franklin and Bud McKinstry had been in the water and hauled me out.

"We just saw your butt show up and start floating downstream," Bud said.

"You okay now, Jim?" asked Bill with eyes full of concern. Bill was the big center fielder who whanged out more hits than anyone on the team. Bud caught when I pitched.

"That goddamn river filled in over the winter," Bill said. "Used to be eight feet deep here, now about two. I tried to stop you but, no, you were hellbent to make the big dive."

I shut my eyes. The sun hurt them. I tried to talk but could manage only one word for each shallow breath. "I'm hurt," I managed to say. "I can't move."

Bill said, "We better get him over to the cottage, Bud. You lift his legs." They carried me to the front lawn of the cottage and laid me down in the shade.

Some of the men lounging on the porch came over and one of them asked, "Now what do we do?"

The baseball coach, Art Dickinson, said, "Maybe we should get a chiropractor." Jack Orr said, "Warren and I will paddle a canoe down to the boathouse. One of you guys phone him and have him meet us there."

Bud sat by me and kept the flies off my face. "Don't worry," he said. "The chiropractor will fix you up."

I just lay there in my wet swimsuit. Time did not matter. Nothing mattered but the effort to breathe. Pete Jorgensen, our number-one pitcher (he went to the Chicago White Sox), squatted beside me. "Can't you move at all?" He begged, "Jim, try it." His voice came from a long way off. I found a slight quiver in my left wrist. "See?" Pete said. "You can move."

Somebody asked, "You want your girl to come over? She's just next door." To me the voice came from nowhere. I heard another voice say, "Better not, she's crying awful hard. Somebody told her."

Then the canoe slid onto the bank. Jack Orr jumped out. He puffed. "We made it as fast as we could. This is Doc Klingman." I opened my eyes. A stranger in a dark suit bent over me. He set up a folding table. "Help me lift him up," he said. I found myself lying face down on a springy table. The man pressed lightly on my neck. "That hurt?" he asked. I did not answer. It hurt but I couldn't get the words out.

"Lay him on a blanket," the man said, "and get him dressed. His skin is cold."

"Can't you fix him up, Doc?" Bud asked.

"We must wait and see," Doc Klingman said. "Now please take me back. Get him dressed."

Together Bud and Bill pulled off my swimsuit and shoved my legs into my trousers. They boosted me up enough to poke my arms into the sleeves of my shirt. The stimulation gave me an erection. "Lookit," one of the men said. "Old Jim can still get it up. He ain't dead yet." A sense of feeling came back. I could feel the wool trousers against my legs, a sweat shirt prickling my arms. I wished my penis would reduce itself. The tension made me uncomfortable.

Earlier that morning I had paddled my canoe up the river. Warm in the sun, I threw my sweat shirt in the bottom of the canoe. My cap and pipe lay there with the extra paddle. Opposite the cottage I called to my friends on the bank, "Let me show you a neat trick." I moved back to the very tip of the canoe and the front end reared up at a forty-five-degree angle. I stroked slowly toward the bank. A light gust of wind sailed down the river, caught the canoe broadside, and pushed it over. Art Dickinson called, "Do you want any help?" I spit the water out of my mouth. "I can handle it." I collected the two paddles, but my cap and pipe drifted down the river. I let them go. It was enough to push the overturned canoe and carry the paddles and my shirt. My trousers and shoes were heavy with water.

Someone called, "Showing off?" It pleased me to be able to handle myself so well in the water. A lot of the men could not do it. I managed to reach the shore. It gave me a good feeling to know that when I tried a stunt and flubbed it I could rescue myself.

I just lay there with my eyes closed. The fraternity brothers took turns sitting beside me. It made little difference. The distance from anyone seemed too great for words. Faintly the sound of a motorboat reached me. I heard new voices and I recognized them. Thank god, it was Father and doctor Uncle George. I wished I could tell my father how glad I was that he had come.

Uncle George bit off his words. "I should think you men would know enough to get Jim to the hospital. Dick, you're one hell of a coach to sit there on your butt and not take charge." He motioned to the group. "Pick him up in the blanket and lay him in the bottom of the rowboat. We knocked out the seats so you can lay him down. A couple of you ride with him. Hold the boat against the side of Lafe March's launch until we reach the boathouse."

I shut my eyes more tightly against the sun as I lay in the bottom of the rowboat. I felt Bud and Bill climb in with me. I heard the exhaust of the motorboat, felt the sway of my boat. Bud leaned over and asked, "Are you all right, Jim?" I remembered that the annual formal fraternity dance was tomorrow night. I whispered, "Bud, get my girl a date for the dance." It took a shallow breath for each word. "Sure," Bud answered. "Sure thing, Jim."

I lay on a hospital bed. Was I sick enough to go to the hospital? Another uncle doctor, Uncle Gregg McAlvin from Waterloo, was cutting off my shirt. "Don't move him more than we must," he said sharply.

I saw my mother's face and tried to smile at her. She stroked my hand and I was thankful I could feel it. My Aunt Mamie tiptoed in and, with tears in her voice, whispered, "It will be all right, James, won't it, if you don't get well?" I roused myself. She sounded too much like Sunday school. I gasped, "Not by a damn sight."

The air sifting through the window felt cool. The bed held me between cool sheets. It was more comfortable than the ground. My body was sensitive to touch even though I could not move. Maybe by tomorrow I could get back my muscle control. I heard my uncles talking about waiting until morning for X rays. X rays for what? Sandbags supported my head. I sharpened my eyes and ears.

A square-shaped middle-aged face with merry eyes leaned over me. I saw a white cap. A voice said, "I'm Miss Hoskins, your nurse. I'll sleep in your room tonight, don't worry." What a funny accent she had. I was more awake now than at any time since the dive. I asked, "Where are you from?"

"I was born on the Isle of Man. It's a little island. . . ."

I interrupted her and gasped, "Short-tailed cats! Hall Caine." Miss Hoskins said, "How did you know? He's our greatest writer."

"No morphine," Uncle George said. "If he can't sleep try some. . . ." I did not know the words. Whatever it was he prescribed, it tasted salty when I swallowed it. I drank from a straw as I had done in ice cream parlors.

My mother kissed me. My father kissed me. I could hardly believe it. Nobody kissed in my family. It scared me. I asked Uncle George, "Am I going to die?"

Uncle George shook his head. "I doubt it, Jim. You wouldn't know how."

I heard his steps going away. Then Miss Hoskins said, "You must rest now. I'll leave the light on. Try to call if you need me. I'll be here." I tried to make a noise like a call. "I can hear you," she said.

The Hospital

NIGHT SHADOWS DISSOLVED in the morning light. I drowsed and woke, drowsed and woke, never deep in sleep. Miss Hoskins bathed my face often. She took my temperature by sliding the thermometer under my arm. I confused dreams with wakefulness.

The morning light showed me the walls of a hospital room (Sartori Hospital in Cedar Falls). I still could not move. I yawned and my left arm bent at the elbow and flopped across my chest. But I could not straighten it again. My left wrist flexed when I tried to move it. I can move something, I thought.

About eight o'clock Uncle George appeared. He nodded at me, picked up a clipboard at the foot of the bed and read something. "Pretty fair night," he said.

"What's that?" I asked.

"Your chart where we keep track of what happens to you."

"Uncle George, how did you know I was hurt?" I still had to gasp out my words. I couldn't take a deep breath.

"Dr. Klingman called me. Thank god for that. What made you stupid lugs send for a chiropractor?"

Miss Hoskins spoke. "Should we turn him, Dr. Hearst?"

"Let's wait until Dr. Roundtree comes over from Waterloo. He's going to take some pictures. We will have to move him to X ray and back."

"If he lies too long on his back. . . ."

Uncle George spoke testily, "I know, I know, we must watch it."

"Why?" I asked.

Uncle George spoke brusquely. "Hypostatic pneumonia." Then to Miss Hoskins he said, "I'll have to catheterize him. Will you get the tray ready?"

Through the open window I heard a car drive up the circular drive and stop in front. I heard a familiar squeak and warmed to the sound. My folks were here. The old Haynes had a loose spoke in the left front wheel that squeaked when the car stopped. Then Mother and Father and Louise and my two younger brothers entered the room.

"Oh, Jim," Louise sobbed. Bob and Chuck stared round-eyed.

I asked in my frail voice, "You kids get the chores done?" And when Robert nodded I smiled, a real smile this time. I liked my brothers. We stood up for each other. Once I had to beat the shit out of a bully who was tormenting Charles by twisting his arm behind his back.

I heard Uncle George tell Father, "Will is coming in this afternoon. He's bringing an army neurologist with him."

Uncle Will was another doctor, a major in the medical corps.

"How soon am I going to get better?" I asked.

Uncle George did not answer. He said to a nurse, "Bring in the cart and we'll take him to X ray. Dr. Roundtree just came in."

The cart and bed were the same height. I thought, that's good. Somebody used their heads. When they lifted me, someone held my head so it wouldn't fall off. I could not support it.

I was conscious of going down in an elevator, of being pushed on to the X-ray table, of being turned on my side while a strange nurse held my head. I did not see Dr. Roundtree. A big glass globe swung over me. It glowed and somewhere something went zzzz-pop, zzzz-pop. The nurse said, "That's all. Take him back."

Back in my own room Miss Hoskins gave me a drink of water. I heard a man's voice say to Uncle George, "Fifth cervical. This is nearly always the vertebrae that fractures. I can see no pressure. No one around here can do a laminectomy but I would be against surgery."

Uncle George said, "This is my first case of this kind. Should he be in traction?"

"I'm just a radiologist. But I can see no pressure. I am sorry about your nephew, doctor."

A new nurse stood by the bed. She was young, had big brown eyes, and she was pretty. She smiled at me. She could not have been much older than I was. She wore rubber gloves and carried a white enamel tray. "Here is the catheter, Dr. George."

Her informality surprised me. I said to Uncle George, "Do you know each other?"

Uncle George said, "We were in school together."

I thought he was ribbing me. He was middle-aged, she a young girl.

"Jim, this is Miss Hopkins, the surgical nurse here at the hospital. We're going to insert a catheter into your bladder. You won't be able to urinate for a while."

He slipped on a pair of rubber gloves, picked up a thin rubber tube and greased it with Vaseline.

It embarrassed me to hear Uncle George say "urinate" right in front of this lovely girl. But worse was to come. To my horror he stripped back the bedclothes and left me exposed right in front of her. Oh, my god, it was awful and humiliating!

I never dreamed such a nightmare. At home no one ever saw anyone else like this. Neither did we talk about the body and its functions. We were modest and shy about such things.

Sure, out in the barn I had cleaned up a calf with diarrhea, brought in the bull to breed a cow in heat, helped an old sow have her pigs. And in the army we had "short arm" inspection every two weeks. We always swam naked in the college pool after baseball practice. But oh, my god, not in front of strange and pretty girls!

Uncle George picked up my penis, gently slid the tube into it, and said, "Adhesive, please." He strapped the tube to me. Miss Hopkins never batted an eye. She just smiled at me and held the tray. Chagrin boiled inside me. How would I ever face her again?

Then my own nurse, Miss Hoskins, asked, "What about his diet, doctor?"

"Make it light but about anything he wants."

She braced my head with sandbags more securely. I did not want anything to eat. I wanted to get up and get out of the damn bed and I couldn't move. Slowly I faced a growing fear that I might not ever be able to move again.

Late that afternoon a thickset man wearing an army uniform walked into my room. "Why, Uncle Will. . . ."

"What have you been up to, Jim?"

A dark-haired man more slender and younger than Uncle Will followed him into the room. He also was in uniform.

"Jim, this is Captain Neubauer. He is the neurologist on our staff at the base. He wants to have a look at you."

Captain Neubauer stepped up and squeezed my hand. "Hello there. Put you on your back, have they. We'll see what we can do about that."

"You want to go over him now?" Uncle Will asked.

"Let me see the X rays first, see what the damage is."

Later I sucked a little chicken soup through a glass tube. Then Miss Hoskins said, "I'm going to supper now. The girls on the floor will look in on you. I'll be back soon. When you can use your hands again, you can use the bell to call when you want someone."

"She doesn't talk as if I won't get well. She said, 'When you can use your hands again'."

It must have been after supper when they came back, Uncle Will, Captain Neubauer, Uncle George, and Uncle Gregg from Waterloo. Mother and Father came too but they stayed out in the reception room.

Captain Neubauer took off his coat. "Now, Jim, I want to do some experimenting and see just where we stand. Bend your left elbow."

By gosh, I could. But it flopped down across my chest. Captain Neubauer straightened it out. "Flex your left wrist." To my surprise I made it bend.

"Now close your eyes and tell me where I am touching you."

"The big toe on my left foot, sir."

The captain smiled. "Forget the 'sir.' You aren't in the army now."

"Right knee."

"Now. . . ."

"Belly button."

"Apparently he has full sensory control. Now close your eyes and tell me if I am pressing you with the sharp end or broad head of this pin."

I tried but gave up. "I'm just guessing, I can't really tell."

"Pain threshold pretty high. Now I have two small glass tubes, one with hot water, one with cold. Tell me which is which when I touch you."

Again I concentrated but it was no use. "I can tell where you touch me but they both feel alike."

He touched the bottles to my shoulder. I said, "Sure, I can tell now."

The captain said, "Below the nipples an absence of feeling. Be careful with bath water. Don't burn him."

Uncle Gregg asked, "Any suggestions?"

"Take away the sandbags. His neck muscles should have recovered from the shock. But when you turn him, place his head on a small hard pillow to keep it from drooping. Turn him often. Watch for signs of pneumonia and bedsores."

Uncle George said to the captain, "His father would like to talk to you."

"Of course," said the captain, putting on his coat.

Father came in. The captain said to him, "This young man is seriously injured. He has damaged the spinal cord in his neck and as a result he is almost totally paralyzed. The central nervous system, brain and spinal cord, does not repair itself.

"But somehow messages get through. He will regain some muscle control. We don't know yet how much. But training, exercise, can do a lot, has done a lot in our VA hospitals."

He paused. "He is fortunate in that his sense of touch seems unaffected which means the posterior side of the cord suffered the most damage. Come out in the office and I will draw a diagram for you."

My spirits dropped like a stone in a well. Did he mean I wouldn't get well? Never again pitch a ball game, jump on a horse and round up the cattle, take the car to pick up a girl for a dance? Can't somebody fix my neck, operate or something? There just had to be some way out of this. . . .

Miss Hoskins straightened my sheet. "That was quite an ordeal, wasn't it?"

I looked past her into space. Bitter thoughts darkened my mind. Never again, just never again. . . .

"You're talking much better. Is it easier to breathe?"

Never again . . . not even stand up to take a leak? This stupid rubber tube in my bladder . . . women looking at me uncovered. I wouldn't believe it. Someone sure as hell had to be wrong.

Father came in, sad-eyed but smiling. "Captain Neubauer thinks you'll be able to plow corn again."

I was sure my father was lying . . . or maybe he wasn't. Maybe

Captain Neubauer had changed his tune. I tried to believe that.

My uncles trooped back into the room, a new face among them. "Uncle Mike, oh Uncle Mike," I cried. Now all four of my doctor uncles were on hand to see that I got on my feet again.

Uncle Will said, "I've got to get back. I pulled Captain Neubauer out of the hospital. I'm due for surgery in the morning. You'll look after him, George?"

Uncle George was younger and resented his older brother's imperiousness. I did grin a little when Uncle George said, "I'll call you when I need advice."

Funny, Father got along well with both his brothers. In fact, I thought we were a close-knit family. There were about thirty of us when we gathered at the river, as one of Aunt Jennie's hymns would have it. That is, when Uncle Mike Thielen brought his family from Grundy Center and those hulking ham-handed Dane brothers came from La Porte City.

This was the first time the family fabric had been torn by an accident. It caused a gathering of the clan.

A banker once said, "The Hearsts may fight among themselves but don't any outsider try to mess with one of them. He'll have the whole family clawing him."

Uncle George said, "Charlie, you and Katharine go home and get some rest. There's nothing more to do here. Miss Hoskins will take care of Jim."

This was the beginning of the long time. I now found myself in a different country, a strange land where I would be a citizen the rest of my life. I began a struggle through quicksands I had never dreamed of, through deserts of despair, through lonely forests where the way was lost. But I would be given enough courage and benedictions of love and the support of a talent I hardly knew I owned to carry me through. Somewhere, perhaps from past generations, I had inherited the will and determination to fight the battles that must be fought.

The care and devotion given me by Miss Hoskins is beyond recording. She went on a selfless twenty-four-hour duty with me. But once routine established itself, she left for a few hours each afternoon and my mother and sister Louise stayed with me. The other nurses kept an eye on me when Miss Hoskins was gone. Until I became strong enough to push the call bell against my teeth to ring it, Miss Hoskins slept in a cot by my bed in her nightdress and kimono.

The next morning Uncle George just stuck his head in to say hello and vanished.

"He's in surgery," Miss Hoskins explained to ease the hurt look on my face.

About eleven o'clock he came back. He looked tired and there were powder marks on his hands from the rubber gloves. "I had a time getting all the gallstones out of that old girl. Then I had to repair Matt Steven's hernia. How are you today?"

He read my chart. "I called the Mayo Clinic last night and talked to one of the orthopedists. He said he would be down this way in a couple of weeks and look at you. He said to keep on the way we are and watch out for pneumonia and bedsores."

Miss Hoskins turned me every two hours. She always called in another nurse to help her. I found that I could lift my head by myself while someone shoved a hard pillow under it.

Soon after Uncle George left, Miss Hopkins came in. She too had powder marks on her hands from rubber gloves. She said, "Hoskins, I'll feed him while you go to lunch." She peered at me. "Wouldn't you like to have me feed you?"

My, she was lovely. She had a kind of bubble in her voice as if she were going to laugh. "You bet," I said.

Miss Hoskins shook her finger at me. "Men are fickle."

Miss Hopkins took the tray and placed it on the bedside table. "I'm going to crank up the head of your bed a bit so you can see Lucrezia Borgia and her poisoned ring. Phooey on Dr. George. He'd be glad to have you sit up a little."

She perched on the edge of the bed. "I ought to shut the door. Nurses aren't supposed to sit on patients' beds." She swung her leg over on a chair for support. It was a good-looking leg. For a moment I forgot my agony. This girl excited me.

"What have we got today? Chicken soup, mashed potatoes with butter. Living high on the hog, my boy." She smiled and tucked a napkin under my chin.

"Did we have a time this morning! You know Dr. George does surgery for some of the doctors in these small towns. The old gal from New Hartford was so fat I thought his retractors wouldn't be long enough.

"If I were your fairy godmother and could grant wishes, what would you wish? Be reasonable, we can't run the film backward."

"To turn over alone and feed myself," I said.

"What? When you've got me? Here, finish your soup. I'll see you tomorrow."

By the third day I could bend both arms at the elbow but I could not straighten them or raise them. I had a strong flexion in my left wrist. My neck no longer pained much when I lifted my head. My appetite picked up. Most of the local doctors stopped in to say hello. One of them said, "What you need is plenty of steak and ice cream."

Now a new problem showed its ugly head. I still wore the catheter to keep my bladder drained. But my bowels would not empty. I heard Miss Hoskins speak earnestly to Uncle George. "He's still too weak for an enema and bed pan."

Uncle George said, "I'll write an order for licorice powder. It's mild but effective."

Later that morning, Miss Hoskins brought me a glass of the dark

brown liquid. It smelled like licorice and tasted like licorice. I had
never liked licorice even as a youngster. "Drink it all," Miss Hoskins
urged. "You need it."

Late in the afternoon, without warning, my bowels erupted right in
bed. I almost died from embarrassment. What was I going to do? I
couldn't expect Miss Hoskins to clean me up.

I remembered reading in *Ivanhoe* how Rebecca nursed Ivanhoe
back to strength after he had been severely wounded. How tenderly
she nursed him. It was romantic and touching to note the care she gave
him. But nothing was said about how she managed his body's waste
products. Maybe heroes in stories did not have any. But this was life,
my life.

"So the licorice worked," said Miss Hoskins cheerfully. "That's
good. Wait until I get a fresh draw sheet and someone to help me."

She stepped out into the hall and I heard her call, "Miss Hopkins,
could you help me a minute?"

Oh, my god, I thought. Not Miss Hopkins. What would I do?

Both nurses came in, Miss Hoskins with a clean draw sheet (whatever that was!). Miss Hopkins wore a gauze veil over her hair instead
of a cap. "Here I step out of the operating room for a minute's rest and
who wants me? Old chicken soup and mashed potatoes here. Over you
go, my boy."

They rolled me on my side. Miss Hopkins said, "I'll get a cloth and
some warm water. Hoskins, can you hold him like that?"

Miss Hoskins rolled a clean sheet behind me with one hand while
she balanced me with the other. "We'll roll you back over this," she
explained.

"All right now?" asked Miss Hopkins "Nice and clean. Almost
time for supper and you can eat with a clear conscience."

"What did she mean 'clear conscience'?"

Miss Hoskins tucked in my napkin. "We were a little worried. Dr.
George *hoped* your bowels would move. Now here is a soft-boiled egg
and some green peas."

A week later my temperature began to rise. First, I had chills. Miss
Hoskins piled blankets on me and stuffed hot water bottles around me.
Still my teeth chattered. Mother and Louise took turns reading to me.
It was the only thing that diverted me. Then, as suddenly as I chilled, I
would grow hot and my temperature shot up.

I heard Uncle George say, "You did the best you could, Miss Hoskins. We are all indebted to you. Jim almost died of flu in the army. It
probably didn't do his lungs any good."

"I turned him every two hours, Dr. George." Her voice sounded
weepy yet firm.

It seemed like months that I burned with no peace. I begged for
Father to come and see me every evening. I knew Father would be
tired from making hay all day but I wanted him close. I was too sick to

be read to, but every morning and afternoon Mother and Louise drove in from the farm to sit with me. Sometimes Bob and Chuck came too.

I wished for a cool stream under overhanging trees that I could lie in. I dreamed this again and again. Day and night meant nothing. What the nurses did meant nothing either. I knew Miss Hopkins stopped by but sometimes I thought she was Norine, my girl at college.

Uncle George said to Father, "Hypostatic pneumonia, Charlie. We were afraid of this. Temperature 106° and Cheyne-Stokes respiration. Not many folk survive that when it appears in a pneumonia case."

It seemed to me more than I could bear and one evening I begged Uncle George to give me something to make me die.

He glared at me. "After all we've done for you? Not on your life."

The end of my torment came soon. One night, after one of the many sponge baths of cold water that Miss Hoskins gave me, I dropped off into a normal sleep. But in the morning my temperature had dropped to subnormal levels and my voice sounded like a weak kitten mewing.

A month later I was able to sit up in bed. My appetite came back, but I still could not feed myself. Folks took turns being with me at mealtime—Mother, Louise, Miss Hopkins, the floor nurses. Miss Hoskins had to have some rest. She went to Waterloo and stayed a few days with her sister.

Mother and Louise still read to me in the afternoons. One of the floor nurses, Miss Petersen, read to me on her hours off. So did another nurse, Miss Kershaw, who had a funny French accent that amused me, especially when she read one of Zane Gray's westerns. It sounded so incongruous.

I began to have company. The fraternity brothers were allowed in once a day in small groups. A few of the men, just home from overseas duty in the army, I had not seen for years. It raised my morale when Captain Glen Edleman, just back from France, dropped in and scolded me. "What the hell do you think you're doing, sacking out like this?"

I had always admired Glen, especially for his aloof and chiseled style. It made him seem more mature than the rest of us. He carried that indefinable air of authority that some men have and never know they have it. He patted me on the shoulder. "I'll be back. Here's a cigarette holder I bought for you in Paris. Don't let down."

The neighbors came, some of them ill at ease and distressed because of my helplessness. A white band across their tanned foreheads showed where their hatbands rested. They moved quietly and looked sober and told me about the crops, the weather, and hoped I would be out to the farm again soon. Only Will Isley joked with me. He said, "You're lucky. It's been hot as the hinges of hell in the hayfield."

When Dr. Perrine, my college physics professor came, he knelt down by the bed and sobbed. It made me very uncomfortable. I told Mother afterward, "I have enough problems of my own."

The girls came too. Some of them kissed me and patted my hand. No one spoke a word of pity. For that I was thankful. Norine had gone home but she wrote me a letter every week.

Mother made a record of my callers and when I read it I wondered that I had so many friends. One of the Christiansen girls said, "We knew it the day it happened. Central put out a party call on our telephone line."

More Routine

FOR THE FIRST TIME in my life I discovered the heady pleasure of being the center of attention. My ego filled out plump as a blown-up balloon. It was a new discovery I thoroughly enjoyed. At home on the farm I had shouldered many responsibilities, at times almost more than I could carry. Even as a youngster, when my brothers and I visited our cousin, James McAlvin, in Waterloo, or if we went to a movie or circus, I was told, "Jim, you are the eldest, look after your brothers."

I took the admonition seriously and there must have been times when Robert and Charles hated me for my bossy ways.

When a neighbor wanted help driving cattle, I was sent. When one of our neighbors and his two sons came down with the flu, I rode to their farm and milked his sixteen Holstein cows night and morning for a week. And I hated to milk. I must have been sixteen years old. That was the same summer I drove the family to the state fair in Des Moines and ably piloted the big Haynes through the fair traffic. But sometimes I felt put upon, as if I was given more to do than I could do.

Now my family gave me their whole attention. Years later I was sure that I usurped some of the concern owed to my sister and brothers. But at that time I craved their support. I needed to know they cared about me. With four uncles who were doctors, I had the attention of the hospital staff. Miss Rehwinkle, the superintendent, later told me, "You've been spoiled. You mustn't continue taking advantage of your family's love." But I did not listen . . . then.

The day came when Uncle George removed the catheter. I could void by myself but I could not control my bladder yet. I knew when I had to go but I could not hold back the flow. This depressed and embarrassed me. When my friends brought their girls for a visit, I held the urinal in place under the blankets. I dreaded to hear a tinkle tinkle as the water hit the urinal. They heard it too.

One morning Uncle George said, "Let's get up in the wheelchair today."

Miss Hoskins brought in the high-backed wheelchair and padded it with pillows. Then she called Miss Petersen and together they lifted me into it. I felt prickles of heat, the room spun and disappeared. When I opened my eyes Miss Hoskins was bending over me. Her face looked anxious. "You fainted," she said.

19

"I'm all right," I said. "Raise up the back again." Then I vomited. "Goodbye breakfast," I said. Miss Hoskins wiped my face.

"Can't much else happen, can there?" I asked. I sat up for two hours. Miss Hoskins pushed me out on the sun porch. It was summer in full bloom, the leafy trees, sun-dappled grass, it all seemed new and strange to me. I almost cried because I was so weak.

After that, I got up each morning in the wheelchair. And every morning I fainted and then lost my breakfast. But I refused to give up. It was better than lying in bed.

One day I found I could give the wheelchair a little push with my hands on the handrails. "My gosh!" I exclaimed. "I gave it a shove." Even the nurses cheered me.

The day finally came when I no longer fainted or lost my breakfast. Bladder control improved very slowly. I had to have an enema to make my bowels move. "Damn it," I said grimly. "Nobody ever writes about this part of hospital care. It's always lovey-dovey stuff. The truth is different."

In late July Uncle George said one Saturday morning, "How about going home for dinner tomorrow?"

"Do you really think I could?"

"Why not? Get dressed too—pants, shirt, socks, shoes. You can skip the necktie."

"But what about the urinal?"

"Take one with you. Bob and Chuck can help you. But try to get it through your head that everyone has to micturate. You just can't get up and go to the bathroom to do it."

"All right as an argument but it doesn't make me feel any better," I thought. But what a joy, to go home. I don't think I had realized before what a wonderful place it was.

Sunday morning Miss Hoskins came back from church and, with Miss Petersen, dressed me and lifted me into the wheelchair. "Now you be good," Miss Hoskins said in her droll accent.

Father and the boys came. They wheeled me into the elevator and it lumbered to the ground floor. There stood the old Haynes. Many times I had driven that car on errands, to take Mother to her meetings, on dates. Though usually on a date I took the Model T Ford, unless it was a special occasion.

Robert said, "Put your arm around my neck. Now. . . ." He lifted me out of the wheelchair and sat me on the front seat of the car. "Man, you've lost a lot of weight, you aren't much heavier than a basket of corn."

Father drove. The fields and the neighbors' houses all looked as familiar as the back of my hand yet fresh and new too, as if I had never seen them before. As we passed the Fred Bast farm, Charles, my youngest brother, said, "Fred lost fifty sows from cholera. Remember, Jim, how you and Joe Cunningham milked Bast's Holsteins when the whole family had the flu?"

I remembered all right. Father had said, "When a neighbor needs help, we help." My, I was glad when the Basts recovered.

When we arrived the dog jumped around and barked as if he had the crazies. He licked my face from ear to ear. Mother and Louise came running out to the car, their faces aglow. I hope I don't start to weep, I thought. Bob and Chuck put me in an armchair and carried me into the house. When we ate I sat at the table and fed myself.

"Here we all are together again." Mother's voice sounded happy. I thought of that Sunday often in the hard days to come.

After dinner Bob and Chuck carried me out into the yard. The dog was beside himself. He licked my hands and then ran in circles and barked. "What do you suppose a dog thinks about?" Chuck asked.

The hired men and their wives came over to say hello.

Chuck said, "We have something to show you." Bob went out to the machine shed and rolled back the doors. I heard a motor start. Then Bob came rolling up on a tractor with steel tracks. "You've got a tractor!" I almost yelled it.

"Sure thing, and a three-bottom plow." Bob drove the machine right up beside me. It throbbed with a powerful beat.

"I'm going to ride that thing some day," I promised myself.

About three-thirty, Mother said, "Maybe you shouldn't get too tired the first time. You can come home every Sunday."

As I hugged her I said, "Mother, you don't know how glad I am to be home."

On the way back to the hospital I said to Father, "I don't need a special nurse anymore. I can sit up and feed myself. The floor nurses can look after me."

"It would cut down on expenses," Father answered. "We finally got a payment from the Veterans Administration on your army insurance. It has a total disability clause. Should we put it in the bank and save it for your education?"

I shook my head. "No, put it on the hospital bill." This was during a depression of farm prices and my expenses must have been heavy. Hoover had pulled the rug out from under farmers by refusing to guarantee farm prices after the war. First he had urged them to plow up every acre, pasture, swamp, and meadow to raise food for our own army and that of our allies. We were told: "Food will win the war." The slogan was everywhere.

Now with huge surpluses backed up on the farms, elevators, and docks we had no markets. Wheat dropped to forty-seven cents a bushel. This was in the early twenties when the rest of the country still whooped it up for prosperity.

I repeated, "Put it on my hospital bill."

Soon I tried standing up beside the bed, a nurse on either side. Then I ventured a few steps. My toes dragged, my left heel would not touch the floor, my legs crossed. Each step meant pulling the foot from behind the other leg. Then it would swerve in and throw me off balance. And I needed balance.

Father had the planing mill make a set of parallel bars with a seat at one end. I tried to walk between the bars. I fell a few times because I needed more grip in my hands.

Acting on the advice of Uncle George, a University of Iowa man himself, I went to Iowa City to the famous Steindler Orthopedic Clinic. A hospital in a medical college, where teaching students is the paramount issue, can be the loneliest place in the world for a patient. It is too big and too busy. Patients become clinical material for teaching purposes.

I missed the daily visits from my family, the cheerful words with the nurses, who were all friends of mine now. A couple of my fraternity brothers were in medical school and made a duty call on me. But it was a one-time thing. They were busy in classroom and laboratory. The hospital seemed full of hurried people, none of them concerned with me.

I was just another case, a young man with a fractured spine. Student nurses, girls just out of high school, bathed me, changed my bed, answered my bell. They were kind, often awkward, always in a hurry to finish and go to their classes. Supervisors walked around, arrogant as army officers, as they ordered the student nurses with cold, impatient words.

A young doctor with a pen and clipboard came in to "take your history." Age, time, place of accident, care, return of function, parents. "All right, close your eyes and tell me if I touch you with the sharp or dull point of this pin." I had to go through that again along with the cold and hot water test. I failed them both. He stimulated my already exaggerated reflexes. Why was he here?

I protested. "Dr. George Hearst has already written to Dr. Steindler about me."

"But my job is to take your history."

"I don't want to be here. The sooner I'm home the better I'll like it."

For a moment the young doctor became a human being. He nodded and said, "I know it's tough but don't worry. The Chief will fix you up."

The next morning I heard a rush of footsteps. Suddenly my room filled with men in white coats, the supervisor on my ward standing behind them. A compact, well-built man with a trim mustache, grizzled hair, and glasses approached my bed. His eyes twinkled and he spoke with a marked foreign accent. "Mr. Hearst, I am Dr. Steindler. Your uncle wrote to me about you. He said you are a brave man."

He turned to his staff. "Mr. Hearst cannot walk because his adductors pull his legs until they cross. The left Achilles tendon has contracted and he can't put his whole foot down on the floor."

"But my neck, Dr. Steindler," I said hopefully. "Can't you operate and cure this paralysis?"

With the benign look he so often wore, Dr. Steindler touched my head. "No miracles. First we must get you on your feet. Then you must train your muscles to do the work you want them to do."

He turned to a man behind him. "Dr. Funston, arrange for the operating room tomorrow morning at eight o'clock."

To me he said, "We will cut part of those strong muscles so they won't cross your legs. We will stretch the heel cord so that you can set your foot down squarely."

"But," I begged, "can't you connect the nerves in my neck?"

Dr. Steindler grasped my hand. "We will see you tomorrow morning." And so I was operated on.

When I woke from the anesthetic my mouth tasted dry, my stomach in revolt. I wore a new suit, a plaster cast that reached from my waist to my toes. My legs were spread apart the width of the bed, a two-by-four between the knees held them apart. The nurse sitting beside me gave me a sip of water and said, "It is called a double hip spica cast."

When Dr. Steindler stopped by on his evening rounds, he asked, "Are you all right? You don't hurt much, do you?"

I answered slowly, "I'm glad I am not a centipede."

Dr. Steindler beamed. "He makes a joke. You can go home tomorrow. Keep the cast on for six weeks. Then I want to see you again."

Father came to get me. With the help of the orderlies, I was loaded into the back of a pickup truck. To my surprise, the supervisor on my floor came to the door and said, "Goodbye and God bless you." I didn't realize she even knew I had been there.

At the station a gang of workmen hoisted me into the front of the interurban car beside the motorman. The motorman said, "We'll get you home. Awkward pair of pants you're wearing."

In my old room at Sartori Hospital I was home again. All the nurses came to welcome me. It was like the return of the prodigal son. A great wave of homesickness suddenly flooded me and then ebbed away. I was home.

Strange how my mental attitude improved when I was surrounded by friends. I lived with adult graduate nurses who treated me like a member of the hospital family. In a way the security of the hospital weaned me from my own family. I no longer needed the squeak of a dry spoke to make my pulse jump. If no one came for several days I did not miss them.

Perhaps for my own family it was better too. I had demanded so much attention. Now Mother could devote herself to the others in the family without the constant pull to be at the hospital with me. Of course, I could no longer go home for Sunday dinners. I was bedbound in my heavy cast. I was strapped in a plaster cocoon.

The nurses levered me over on my side to change my bed or put a bedpan under me. I controlled my bladder now with some success though when the urge came I could not hold back long. This puzzled my uncles. "It should be the other way," Uncle Gregg said. "You should have trouble starting."

I read incessantly. I abandoned Zane Grey and the mystery and adventure stories that had calmed me when read aloud. First I tackled the French authors—Flaubert, de Maupassant, Mérimée, the poets Baudelaire and Verlaine. Aunt Jennie Curtis, Uncle Will's wife who would soon divorce him, brought me a small portable typewriter. It was placed on my bedside table. With the headrest raised and the bedside table swung in front of me I hammered out short letters with my index fingers. I could not sit up very straight because of the cast. But it gave me great satisfaction to type out notes of thanks to people who remembered me with flowers and books.

I had two regular callers. Mrs. Doctor Hansen had lost a son to the flu at the Great Lakes Naval Station during the epidemic. She always brought me flowers. Mrs. H. N. Silliman (whose husband had the first automobile in Cedar Falls) brought me old books from her father's library. These elderly ladies, both widows, made the long walk up the steep hill to see me every week. I was a bit abashed by their kindness.

My high school principal, Mrs. Hope Graham, brought me some books about which she had some reservations. She said, "Here are some contemporary novels. The sex scenes are explicit. I don't want to rouse your passions." One of them was called *Salt*, written by Kathleen Norris's husband. They were daring books then. Today they would not make a Sunday school teacher blush.

A month went by. The cast hurt. I could not sleep. The spasticity in my legs made them jump. Miss Hoskins had gone on general duty but she still kept an eye on me. One day she spotted a damp place on the cast. She told Uncle George about it. He looked at it and said, "There's trouble here. Bring me a cast knife and some water. We've got to get this thing off.

Uncle George cut through the plaster and spread the cast shell. He and Miss Hoskins lifted out my legs. It hurt to move the legs close together after weeks of being spread-eagled. On the outside of each leg, just above the calf, was a small ulcer. There was one on my left heel too. One of them had leaked through the cast. No wonder I could not sleep. But these were the only sores I ever had. Doctors who saw me later were amazed that I did not have chronic bedsores. "Man, they sure took good care of you," a man at the Mayo Clinic told me.

I began my exercises. I stood between the parallel bars. I could take a step without my legs crossing. My left heel came down flat. To exercise took everything I had—muscle, will, balance. Everything was just barely enough. I could just barely stand after the nurses helped me to my feet, just barely place one foot ahead of the other, just barely grip the bars with enough strength to keep from falling.

The nurses encouraged me, taunted me, called me lazy. It was much easier to sit in the wheelchair than to fight my incorrigible muscles. The spasticity would shoot out a leg and throw me off balance. If I pulled my abdominal muscles too tight I had to use the urinal.

There was improvement, even though it was like setting stakes to see if a glacier moved. I could not or would not face the fact that there was no way to repair my damaged spinal cord. I stubbornly clung to the belief that there was some way of freeing me from this paralysis. I could not face being crippled.

Once in awhile, when Bob and Chuck took me for a ride, we would stop on College Hill. There I held court while friends, businessmen, fellows from the different fraternities, and girls I knew came to the car to visit with me. I saw a student in front of the drugstore do an excellent imitation of an old man suffering from a stroke. "The son of a bitch," I muttered. "I'd like to break *his* goddamned neck."

At times, I sank so deep in depression that even the raillery of close friends could not pull me out of it. I would say in low tones to Tom Anderson or Colin Shillinglaw, "I don't have to stand this. Why the hell should I keep on living like this!"

My brothers in the front seat must have shuddered. But I did not mean it. The will to live flooded me with purpose, overwhelming any notions of self-destruction. These spoken thoughts were a kind of unconscious blackmail to keep my brothers concerned about me. Years later I wonder why they did not call my bluff and say, "Okay, go ahead, quit."

My brothers treated me with care and affection. They carried me to and from the car to make visits home or to the homes of relatives. Maybe for them a big brother was someone special. The affection was mutual. I did insist that my fraternity pledge both my brothers. And I persuaded Father to let them play football. They played on a championship high school team and won both local and state honors.

Father took me to see my brothers play football. They played on the same side of the line, Chuck at left end, Bob at left tackle. They worked beautifully together. Occasionally, on a tackle-around play, Bob would get the ball. I loved to watch him. He started slowly, but once under way he moved like a freight train and mowed down the opposing tacklers. He loved contact, Bob did. He was big—six feet tall, two hundred pounds. I remember the gleam of triumph in his eye the first time he could put me down and sit on me. Both boys were chosen for the all-county team.

Bob sang in the high school glee club, dated a lot of girls. Father confessed to me that he found a condom in Bob's wallet and asked me what he should do about it. I grinned. "Nothing, Dad. Let him alone." It was a small cloud compared to the storm gathering on the horizon.

Bob complained of a pain in his neck. A gland just below his ear swelled as if he had the mumps. Uncle Will, now out of the army, examined him and advised Father to take him to Iowa City. There Dr. Lee Wallace Dean, head of the ear, nose and throat department, took him in charge.

He suggested a biopsy. A small incision was made in the gland and a thin slice of tissue extracted. A few days later Uncle Will drove out with the report. Uncle Will said, "Lymphatic sarcoma, cancer of the lymph glands."

Robert rode the interurban to Iowa City to begin X-ray therapy at the state hospital. He never uttered a word of complaint. He still helped me whenever he could. Robert still looked strong and healthy and I refused to accept the verdict. But the whole family was wrapped in a blanket of anxiety.

We both went to the state hospital, Bob for more radiation therapy, I for some physiotherapy. Once, when Bob and I rode up in an elevator, Dr. Dean put his hand on Bob's shoulder. "I'm terribly sorry, young man," he said.

I thought, "Oh Jesus, is it really true?" I was chilled by this revelation.

In physiotherapy I sat in a wheelchair facing the ends of parallel bars in the gymnasium. Every hour a gray-haired woman in a white smock came in and helped me stand. I stood for five minutes and then sat down and waited an hour. I rode an electric bus from the hospital to Children's Hospital across the river where the physiotherapy rooms were. Twice a day Bob lifted me on and off the bus. He could do it better than the orderlies.

After the third day I said to Bob, "Hell, I can do this at Sartori. I'm going home."

The old hospital crawled with bedbugs and cockroaches. I found bumps on my arms and neck from bedbug bites. I roomed with Doc Wells, a young man who had just graduated from the dental college. He had been afflicted with septicemia and his joints had ankylosed (frozen). Now Dr. Steindler operated on elbows and hips, one at a time, chiseling away the bone to give Doc enough motion to practice his profession.

The tedium of the routine weighed on my spirits. Bob finished his radiation treatments and went home. One of the orderlies said to me, "Do you think you could swim?"

I hadn't thought about it but I said, "Probably."

"Want to try it? Tim and I can take you down to the river and see."

The two medical students wheeled me down to the river. They took off my hospital gown, clasped me under the arms and knees, one on each side, and heaved me in. I landed with a splash, sank, rose, turned on my stomach, and struck out for the bank. Then I turned on my back and floated. "No problem," I said.

But the hospital did not take a light view of this. I was severely reprimanded. "We cannot take responsibility for such rash acts," I was told.

It was the only fun I had. Oh, not quite. A student nurse took a fancy to me, and when she was on night duty she would slip into the room, bare her breasts, and let me kiss them. She gave me a snapshot of herself in her nurse's uniform. I kept it for a long time.

Bob slowly went downhill. His buoyant, aggressive health began to wither like a stalk of corn attacked by wilt. But he never complained, never lost his composure. I tried hard to ignore his affliction.

One day Bob and I were driving out to the farm. The rural mailman, Everett Hughes, stopped us. "Bob," he said. "How are you getting along?"

I answered, "As best I can." I was so used to the question that I answered almost automatically. Then I realized that the question had been addressed to Bob. The mailman gave us a queer look and drove on. Bob didn't say anything. He was used to playing second fiddle. But I never forgot it or how ashamed I was. I thought, "For Christ sake, I'm slowly getting better and Bob is slowly dying. Couldn't I let him have the attention he deserves?"

Late in my second year at Sartori Hospital I became almost a member of the hospital family. The nurses helped me dress each morning. My arms had recovered a good deal of strength and motion. I could hold a book, brush my teeth, comb my hair, feed myself. But my hands were still weak and lacked control.

Miss Rehwinkle, the superintendent of the hospital, insisted that I eat lunch and dinner down in the nurses' dining room. Someone would stop and help me to my feet. I would shuffle across the hall to the elevator, holding a nurse's hand and arm, and ride down to the dining room. There I sat in a straight chair at the table. Miss Rehwinkle said my presence kept the girls from talking hospital talk. I could manage to walk if someone held my hand and arm and could use the other to grasp a doorknob, chair back, wall, or even use a crutch on that side.

I could not rise from a sitting position without help. I tried using crutches but the tips tended to slip on the waxed floors and I fell down a few times. I really was not strong enough yet in my hands to manage crutches.

How many weary hours of exercise to gain one inch of progress! Sometimes only half an inch, a quarter of an inch, and maybe the next day I had slid back my gain. Yet I persevered and my confidence and strength increased.

I tried to forget about my condition and think of other things. I fretted about the money my hospital stay cost my family. Twenty dollars a week for room, board, and nursing over two years seemed like an enormous sum. Now Robert needed expensive treatments.

My family sacrificed for me because they loved me. I loved them dearly, even though I didn't often show it. But there was much about love I had yet to learn. Like so many other things, I learned the hard way about love.

First Love

TWILIGHT FILLED THE ROOM. Miss Hopkins sat wearily on the broad window sill. I could just distinguish her features. She had removed her nurse's cap and it lay in her lap. I saw her dusky hair as a frame around her face. The white and dark contrast excited me. My backrest half raised, I stared at her with cowlike admiration. I knew she was tired. She had been on her feet for hours. Our small hospital could only afford one operating room supervisor.

She came to see me every day. Her visits always lifted my spirits. I waited for them. Sometimes she just peeped around the corner and smiled. Sometimes she sat with me while Miss Hoskins rested. This evening Miss Hoskins had gone for a walk.

I craved this time with Miss Hopkins. The hospital was a place of illness, operations, doctors, and nurses and I felt an alien. But Miss Hopkins pretended that I was her special friend and I longed to believe it.

She half-turned on the window seat. "Hoskins is coming back," she said, her voice low and lovely. As if she had suddenly come to a resolution, she rose swiftly, put her arms around me, and kissed me full on the mouth. "Sleep well, my dear," she whispered. Then she fled.

I sailed into a region of pure joy. I quivered with the vibrations of a music played in my pulses. My helpless flesh with its embarrassing needs, the misery of self-loathing, thoughts of a grim future—all melted away in the warmth of my new happiness. All around me the air seemed to bloom. I scarcely noted that Miss Hoskins had returned. When she asked, "Are you ready to go to sleep?" I was too dazed to answer her. She snapped on the light to see if I was all right.

But I seemed to exist at a great distance from a plain answer. My reply seemed spoken by another's voice. I went to sleep, rocked in the assurance of a beautiful tomorrow.

The morning brought sober routine. When I ate breakfast I made my fumbling shadowy hands grip knife and fork with a new determination. The sun shone and back in the orchard a meadowlark sang. My thoughts sang to me, "I'm not so repulsive after all."

When Miss Hoskins went to get the bathwater, the beloved face peeped around the door. "Good morning, Jim. Be a good boy. I won't see you again today." She vanished. She had never called me "Jim" before.

Miss Hoskins set my breakfast tray in the hall and shut the door. "Ready for your bath? Did Miss Hopkins stop? She has a big morning in the operating room. Then she has her half day and she is going to Cedar Rapids to visit some friends."

A twinge of jealousy seized me. Visit friends? Well, why not? But I saw a lonely day ahead for me. I took a nap after lunch and was helped into the wheelchair.

Mother and Louise came to see me. I greeted them so fervently that Mother asked if I felt all right. She brought letters and a book, *Innocents Abroad* by Mark Twain. Mother said, "Uncle George is coming for dinner Sunday. He said he would bring you."

Sunday meant home for dinner, a day to look forward to. Mother said, "I wish George would find a nice woman and marry her."

That evening after I had been turned on my side, a cushion between my knees and the call bell beside my face, Miss Hoskins went to the office to do her charting. The door opened, a figure tiptoed in, leaned over, kissed me, and whispered, "Sweet dreams," and was gone.

I wondered if Mother would invite Miss Hopkins for Sunday dinner . . . probably not if Uncle George was coming. I had been in the hospital long enough to realize that a kind of hierarchy existed between doctors and nurses. Well, maybe next week. . . .

It was afternoon of the next day before I saw *her* again. I sat in the wheelchair trying to read, my thoughts jumping around like sparrows after crumbs. Suddenly she stood in the doorway. "Come on, Jim," she said. "I'm going to take you up to the operating room. After I clean the instruments I'm going to wrap pads. You can help me. Dr. George said it would be good exercise for your hands. Want to come?"

"Oh, yes," I answered. She smiled at me with her warm, lovely brown eyes. Her voice, with its low bubbly sound, made me feel woozy.

In the elevator she stood behind my wheelchair. She placed her hands over my eyes and asked, "Who is this?" Before I could answer she leaned over and kissed me. I was so aflame I could not speak.

She wheeled me down the hall into the operating room. "This is my domain," she said. Curiously I looked at the gleaming white walls, the operating table, the stool for the anesthetist, the glass shelves loaded with shining instruments, the sink where faucets are turned on and off with an elbow.

She explained the faucets. "That is so a doctor, after he has scrubbed, won't have to touch anything and can slip on sterile gloves."

We went into a small room lined with drawers and cabinets. "Here is where we keep our supplies, pads, bandages, sponges, adhesive tape, sheets, and pillowcases. The OBS room is right next door."

"What's OBS?"

"Obstetrical. Where women have babies."

She stood beside me. I put my arm around her waist. She pressed my head against her. "Do you like to have me love you a little?"

"Oh, yes," I whispered. "I didn't think any woman would ever care for me again."

"You had lots of girl friends in college. Some of them still come to see you."

"Not like this," I murmured. "I never felt like this before."

She pushed me up to a table. "Let's get busy or Miss Rehwinkle will think we've eloped. Now put this folded pad inside a cloth wrapper and fasten it. See if you can do it."

I dropped my wrists so my fingers would open, grasped the pad, placed it on a square of brown cloth, and turned the corners over. She said, "Good, you can do it."

"I can't fasten it. A safety pin is small for me to pick up."

We worked in silence a few minutes. "I don't even know your first name."

"Prudence. Isn't that silly? Call me Prue. We're Quakers. I was brought up in a tiny town called Hopewell. It's a community of Friends. We're poor as church mice."

"Do your folks still live there?"

"Father and Mother are gone. But I have a brother who farms near there. He's married and has three children."

"Where did you go to school?"

"After high school I attended Coe College in Cedar Rapids for two years. Then the way opened for me to become a nurse. So I went to Battle Creek, Michigan, to the nursing school in the hospital there."

"Battle Creek? Cornflakes?" I smiled.

"Yes, Dr. Kellogg was chief of staff at the hospital."

"Who does the cornflakes?"

"It seems to be a family affair. There is a Post family that intermarried with the Kelloggs. The people are all vegetarians. We ate meat substitutes, soybeans and nuts shaped like turkey legs and pork chops. Very good too." We laughed.

"What are you going to do with these pads?"

"Put them in the autoclave. That's the sterilizer. It's that big shiny drum just outside the operating room."

"Do you sterilize other things?"

"Of course—instruments, urinals, bedpans, gowns, rubber gloves, nearly everything."

I looked at her in admiration. What a lot she knew.

"You look droopy," she said. "I'll take you downstairs."

In the elevator, before she pushed the button, she looked earnestly at me. A kind of glow shone in her face. After I had seen it several times I called it her "inner light." She said, "The body is not the person, be it broken or whole. Do not grieve over what you cannot help."

After supper she came into my room. I was sitting with the head rest raised so I could feed myself. Miss Hoskins took her chart and went to the office. Prue pushed the door partly closed and sat on the bed. "I love you, Jim," she said. "I love you for your courage and determination. All the girls talk about it. But most of all I love you because you are yourself. I want to help you."

Even many years later, as an old man, I remember this scene. The window was open, a breeze blowing the curtains slightly, lines of blackbirds drifting past on their way to the pine trees by the hospital, a smell of windfalls from the orchard, the covers of the bed smooth over my legs, the hush of twilight filling the room. I could make no reply. I lay there and trembled.

It has been said there is never a love like the first one. I view that statement now with suspicion. The truth is that there is never a love like any other love. Each has its own emotions. I prayed silently, if God spares me and heals me I shall forever be in debt to this girl, this marvelous girl with warm brown eyes and soft dark hair.

Finally I said, "I'm not much to love but what I am is yours."

I reached out my arms and held her. I kissed her with all my desire ripe on my lips. She lay lightly on my breast a minute and held my hands tightly. Then, without a word, she slipped off the bed and turned on the light.

"I'm going to sit here in this chair and we'll talk. When Hoskins comes back she'll fix you for the night."

I could find no words. I looked at her as a beggar might, who, hoping for a crumb, had found the Lord's Supper.

She said, "Tomorrow morning, starting at eight o'clock, Dr. George has six tonsillectomies. Then Dr. Mead has an appendix to remove. Dr. Corsaut from Dike wants to amputate the hand of a young boy who caught it in a corn sheller. It's become gangrenous. This will keep me busy."

I tried to match her factual tone. "Do you let outside doctors use the hospital?"

"If they have local help. Dr. Will is going to help with the amputation."

Miss Hoskins bustled in. "All ready to go to sleep?"

Prue said, "Good night," and disappeared. My elation went a little sour. I wanted to go with her, to walk off down the hall with her. She could go and come as she pleased, but I was the bed's captive, prisoner of a body that would not obey me.

I nodded to Miss Hoskins. She put out the light. Let her put out the goddamned light forever, I thought darkly.

Each morning Miss Rehwinkle stopped to say good morning and ask how I slept. She was the superintendent. It seemed to me that she did everything—hired nurses, kept an eye on the janitor, made out menus, ordered supplies, scheduled surgery. She kept all the narcotics and opiates in an old-fashioned safe in the office and doled them out when they were prescribed.

She was tall, erect, with fine yellow hair and blue eyes that were a bit chilly. She seemed impersonal and aloof, yet she was friendly in a professional way. I was sure no one would call her by her first name. I wondered if she had ever been a little girl.

This morning she wore a gauze veil over her hair and a short-sleeved gown. "I'm going into the operating room today," she said. "It's Miss Hopkins's day off. But she's going to take care of you while Miss Hoskins does some shopping."

It shocked me to silence. The girl I loved would give me an enema, bathe me, help lift me into the wheelchair. What new humiliations did the days have in store for me? I overlooked the fact that she gave up her day off to look after me.

Then she came in the door. Her rubber-soled shoes never gave me any warning. She carried the enema can and a bedpan. She shut the door and smiled at me. "Here we are. Let's get the work done."

Embarrassment must have been written all over my face. "Don't worry," she said cheerfully. "I'm a good nurse."

When it was over and I was bathed and Miss Petersen had helped lift me in the wheelchair and the bed was made, she put her arms around me. "Don't be foolish about what must be done. I want to take care of you. Don't you know that?"

I held her hand. "I nearly died. I was ashamed to have you do things like that. I'm so helpless." I was about to cry.

That evening she came to sit with me again. Miss Hoskins took her chart and prepared to leave. "You two be good," she chuckled.

For many evenings we were content to be near each other with a few kisses and caresses before parting. But as the days grew shorter, the evenings darkened early and Prue did not turn on the lights. The dusk woke fires in us both.

Prue warmed at once to my touch. Touching roused appetites for further explorations. One night she lay on me and I whispered, "Come on . . . dear . . . come on." And I entered her.

"Oh Jim, oh Jim," she whispered. "What have we done?"

"I couldn't help it," I breathed. "You excite me so."

"Oh, let's pray or something," Prue said. "Pray we won't do it again."

"We could say the Lord's Prayer together," I suggested.

We found prayer not an easy answer. Before long we were united again. And again. And now, prayers or no prayers, guilt feelings or no, there was no stopping us. I wondered that I could perform, as helpless as I was.

So I asked. "Uncle George, I can get an erection but I can't walk. How come?"

Uncle George shook his head. "Don't ask me. Nature tends to propagate the species come hell or high water. But keep it under your hat, all these women around."

We tried to be casual around other folk. Prudence took me up to her quarters every chance she had. And I did exercise my hands.

I washed and dried instruments, learned about scalpels, hemostats, retractors, different kinds of curved needles, and sutures. I turned rubber gloves inside out and blew in the wrist to make the fingers pop out. I found leaks in gloves that Prue patched with pieces of old gloves and rubber cement.

I folded pads and rolled bandages. I learned some of the habits of the different doctors. I discovered that Uncle Will's instruments came from Vienna and were made of German steel. He bought them when he was a student there. "By far the best set here," said Prue. "He lets the other doctors use them too."

Prue would stop and sit on the arm of the wheelchair. I would hug her and we would kiss long and fervently. We tried French kissing but Prue said she didn't care much for it unless she was really worked up.

I discovered what "worked up" meant. I also became aware of a woman's menstrual periods. "Funny," I said, "we boys talked about the 'monthlies' but we didn't know what we were talking about."

One night I begged Prue to show me what she looked like "down there." She considered a moment, then sat on the bed and pulled up her uniform. I stared, then averted my eyes quickly. "It's about the way it should be, I guess."

Prue looked hard at me to see if I was serious. Then she giggled. "You are the prize nitwit. 'The way it should be.' What a statement."

We did not turn on the lights in my room until time for Miss Hoskins to appear. Bless her heart, she kept to schedule and never surprised us. Prue reported that Miss Hoskins said to Miss Rehwinkle, "Time I disturbed the lovebirds."

I took Prue home with me several Sundays for dinner and then did not ask her again. Mother did not show the friendliness I hoped for. I suppose word had reached home of our attachment. I got the message that a person in my shape had no business becoming infatuated with a girl.

I worked at my exercises every day. I stood up beside the bed. If they had time, two nurses supported me by the arms and I walked a few steps. Some obstetrical straps fastened to the end of the bed gave me something to pull on to exercise my arms and hands.

"I've a reason to work hard," I told Prue one day. "If I'm going to get well enough for us to be married."

"Whoa there, son," Prue said. "Back up. Who said we're going to be married. I'm several years older than you are and your folks don't approve of me. Right now you must consider your family."

"You aren't marrying my folks."

"Listen, Buster, your family have laid themselves out for you. You can't wave that away. They didn't make you dive into the river but they have been at your beck and call ever since you came here. You think about them a little."

I sulked. I knew she spoke the truth. Damn it. Why couldn't I just get up and go my own way? The hell with everybody, I thought. I'll go to South America.

Prue laughed. "Tuck in your lower lip, sweetheart, and get that mulish look off your face and I'll kiss you."

I did not know when it started or why it started, but I began to weary a bit of the attention Prue gave me. She seemed to smother me in blankets of affection. The light no longer leaped into my eyes when she entered the room. I no longer felt embarrassed when she attended to my intimate needs.

I liked to have Miss Hoskins or Miss Petersen perform the morning ritual. I joked with them as friends with no emotional tax to pay. Miss Petersen could handle me better than anyone. She could even get me up alone. She would put her arms around me, slide me off the bed, stand me on my feet, turn me around, and sit me down in the wheelchair. Even Prue could not do this.

They were just little things at first. Prue always stopped on her way to the dining room to see if I needed help with my tray. One evening when she stopped she looked tired, weary. It had been a busy day in surgery and she had assisted at a hard delivery in the obstetrical room. "Do you need any help?"

I saw how worn she looked. Almost as if I intended to hurt her, I said, "You're the one who ought to have help." Her forehead creased in a puzzled frown and she left without more words.

She did not return after supper. I wheeled out to the sun porch and read for an hour. I moved to the office to visit with Miss Rehwinkle and Miss Kershaw. They were surprised to see me. I went back to my room and waited to be put to bed. "Let her stay away," I thought, trying to dull the sting of conscience.

I wore her class ring on my little finger. One night when she bent over me to say good night, the ring slipped off. She saw it and half sobbed, "You're even throwing away my ring."

This irritated me. "Quit making up trouble. It just slipped off. Don't be so touchy."

Once in the operating room when I washed the instruments after surgery I nicked my finger with a scalpel. It bled. Prue swabbed the cut with iodine. Of course it stung. I jerked my hand away and snapped, "Don't get so busy."

Prue glared at me. "You fool. Don't you know the risk of infection from a dirty scalpel? Why do you think we do all this scrubbing and sterilizing? You're just stupid."

We always made up—kissed, apologized, and rubbed noses like Eskimos. Each took the blame. But the bloom was off the rose and we both knew it.

A climax developed one afternoon when Prue took me with her to set up a room for an OB patient. I watched her make the bed. When she bent over I could see the tops of her stockings. "Nice legs there, pal," I said.

"Thanks."

"Many a merry time I've had. . . ."

"Don't be coarse."

"Here I am alone in a room with a lovely woman and safe as if I were in church."

"Don't be so sure."

I taunted her. "What could you do about it?"

"Why you damn little squirt." I had never heard Prue use a cuss word before. Her language always seemed on a cleaner level than mine. We looked at each other and we both smiled.

Then Prue took a straight chair and locked the back of it under the doorknob. She took off her cap and unbuttoned her uniform. She turned to me, her large brown eyes glowing. She lowered the back of the wheelchair and raised the feet so that I lay almost horizontal. "Hey, what do you think you're doing," I protested.

She did not answer. She began to kiss me with long hot kisses, her tongue moving back and forth in my mouth. She slipped her hand under my blanket, inside my pajamas and began massaging me slowly with a squeeze at the end of each stroke. When she had me ready she pulled down her pants and straddling the wheelchair forced me into her. She bit my lip and cheek. She made a growling sound deep in her throat.

She lay on me with a fierce purpose as if I were prey she had just captured. She worked me without mercy.

I gripped her tightly, eyes shut, skin damp. "She's pumping me dry," I thought. "She's sucking it all out of me."

Then it was all over. She rested lightly on me for a few minutes to catch her breath. She closed my pajamas and rearranged my blankets. Then she hoisted up her pants and fastened her dress. She went to the mirror to tuck back her hair and put on her cap. She was Miss Hopkins again.

"How about being as safe as in church?" she asked, her voice trembling.

She raised the back of the wheelchair and put down the footrest. She kissed me softly.

"For the love of Mike, Prue, talk about being raped. What if someone had come in?"

"But no one did. They would not have been able to open the door anyway."

"What would you have said to explain it?"

"How do I know? No one came."

This was our last real surge of sex. Later encounters to both of us seemed a ritual to be gone through because it was expected. We hurt each other when we quarreled.

"What's the good of all this if we aren't going to be married?"

"Jim, look at me. How can we be married? We couldn't live with your family. If we had our own place I could not work and look after you too. Be sensible."

Her face glowed with her "inner light" and there were tears in her eyes. "Don't you believe in love for love's sake?" Her voice became solemn. "For two people to be so blessed with caring for each other and to trust in cleaving to each other so that their lives are enriched?"

I was humbled but not silenced. "I know but I won't always be like this. Some doctor somewhere will cure me."

Prue smoothed my hair. "You don't want to go on like this?"

It irritated me to answer a question like that. "I don't know. Probably I am a selfish bastard, but more than anything else I want to get well."

Our last quarrel came about in a trivial way.

It was Christmas and the whole family had been invited to dinner with the McAlvins in Waterloo. Uncle Will brought a new contraption for me to try. It was a rubber urinal to be worn inside my trousers so I would not need to use a regular urinal at the party. It strapped around my waist with a receptacle for my penis and a rubber tube running to a bag strapped to my leg.

I was all dressed except for this gadget when my folks arrived to pick me up. Mother said, "We're a bit late. Father and the boys went to get the car filled with gas. Are you ready, James?"

"All but this new urinal and I want Dad or Bob to help me put it on."

"Can't Miss Hoskins do it?"

"No, I want Father or Bob." I was a little angry.

Prue came in and said, "If you and Louise will step out a minute, Mrs. Hearst, I'll put it on."

Her tone of assurance set me off. "The hell you will. Keep your hands off me."

"Why, Jim, your Mother said they were late. You know I've done everything for you."

"Well, you aren't going to do this. I'm tired of having you think you can do what you want to with me. Just keep away."

"Yes," she said in a low voice. "I will."

When I returned from the McAlvins that evening she did not come to kiss me good night.

I saw little of her the next few days. Then I received an appointment from Dr. Steindler in Iowa City. Prue said goodbye to me but she did not kiss me. She said, "I hope you get the benefit from this trip that you deserve. I wish you well with all my heart."

I never saw her again.

After two weeks in Iowa City, learning exercises in the physiotherapy department, I came back to my room at Sartori Hospital.

I was tired. I stayed in bed until after lunch. Miss Rehwinkle came in and sat by my bed. She had not ever done this before.

She said, "I suppose you know Miss Hopkins has gone." Startled, I said, "No! Where?"

"She's taken a position in a nuns' hospital in France, just outside Lyons."

I couldn't believe it. I lay there stunned. "You mean she has gone to France?" I couldn't even comprehend my own words.

"Yes, she should be there by this time." Miss Rehwinkle gave me an envelope. "She left this note for you."

I tore it open. It said:

JIM—We are not good for each other anymore so I am going away. I wish I could say I leave with kindness but I do not, I leave with bitterness. I missed my last two periods. If I am pregnant and I think I am, our child will be born in France. You will never see the child. You did not want me and you would not want my child. Miss Rehwinkle has my address but I will not answer letters from you. It is better to make the parting final and clean. PRUE.

I lay there a long time looking at nothing. An instant relief was followed by a great emptiness. I sank into a deep depression. I knew I had lost something I would never recover. And I knew now how precious it was.

Last Hospital Days

TOWARD THE END of the second year, Sartori Hospital began to seem like home for me. Miss Rehwinkle kept my room for me when I was in Iowa City so things would be just as I left them—books, typewriter, letters, clothes, even vases on the dresser Mother had brought from home for flowers. My feelings turned against flowers. They reminded me too much of funerals. The fact was that whenever a funeral home had a funeral, the leftover flowers were sent to the hospital to be distributed among the patients.

The nurses disliked the practice. They had the work of trimming and arranging them and evading questions about who sent them. The flowers always looked wilted and secondhand. I would not have them in my room.

I settled in after my last trip to Iowa City. My stay there had been strenuous. Many of the exercises were still beyond my strength to perform. It was a relief to be back in my own room. The nurses seemed pleased to see me. Miss Rehwinkle introduced me to the new operating room supervisor. She was a red-haired, wholesome appearing gal with a friendly, wide smile. I hoped we would be friends.

I missed something. The days ran on bare feet into a dwindling future. I dove into shallow pools of depression and no one came to rescue me. The nurses had their own families and problems to contend with. And my friendship with Miss Hopkins had tended to isolate me from the other women. In a way I had shut myself off. I even rejected some of Miss Hoskins' well-meant approaches. My indifference sometimes shamed me. My family and Uncle George felt indebted to her for the care and devotion she gave me in a critical time, days when I was in a live-or-die condition. My life had depended on her ability and professional skill. But we had lived intimately together too long. I was weary of her solid virtues, her half smile, her knowledge of my weaknesses.

I missed Prue even though I had to eat humble pie to admit it. It was no use trying to persuade myself that I was relieved not to have her hovering over me. I missed her terribly. At times my sky so clouded over with guilt that no sun could burn it away. What a cruel stupid bastard I had been to throw away, like Othello, the pearl of great price. She would have given her life for me and I had pushed her away. Now I had no one, no one who looked beyond the care of my crippled body. "God," I pleaded, "what was the matter with me?"

My family had more sorrow to contend with. In spite of X-ray and radium therapy, Robert slowly slipped downhill. He lost weight and his face changed into worn and haggard features. Sometimes he could not be roused in the mornings and Father would come in from the field to help get him up.

But Bob never whimpered, never complained. He acted as though my accident was more important than his doom.

"He's only twenty-two," I protested. "God can't let him die."

What did the chorus in *Antigone* say? "When once a house has fallen from heaven, there the curse lies evermore." It seemed true to me.

I wished I could let Bob know how awful I felt about his illness. But I did not know how to say it. My family seldom expressed their emotions. We were a stoic folk. "Dumb Scotch-Irish Calvinists," I thought. "Unable to say how much we love each other." I walked the plank many times when I thought of Bob and my inability to comfort him. Now Chuck lifted me in and out of the car when I went home on Sundays.

I wondered how the family found money to pay for all the treatments and hospital bills. My army insurance check came every month. It wasn't much, but it helped.

I interested myself in the hospital's ability to survive. My twenty dollars a week for room, board, and nursing might be a lot to me but could the hospital thrive on it? No doubt the two- and four-bed wards were cheaper. I knew every precaution was taken to keep down expenses. The thermometers in their jar of disinfectant were scarcely ever broken. Rubber gloves were patched and reused. Urinals and bedpans, iron under baked enamel, were sterilized and did not wear out. Sheets were mended, hypodermic needles saved and resharpened. In the fall, if the house was not full and the nurses not busy, they helped Miss Rehwinkle can fruits and vegetables from the big hospital garden. The janitor looked after the garden.

He was a character, the janitor. Everyone called him "Uncle Fred." He was a short wiry man, all muscle, with bowed legs and arms, always moving at a trot. He cleaned rooms and halls, mowed the lawn, tended the heating plant, washed windows, put on storm windows. He carried me downstairs one day when the elevator stuck. No one could turn out work like Uncle Fred. And if Miss Hopkins needed help to clean up the operating room, Uncle Fred was Johnny-at-the-rat-hole.

Sometime after Christmas Miss Rehwinkle stopped to see me. "Do you ever hear from Miss Hopkins?" she asked. I shook my head no.

"I had a letter from her. She seems well, enjoys her work. She's learning to speak French. Some of the older nuns don't speak English. She works in obstetrics, not in surgery as she did here."

As she stepped to the door, Miss Rehwinkle recalled something. "She's adopted a baby. She named it Prudence Jamesina, probably for you. I thought you might have heard from her. It's just like her to care for some poor little illegitimate waif."

"I wonder if she knows," I thought. "Probably not or she wouldn't be so open about it." Then I said, "She always had a big heart for someone in need."

When she had gone I turned a furious anger on Prue. She couldn't do this . . . my own child . . . not ever to see her . . . damn her. When I cooled down I wondered if Prue really meant what she had said. But I knew she did.

One day I told my mother as much of the story as I could. Her eyes brightened, "A granddaughter?"

"But a bit of a truant," I said.

"Do you think I could write to Prudence?"

"I don't know. Miss Rehwinkle has her address. You could try." Then I added, "We're not in good standing with Prudence Hopkins at this moment." I never asked Mother if she wrote or not. I assumed she would tell me if she received an answer.

Several times I visited Ina Trus in the operating room. She let me wash instruments and fold pads. But the fun had gone out of it and I did not visit her very often.

Each day I worked at my exercises. God, how I hated to exercise. At the slightest stimulation, spasticity would stiffen my legs. My reflexes were so sensitive that my legs jumped every time I bumped them. I gritted my teeth and *willed* the rebellious muscles to obey. Sometimes they would respond but the effort exhausted me. "I've got to get out of here," I told myself.

"Exercise is the only way you will get anywhere," Uncle George told me. "Reeducate the muscles. No one knows how to patch a spinal cord. You're lucky to have as much control as you do."

I didn't believe him. Somewhere I knew there was a doctor who could make me well. Meanwhile I worked as hard as I could.

Late in the spring Miss Rehwinkle came into my room and sat down. "We're getting chummy," I thought. In a way we were too, as chummy as Miss Rehwinkle ever got. She respected my family and I think she liked me. We had been together almost two years.

"I am taking a month's vacation," she told me.

"About time," I said. "I've admired the way you run the hospital. I don't see how you keep it up."

"I'm going to visit my brother in Indiana and some cousins. I want to attend a convention of my church in Kentucky. Some returning missionaries are going to give an account of their service."

I knew she was a faithful member of her church. She always said grace before meals. "Who'll run the place while you're gone?"

"A Miss Eric, Isabel Eric. She's the operating room supervisor and temporary administrator at St. Francis Hospital in Waterloo."

"A good Lutheran bringing in a Catholic?"

"Oh, James. Let us not be narrow-minded. Miss Eric has a fine reputation."

"I'm just joking."

Miss Eric arrived, a black-haired, dark-eyed, compact bundle of energy. "On the young side," I thought. "And I'll bet she doesn't run as tight a ship as Miss Rehwinkle did."

She didn't, though she managed well enough. But I noticed a relaxed air among the nurses and maids, a little letdown as shifts changed and reports were made. But Uncle George said she was a whiz in the operating room.

One day a patient wheeled into my room, a small man with a wizened, old face. "I say, chum, can I come in?" He had a broad British accent.

"Sure, come in. I'm Jim Hearst."

"George Maynard here. My first visit to the States. My brothers farm south of Hudson. I stepped in front of their beastly old mower and it snipped a tendon in my heel."

I nodded. "From England—you a cockney?"

"Not really. My mother didn't give me that fortune. A true cockney must be born within sound of Bow Bells."

I seldom visited other patients. They came and went. A week or ten days and they disappeared. I usually stopped in to say hello to folk I knew. The older nurses used to bring babies and lay them in my arms. They joked about it. "When these babies grow up you can say that you held them."

But George Maynard sounded interesting, with an accent so broad you could walk on it. I asked, "You a farmer in England?"

"Not hardly. I was a jockey." He smiled a thin smile, skin tight over his cheekbones. "I'm too old now and too heavy."

You don't look very heavy to me, I thought. "In the army?"

"Four years in the mud in France. Perishing in the trenches. You Yanks made it just in time. We'd come to the end of our rope."

The depression that weighed on me lifted with this new acquaintance. George Maynard showed me a new side of life: the sporting world. I heard tales of English racetracks, of the way horses win or don't win, of bribing jockeys, the way bookmakers juggle the odds. I heard how George won the Irish Sweepstakes and was disqualified because he struck another jockey in the face with his whip.

"The bugger crowded me against the rails," George explained. "He knew my horse could win. I slashed him across his dirty face." George paused. "I never went in for dirty tricks."

We met every day, either in his room or mine or on the sun porch. George and his stories eased me out of the mire of introspection. We played cards. George showed me half a dozen card tricks. I found I could use my hands well enough to work them with fair success.

"Keep practicing," George said. "Do your bloody hands good."

He showed me a game called "three-card monte," a game gamblers played with suckers on trains. "I can't do it very well but you should see a real tout do it."

He could fool me. He shuffled three cards rapidly, then asked, "Which is the king?" For the life of me I couldn't outguess him, even when I saw the king before he started to move the cards around. It was like betting on which shell the pea is under.

George persuaded Miss Eric and Miss Trus to play bridge. Nearly every evening after supper we played bridge until bedtime. I looked forward to these evenings and dreaded the time when George would leave.

But George did not leave. The Achilles tendon did not heal. He needed more surgery and another cast. "I'll play in your yard a few more weeks," George said.

George, with his good-natured fatalistic attitude, helped me over the pain of Prue's absence, Robert's illness, and my slow progress.

I noticed a shy companionship beginning between George and Miss Eric. I thought, "Both Catholics, why not?" But the break-up was my own fault.

I hadn't had much experience with liquor. Alcoholic drinks were frowned on at home. Sometimes at fraternity meetings somebody would provide bootleg booze. It was the fashion to evade the law during Prohibition.

One day a fraternity brother brought me a pint of whiskey. I didn't think about it as illegal possession. I mentioned the whiskey at one of our bridge games. I invited George to have a few highballs before supper. But when I went to get it, it was gone.

I called in Miss Eric and said, "Someone took my whiskey."

"Yes," she said. "I did."

I digested this fact a minute. It seemed a breach of confidence that I thought had been established at the bridge games. My temper flared. "It's none of your damn business. That is my whiskey."

"It is my damn business. As long as I'm running this hospital I'll not be guilty of breaking the law. We even have a federal inspector who comes each month to check on our narcotics and opiates."

"I could have one of my uncles prescribe whiskey for me as medicine."

"Yes," Miss Eric said. "You just do that."

But I had the last word. I overheard one of the nurses chatting in the hall. She spoke of Mr. Maynard going for a ride the night before with Miss Eric.

The next morning when Miss Eric stopped to check the linen, I said, "I hope you and George enjoyed my whiskey during your ride last night.

She froze. Then her face flushed and her eyes dilated with shock and anger. She left without a word.

"That'll give her something to think about," I said to myself. But I knew it was a low blow and not true. That was the end of our bridge

games and almost the end of the friendship between George and Miss
Eric.

I renewed my exercises with desperate determination. If one of the
nurses had time, she would help me walk around the room. There were
times when I could rise to my feet from a sitting position all by myself.
Then there were times when I could not. But I persisted.

I stopped going to the nurses' dining room for my meals. I am
afraid I let my antagonism toward Miss Eric make me unfriendly. I
cooled toward George.

I slept badly. My appetite declined. I snapped at the nurses. Visitors often irritated me. I thought more and more of self-destruction.
Who would really care, I argued. Who would miss me? I did not realize
how self-centered I had become.

One noon when most of the nurses were at lunch and the remaining
floor nurse was busy with a patient, I rolled into the superintendent's
office and opened the safe. This knack of being able to open up simple
combination locks showed up at college. I discovered I could open any
of the combination locks on the lockers. The coach warned me not to
mention this. If something was missing from a locker I might be accused.

The safe was only a three-digit combination lock and I opened it
easily. I had seen Miss Rehwinkle take out the morphine vials and I
knew where they were. I picked up a vial marked "one quarter grain"
and stuffed it in my shirt pocket. No one would miss it until the federal
man made his check of the inventory against use. And it was enough to
put me away. I hid it in my dresser drawer behind some letters. It
eased my mind to know it was there.

George would not let me cast him off. He came for a visit every
day. He asked me to go out to the Maynard brothers' farm for supper.
He arranged it with Miss Eric.

His brother Alf came to get us. He was a tall, limber, horse-faced
man who picked me up as if I were a bundle of straw and stowed me in
the car. George hobbled from his wheelchair and away we went.

I had to admit I enjoyed the trip. The three men lived in an old
farmhouse. Inside it was bare and bleak as if a family had just moved
out. But the raucous good humor of the brothers, their quick, sharp
talk, the British slang I only half understood, and their solicitous concern for George and for me made me forget my depression.

"My gosh," I said to Tom, a square-faced, slightly stooped man.
"You guys don't look like farmers to me."

"Blimey, old chap," Tom said. "After the war the streets of London were crowded with ex-soldiers hunting jobs. The dole wouldn't
even wipe your ass. So we came to America and here we are."

Albert, the youngest, said, "We've got money in the bank, credit
at the stores, and girls on Saturday night. What more do we want?"

They pushed me up to the table to share scrambled eggs, fried potatoes, bread and butter, applesauce and cookies. They all drank strong hot black tea. It tasted good.

"Old Tom here throws up a bit of good food. I think we'll keep him," Alf quipped.

Tom said, "I cook, wash up, clean the floors. Somebody could hire me for a housekeeper."

George told me, "Tom was gassed pretty bad in the war. His lungs are eaten away. He can't do hard work."

After supper they all sat around and smoked—all except Tom. He coughed a lot. I wondered why they did not wait until they were out of doors. But they were a jolly group and Tom did not complain. After a while Alf took George and me back to the hospital.

Alf told George, "I'm stepping on your heels, lad. I'm riding Griffith's saddle horse in the races next month."

"I'll come and see you," George said. "Don't break your bloody neck."

That night I slept well. "Maybe I just need to get out more."

I did but in a stranger way than I expected. One afternoon George and I took the elevator to the ground level and wheeled out under the trees. It was a hot summer day with no wind. The air shimmered, gnats buzzed. George tossed his magazine onto the yard swing and yawned. "Let's go downtown and see the sights," he said.

I closed my book. "Are you crazy? I wouldn't dare go down the hospital hill. Too steep for me to hold the wheelchair. My hands aren't strong enough."

"No danger, me boyo," George said. "Let me lead. I'll stop every five feet and let you bump into me. Nothing risked, nothing gained."

What the hell, I thought. "Push on. I'm right behind you."

We wheeled along the drive to the top of the hill. The hospital stood on a rise of ground. The hill was only a block long but it was steep.

"Right behind me," George said over his shoulder. "Never fear, I'll catch you."

He did. George rolled down a few feet, then turned into the curb to brace his chair. I came behind and bumped into him. Like mountain climbers, we rappelled our way down the hill.

When we reached the street I said, "Whew! We made it. But how will we get back up again?"

"Sufficient unto the day thereof," intoned George. "How far downtown?"

"Six or seven blocks. Let's push on." I gave my wheelchair a shove.

Brother, I thought. This is slow going. George could roll along at a fair gait, but I had to hook my thumbs in the spokes of the wheel. But push by push we made our way. The asphalt paving was so warm that the narrow tires of the wheelchairs cut in and left a track.

About halfway downtown a middle-aged woman came from her house with a tray bearing a plate of cookies and two glasses of lemonade. She said, "I saw you coming. Why, James Hearst, who would ever think you could be strong enough for this?"

I recognized her. She attended our church. "Mrs. Thomas, how nice of you. This is George Maynard. We're runaways, bound for the bright lights."

"You boys be careful. Keep to the sides of the street. Though, goodness knows, you're safe enough in this town."

We stopped at Sixth and Clay for a minute to rest in the shade. A car pulled up behind us and stopped. The Hilton sisters came around to where we sat. I had dated them both in high school. I introduced them to George.

"What do you think you're up to?" Leta asked.

"We're on our way downtown. Tired of hospital life."

"We'll do our good deed for the day," Neva said, "and push you to Washington Street. If you turn there, it's downhill."

"Never deny a woman her privilege," George said.

I grinned. "You're full of pithy sayings today."

The girls pushed us to Washington Street, said good-bye, and went their way. It was downhill until we came to the Rock Island tracks. George said he could make it. I did not think I could. While we sat there arguing, the head mechanic from Rasmussen's Chevrolet Garage came over wiping his hands on some cotton waste. "Jim Hearst, you bugger you, how are you?"

"Better than I expected but not as good as I hope. Listen, Frank, do us a favor. Boost us over the tracks."

"No sooner said than done."

He pushed me across, then did the same for George. "Jim, turn down toward Main at the next block. It's downhill. You can park in the shade of the Olympia Candy Kitchen across from Berg's Drug. You boys have gone far enough. You look tired, Jim."

We stopped by the side of the Olympia, about fifty feet from Main Street. I was glad to rest.

Gus Rejos, the Greek owner, came out. "You want ice cream? Soda pop? I get you a watermelon."

From across the street John Berg left his drugstore to bring us a carton to put our melon rinds in. George looked at me. "Do you know everybody in this town?"

"Damn near, George. It's getting late. We ought to go back."

From the circle of friends around us, two young men offered to push us back. Earl Miller pushed me and Tom Waugh pushed George. We had just turned up Sixth Street toward the hospital when a car pulled up behind us with squealing brakes. An elderly man staggered toward us.

"Isabel said you were gone and I said I would find you." He steadied himself by grasping one of the chair backs. "She's my daughter, you know."

Earl looked bewildered. "Who is Isabel?"

The man shouted, "She's superintendent of the hospital."

Earl said in a low voice. "He's pretty well loaded."

I turned to George. "You know anything about this?"

George squirmed as if in discomfort. "Only that she once said her father had a drinking problem."

We heard the car start behind us. The motor roared. I looked back in time to see the car bounce against the curb, head out into the street, and bounce back toward us.

"Jesus, watch out!" Tom Waugh yelled. He tipped George out and leaped for the parking, dragging George with him. Earl tipped me out of the wheelchair and dragged me up on the grass.

The car stopped suddenly but not before it had run against both wheelchairs. Earl braced me against his legs so I could sit up. The old man sat still behind the wheel. Then he slowly backed up and drove down the street.

I said, "You guys were sure quick on the trigger or George and I might be lying under those wheelchairs. Now what?"

Tom said, "I'll call Dad's garage and have somebody bring a car. Then we can get you back to the hospital."

Supper was long past by the time I reached my room. The maids and cooks had gone home. But I was more concerned about our narrow escape. Miss Hoskins brought me a sandwich and a glass of milk.

"Where's Miss Eric?" I demanded. "I want to see her."

Miss Hoskins shook her head. "Calm yourself. I guess her father has been a problem ever since her mother died."

"Damn him. He might have killed us."

"Would he have hit you if you had been on the hospital grounds where you should have been?"

I stumbled over that. "We just took a little ride."

"The hospital is responsible for its patients, James. You should know that. You've been here long enough."

I cooled down when I thought of what Miss Hoskins said. Of course she was right.

"I hope the hospital carries insurance on those chairs. They looked pretty sad to me."

Miss Hoskins pursed her lips. Just then Miss Eric came in. "I'm glad you both are not hurt. My father is at the police station. We'll see what should be done about your absence from the hospital grounds. That's my responsibility."

Her eyes, still bright with tears, held me in a steady gaze. Her drawn face made her look old. The pathos of the situation touched me.

"I'm sorry," I said. "And I apologize for leaving the hospital without permission. I'm sorry about your father too."

She stood straight, as if she had a ramrod down her back. Her voice was cold. "I'll discuss the destruction of hospital property with the trustees."

I saluted her and said under my breath, "Atta girl, Isabel. Never say die."

The next day I told Mother about our escapade. She said, "Maybe you had better come home, James. Robert keeps asking for you. He says he wants you to talk to. And he would like to have you read to him when the pain is bad, those Wodehouse stories that make him laugh.''

"I spoke to Father about this. I still need lots of help."

"I think we can manage. We've talked it over. It would be good for all of us to have you home."

The next morning Miss Rehwinkle came in. "Good morning. What's this I hear about you?"

"You're back," I said. "About time. Did you have a good vacation."

"Splendid. My family are all well. I hear you had an accident."

"Maybe it's time I left the hospital. I've been here two years. I'll miss you and Miss Hoskins and the other girls. I can never thank you for all you've done for me."

Miss Rehwinkle smiled. "You taught us something too. We won't forget you."

I said, "You in particular have made me feel at home here and that isn't easy in a hospital. But I ought to go home now."

Miss Rehwinkle sighed. "Yes, and it's time for me to leave also. I must submit my resignation to the board before it's announced publicly. Please don't mention it, James."

"Do you mean it? Are you going to leave?"

"I've decided to serve my church by becoming a medical missionary to India. I leave the States on November first."

"You're a dedicated person and I admire you. But Sartori will not be the same. No one can run this hospital the way you do. If you leave, I'm glad I'm leaving."

"You have work to do too, James. You can be a support for your family. I grieve for your parents. Help them keep up their courage and poor Robert's."

I was a bit embarrassed. "Mother will want you to have dinner with us before you go. When you get to India will you write to me?"

She nodded and left the room.

But I had a duty to perform. When I knew Miss Rehwinkle was alone in the office, I took the vial of morphine from its hiding place and wheeled in to see her.

"This belongs in the safe," I said. "I want to return it."

Miss Rehwinkle raised her eyebrows. She looked surprised. Then with a voice full of suspicion she asked, "James Hearst, where did you get this?"

"Out of the safe."

"But the safe must always be locked. Who was careless?"

"No one. I opened the safe myself and took it. There's no one else to blame."

I could tell she did not believe me but I could not help that.

Home Again

HOME AGAIN, this time to stay. I hid a stab of apprehension under my feeling of welcome. I eyed the bedstead set up in the parlor and the commode and urinal beside it. I was glad to be home but disturbed by the intrusion of hospital features into the parlor's gentle formality. I kept asking, "How will we manage? How can I be taken care of?" I tried to keep these questions out of my smile.

I knew that each member of the family had work to do. I wondered how much my routine would add to the established ways. I told myself that it was a little like having an idiot grown-up child. But perhaps my family worried about me as much as I worried about upsetting them.

"Oh, shit," I said aloud. "I've been too long in the hospital. Time I was weaned."

Father said, "You'll have to tell us, Jim, just what help you need. We don't know how much you can do for yourself."

"I still can't do an awful lot," I confessed. "I can't even undress myself."

When bedtime came, Bob and Chuck helped me to bed. "Leave the duck on the floor where I can reach it," I said. "Sometimes I pee in my sleep and don't wake up in time. I hope Mother put a rubber sheet on the bed."

Just as they were leaving with the lamp I called to them. "Listen, you guys. It's one thing to have me come home for Sunday dinner and everybody scurry around to help. Now I'm here all the time. Don't get mad when I want something."

I slept restlessly. I did not wet the bed. Just before breakfast my brothers came in and helped me dress. They brought a pan of water so I could wash my hands and face. Then leaning on their arms I walked to the table.

I made it through the first night, I thought. At the table I ate my bacon by picking it up with my fingers. I asked for unbuttered toast to save someone the job of spreading it for me. I was determined to pare my needs to the bare essentials.

I knew that no matter how devoted the family was and how they all wanted to help me now I must not impose on them. Right now I was treated as a guest and this would not last. I did not want it to.

49

It saddened me to look at Bob with his thin face and the wasted muscles on his hands. Bob ate a good breakfast and joked with me. But the signs were on him. As a sturdy tree begins to wilt from dry rot, so Bob's healthy body began to crumble. I could see it. I had lived too long in the hospital not to be aware of symptoms. I wondered how much my parents noticed. Bob still pretended to handle me with a rough touch but the spark had gone out of our play. The skin on his neck showed the deep brown color that came from many X-ray treatments. This was the site of the original lesion.

Monday morning started the week. Louise hurried off to the college high school where she supervised student teachers. Chuck helped finish the chores, leaped into his clothes, cranked the Model T, and hoped to make a nine o'clock class. This was his senior year.

Father sent the men silo-filling and he nailed boards on the corn-crib to get ready for the harvest. Mother made beds, washed the dishes, and went out in the garden to clean up her flower beds and prepare for winter. A typical fall workday for the family.

Bob helped me to a chair in the living room and then lay down on the couch. "If you want anything, just holler," he said. "I lie down for awhile in the morning. Don't have much poop these days."

"Just one thing," I said. "When I have to take a leak will you empty the duck? I can't get used to the idea of having Mother do it."

Bob took a short nap. When he woke up he said, "Why have we always been such a Puritan family? We seem to pretend that no one ever goes to the can or screws girls. Hell, Jim, you and I weren't out of short pants when we led in the bull to breed cows and helped the old man sort sows for the boar. But when it comes to people . . . I just don't know."

"Probably inherited it from Grandfather Hearst. He had New England coming out of his ears. You know, Bob, once Father tried to give me sex instruction. I was just a little kid, but mean. He asked if I knew when a cow had a calf did it come out of her rear end or her side. Of course I said her side just to see what he would say."

Bob chuckled. "I'll bet that shut him up. We didn't need any sex education around the farm. In the spring we saw colts and calves and pigs being born. Remember how we peeked in the incubator to watch chickens hatch out of the shell? We knew what the stud horse and bull and boar were for."

He stretched and yawned. "I'd give a lot for a good fuck right now. But I don't suppose the girls will go near me with this thing I've got."

"Sure they will. You look better than you feel. You always had lots of girls. They won't desert you. Gosh, Bob, remember the dirty trick you played on Chuck when you took his girl home from a fraternity dance because you liked her better than you did your own date? Man, was he hopping mad."

Bob grinned but he said, "I really feel awful some days."

I said to myself, "Jesus, will we talk about it now? What can I say to encourage him that won't make him mad?"

After awhile Father came in. "You need an enema, Jim?"

He pushed the commode out into the middle of the floor. "Let's get you on this thing. Then I'll get the syringe and soap suds."

I gritted my teeth. "Oh, goddamnit, goddamnit all. Why do I have to go through this? No privacy at all!"

Bob said, "Jim, your guts should work. Your heart does and your lungs. Bend over, push your belly against your knees."

I tried it and it worked—not easily, but it worked.

"Wait a couple of days," Bob said, "and when your ass end feels heavy Chuck or I will carry you down to the privy. The hell with this stuff."

There were no more enemas. I was rid of one ball and chain.

The next morning Father put the parallel bars out in the yard. He fastened a seat at one end, high enough so I could slide off it and be almost erect. I could rest there when I got tired. I could get on my feet alone when I wanted to start exercising again.

Every morning while the warm weather held, Bob carried me out to the bars. "Sure it's tough, but concentrate, make the muscles go. Remember you had to warm up before you pitched a ball game. Well, take a few years and warm up."

The man who delivered barrels of gasoline for the tractor came over one morning when I was trying to walk. He said, "Don't make much progress, do you. Too bad."

Bob was sitting on the porch and called out, "Even slower, Fergus, than getting over a dose of clap."

Later I asked, "What was that about?"

Bob laughed. "The boys tell me that Fergus picked up a doll over at Electric Park and she gave him a little present he can't get rid of."

"I wish I had your guts, Bob," I said.

"With Fergus? Tell him where he can stick it. What a crow."

It shamed me to see my brother rise so easily above his illness. My thoughts crept around like a beggar with a tin cup. I labored at my exercises without much hope yet determined to do what I could.

I sat at a desk in the house and poked out letters on the portable typewriter Aunt Jennie Curtis had brought me. Deep inside me, like a spark in a bed of ashes, burned the idea that maybe I could write something. I remembered how in country school I had made rhymed couplets out of the short stories in our reader. Even though the teacher encouraged me, it must have been pretty bad stuff.

The problem of how to make a living began to haunt me. I wanted to free myself from dependence on my family. Chuck would probably farm or teach. But what could I do?

Bob was the farmer. He was big and strong, and had a knack with animals. It was hard to believe he could not get well. I tried not to think about it. Bob and I had always worked well together. We had a room together, slept together, even double-dated together. I believed that there was a chance for him in spite of what the doctors said.

The year deepened toward winter. Farm work crowded to the end of harvest. Father, always involved in farm organization work, was elected president of the Iowa Farm Bureau and moved to the Des Moines office.

Farm prices had dropped into a well. After the war, Herbert Hoover, in charge of the food program, withdrew support for farm prices and the markets collapsed. The huge food factory farmers had built at the government's insistence—all those plowed up acres of grasslands and hill country—closed down. Farmers suffered a depression all through the twenties while the rest of the country went on a stock market spree.

"It's a good thing the old man got the job," Bob said. "We need the money."

I agreed and said, "At least we don't have to pay my hospital bill every month."

Chuck quit college at the end of the winter quarter. "I can't go to school and keep the farm going. With Dad gone, it's more than I can handle."

Perhaps he was too young and inexperienced in handling help or perhaps the men after the war were too restless, but hired help came and went. It seemed to me we were always looking for hired men.

"Don't throw your weight around," I told Chuck. "Tell them what to do but let them do it their way."

"Yeah," Chuck answered, "and have a half-assed job."

Bob just shook his head. He had enough problems of his own.

It bothered me, this procession of hired men. "Don't be so damn bullheaded," I growled at Chuck. "Just get the work done. It doesn't have to be done your way."

Chuck glared at me. "If you're so smart, you come out and run things."

I was hung up on a dilemma. I was dependent on Chuck and Bob for help. I couldn't afford to alienate them. I had to pull my punches and not say what I wanted to say.

I knew Chuck worked hard. He worked too hard. He would do better if he planned operations more carefully and did not try to do everything himself.

"If I could just get up and around by myself!" I often thought. Each time Chuck and I argued, I tasted the sour fruit of my dependence. My experience in the army had taught me when to enforce an order and when to lay off.

The farm buildings and fences began to deteriorate. Barn doors swung on one hinge. Fence posts rotted off and left gaps for the cows to get through. Disease spread in the hoghouse and pigs shriveled and died and the brood sows aborted. A water pipe froze and burst because the water had not been turned off.

I exploded, "Jesus Christ, Chuck, can't you look after things any better than this?"

Chuck turned a stoney face to me. "Aw, shut up. I'm doing the best I can."

Bob said, "Don't ride him, Jim. He's too young to handle all this responsibility. He's got more on his plate than he can eat. He helps you, drives me to X ray, takes Mother shopping, tries to run the farm. He can't manage all that."

"I suppose not," I admitted.

Bob said, "Don't forget this either, Jim. You and I got out of the house pretty young and helped Dad and the hired men. Mother needed help and Chuck stayed a long time helping with the chickens and garden. He never worked with the men like we did."

I redoubled my efforts at exercise. I needed to get out and around.

Spring came and moved toward summer. Somehow the oats were sowed and the corn planted. The county extension office mailed out reports of a new hay crop called alfalfa. It sounded too good to be true—three crops in one year. But it would not grow in acid soil.

"It's not really new," the county agent said. "It's been grown in Europe for centuries. Thomas Jefferson grew it on his plantation. But it was called 'lucerne'."

Chuck took soil samples and had them tested. Our Tama loam all showed an acid bias. But an application of lime would correct it. Bob and I studied the reports, talked it over with Chuck, and decided to try alfalfa on a ten-acre plot. The soil needed three tons to the acre to correct the acidity. Thirty tons of lime would be a carload. The county agent said the limestone quarry at Dubuque had the best lime—soft and easily dissolved. It would change the pH of the ground most quickly.

I ordered a carload and asked the railroad agent to have the car spotted on the Iowa State Teachers College siding three and one half miles from the farm. This was as close as we could get it. Chuck borrowed dump boards for the wagons from one of the county supervisors. The county used them when gravel was hauled for the roads.

Chuck hired two extra men when the car came in and went at it. The lime was shoveled out of the freight car by hand and into the wagons. Horses pulled the wagons to the farm. There the dump boards were drawn away one by one and the lime fell on the ground. This saved the men from having to shovel it off. At that, it was backbreaking work. These were days when men worked harder than machines. Chuck then sowed the alfalfa seed.

The neighbors poked fun at us and all our work. Why not stay with timothy and clover? They were good, dependable hay crops.

I said to Bob, "Somebody has to be the pioneer. And wait until we plow up this sod and see the corn crop it will raise."

Fifty years later, I wonder how many farmers now would go to all that work. Today, when a farmer wants lime, he calls a lime hauler who spreads it from his truck. No one lifts a shovelful.

By midsummer Bob began to fail rapidly. He no longer felt strong enough to go for X-ray treatments. Some toxic substance in the disease gave him a terrible case of hives. His whole body broke out in blisters and the itching drove him half wild. Some days he wore no clothes at all, just covered himself with a sheet. Mother cared for him tenderly. The doctors could give him no relief. Then, as suddenly as they came, the hives disappeared. But Bob was weak and spent most of his days lying on the couch.

After many struggles, I gained enough strength to raise myself to my feet from a sitting position. I needed a chair with arms so I could boost myself up. Then with a pair of crutches I could shuffle from one room to another. When a crutch tip slipped I went down. Chuck or one of the hired men would have to come in and pick me up. If the men were in the field I had a long wait. "But," I said grimly, "I'm getting there."

One day after lunch Mother opened the door for me and I struggled over the threshold to the porch. The railing circled two sides of the house. A rambler rose that climbed one of the pillars bloomed furiously. Grandfather Hearst had located his buildings on a rise of ground. I could see the college smokestack and, ten miles across the fields, smoke from the John Deere foundries.

The sun warmed me. Patches of sun and shade dappled the lawn. Warm air eddied around me with a light touch. I went in the house and sat beside Bob as he lay on the couch.

"I wish we could drive off in this room to the top of the next hill and take off the roof," I said to Bob.

Bob did not answer for a few minutes. Then he said, "You know, Jim, we always worked too hard or were too busy to appreciate the out-of-doors. Now it's too late, at least for me."

"I know, Bob, I know. Hard work seemed our mission in life. I hold it against Grandpa Hearst that he could never see any sense in fun—in just loafing, playing or fishing or just inviting your soul. Church and work were his goals."

"Don't let it get Chuck, will you. He works awfully hard," Bob said. Then he added, "You were pretty bossy, Jim, when we were kids."

"Yeah, cousin Helen always called me 'Grandpa Hearst' whenever I sounded off. I didn't know how to make suggestions. You know, Bob, every time we boys went anywhere, Father or Mother or both would say to me, 'Remember you're the oldest. Look after your younger brothers.' And so I ordered you and Chuck around because I took responsibility seriously."

I paused and then went on, "It cramped my style too. Lots of times when we visited Jim McAlvin in Waterloo, I wanted to run off with the boys my age but I stayed with you two."

Bob shut his eyes and rested. "We never knew that. I wish you had told us. Maybe it wouldn't have made any difference. All the Hearsts are great for telling someone else what to do."

I touched Bob's shoulder. "I wish I had known how to be more kind."

Bob thought a minute. "People aren't as decent to each other as they are to animals. A horse breaks a leg and we put it out of its misery. But I've got to go through this business to the end."

He shocked me. The whole family conspired to make Bob and ourselves believe he would recover. We had to pretend Bob believed us. I groped for an answer. "You do feel better some days, Bob."

"I'm going downhill, you can all see it. Do you suppose I jerked myself off too much? Would that cause cancer?"

"Good god, no. We all did it. All boys do it. Nobody knows why you got this, why anybody gets cancer. Don't torment yourself. Why, Bob, you have more guts than all of us put together."

"Skip it, skip it. Let's just hope I can hold out without going to pieces."

"Oh, Bob, goddamnit. Goddamn everything in this stupid world."

Bob shifted to a more comfortable position. "Let's cut it out. We're getting maudlin. Read me some Wodehouse. I can still laugh at Bertie and Jeeves."

We never talked this way again. It seemed a kind of farewell. We did not easily expose to each other our inner thoughts and feelings. We went on as before, being as cheerful as we could, trying to conceal the heavy weight on our spirits. Bob slowly withdrew to some other world where he lived out the part he was called for. Farther and farther he drew away until he no longer responded when I read to him.

One afternoon Chuck said, "I've got to run downtown for a new plow lay. Come on, Jim, go with me." He carried me out to the car.

When we returned Mother met us at the door. "Robert is gone," she said. Dry-eyed, empty-handed, she seemed to me like a tragic figure in some elemental drama. There was nothing left to say.

A farm does not wait on human suffering and despair. It has its own round of births and deaths to consider. Whether the work is done or not, the land and animals keep their place in the rhythms of the seasons.

We attempted to close the gap left by Bob's absence. We shared a burden of grief, though we seldom spoke of the wound we would carry the rest of our lives.

It was a time of uniting our forces. The drain had been severe on our emotions and finances. The returns from the sale of grain and hay were not enough to meet the bills owed. Farmers who lived through the twenties never forgot the vise that squeezed them.

The Hearsts joined forces and met the crisis with all the muscle we could muster. We set up one account in the bank and all income was fed into it. Louise gave her salary and Mother the money from the sale of eggs and cottage cheese. I gave my insurance check and Father his salary and the income from the farm.

First the hospital, medical, and doctors' bills were paid. Then the insurance, back taxes, and feed bills. The hired men's wages had been paid monthly because they had their own bills to pay.

"It seems strange," I wrote in a letter to my doctor aunt in Milwaukee, "to see one of our hired men who lost his farm still driving his Cadillac. We drive a secondhand Model T Ford. The old Haynes sits in the shed on four flat tires. We go out and look at it when we need to feel important."

The Hearsts did not give hostages to fortune. Louise brought her friends home on weekends. They roused the house with songs, chatter, and midnight snacks of sardines and cheese on rye bread. Some of Louise's men friends brought bootleg alcohol and they spiked near beer with it.

Chuck loved to sing and he brought home some of his friends. Mother and I joined the groups. The festivity, the parties helped us over the loss of Bob and put up a "No Admittance" sign against our financial problems.

One of Louise's friends, Olive Barker, taught in the music department at the college. One weekend she "borrowed" a set of musical instruments. She brought them out to the farm. I could hook my fingers over the slide, so she gave me a trombone. Chuck had a clarinet, Olive a French horn, Peg Fullerton a violin, and Louise the piano. We seemed at our best in "Moonlight and Roses," though Mother said it sounded better from the garden than it did in the house.

But we were not through with disaster. I reminded myself how, in the Greek tragedies, Fate dogged the characters. On a hot July afternoon of the following year Mother cleaned the basement. She piled the trash in the furnace and lit it. Then she took a bath and changed her clothes. She came downstairs quickly and said, "I hear a rustling noise overhead in the attic. Oh, oh . . . look out the window at the smoke."

Now I heard it. "The house is on fire, Mother."

She stared at me. "What shall we do? How can I get you out of the house?"

I waved an impatient hand. During the past year I had learned to get to my feet and reach for the crutches by myself. "Don't worry about me. Call central and have her ring the neighbors. Then call the fire department." I didn't know if they would make a run outside the city limits, but they did.

Father was home for the week helping Chuck and the men make

hay. They were out in the hayfield but they must have seen the smoke almost as soon as Mother heard the fire. The wagons came clattering into the yard behind the galloping horses. A neighbor, cultivating corn just opposite the house, came running across the road. He swept me up, crutches and all, and carried me across the yard.

Then the neighbors began to arrive. They stripped the inside of the house as quickly as they could and carried out beds, blankets, clothes, dressers. When the fire drove them downstairs they saved almost all the furniture there. Chuck and Nels picked up the piano as if it were a toy and carried it out on the lawn. A big man ran out of the house carrying a salt shaker in one hand and the pepper shaker in the other and stood yelling, "What shall I do with these?"

When the frame of a bed cracked a window as it was turned on the stair landing, a man shouted, "Careful of the window." In a few minutes the glass in the windows ran down like melting ice.

Somehow Aunt Clara in Waterloo got word of the fire and she came as fast as she could. She sat by me on a bank of grass across the road and we watched the house burn. "If we just had some weiners," I suggested.

She gave me a queer look. "You don't feel bad?"

"No, now we can have a house with an indoor bathroom, an oil furnace, a large kitchen sink with hot water. And, if I have my way, a fireplace."

Aunt Clara sighed. "It will be a godsend to your mother."

"We can live in half of Grandpa's house while the new house is being built. Nels and his family will squeeze into the other half. It shouldn't take forever to build a new house."

"How about money?"

I snorted. "No one was hurt. We saved most of our furniture. We can worry about money later."

That evening the president of one of the local lumber yards came to the door of Grandfather's house where we were eating supper. He said, "Don't get up. I just wanted to tell you, Charlie, that when you're ready to build, order what you need and we'll deliver it. Pay for it when you can." He cheered us with his words.

Another surprise came to me. It helped lift the dark cloud of my despair. One day while riding with Chuck, I shoved over behind the wheel of the Model T Ford, lifted my leg up on to the pedal, and shoved down. Away we went.

"I have plenty of shove-down strength," I told Chuck, "or I couldn't stand up. But no pull-back and not much direction."

"Learn to relax," Chuck said. "There's enough spring in the pedal to bring it back if you quit pushing. If you get in a jam, turn the key and shut off the motor."

The gas and spark operated from hand controls. There was no foot accelerator in those days. Soon I was driving round the yard. Then I ventured out to the fields. Sometimes I carried water to the men or a tool or part needed for a machine. Once I ran into a haystack and once a closed gate. But I soon found I could stop the car with the hand brake.

One afternoon I took a jug of water out to Chuck, who was disking cornstalks. I drove up beside the panting tractor that looked big as an engine on the railroad. "Do you suppose I could drive it?" I asked.

"One way to find out," Chuck said. "Let me boost you up on the seat."

I sat on the seat and looked around. Everything was big, powerful, and made of steel—even the seat and steering wheel. It made the front seat of the car seem like a baby carriage.

"Get your right foot up there on the clutch," Chuck said. "Now shove it down and I'll shift into low." My foot slid over the top of the clutch but the heel of my shoe caught and held. I shoved it down. What a strong spring! "Now when I open the throttle, ease back on the clutch," Chuck said. He gave the throttle a flip and the motor roared.

I let the clutch back too quickly and the tractor leaped forward. I grabbed hard on the steering wheel to keep from falling backwards. "Scared the shit out of me," I yelled at Chuck. But I could steer it, by gosh! I could steer it.

The tractor ran down the field with me holding it on the row.

"Can you shove in the clutch again?" Chuck asked.

I pushed. Again my foot slid over the top but the heel held. The tractor stopped abruptly. "I'm going to shift into second gear," Chuck said.

I nodded. The gears clashed. I tried to ease back on the clutch but the spring was too stiff. Again the tractor leaped forward, this time going faster. It was easier to steer. As we approached the end of the field Chuck called, "Start turning in plenty of time, don't get hung up on the fence."

I gripped and pulled. The tractor turned slowly in a wide arc. Chuck reached over from where he rode, braced against the fender, and gave the wheel a twist. "Now straighten her out. She's all yours."

Back we came to the end of the field where the car was. The big drive wheels were chopping into the ground with the steel lugs, the disk tumbling behind chewing up the cornstalks.

We stopped at the end. Chuck shut down the throttle. "Enough for the first time," he said and carried me to the car.

I sat in the car dazed with my success, my muscles all atremble. I could do it. I had driven the tractor. Maybe, in time, I could work again.

I drove back to the house, called a greeting to Grace, the hired man's wife, who was feeding the chickens. "What's happened to you?" she called.

Landscape— Iowa

No one who lives here
knows how to tell the stranger
what it's like, the land I mean,
farms all gently rolling,
squared off by roads and fences,
creased by streams, stubbled with groves,
a land not known by mountain's height
or tides of either ocean,
a land in its working clothes
sweaty with dew, thick-skinned loam,
a match for the men who work it,
breathes dust and pollen, wears furrows
and meadows, endures drought and flood.
Muscles swell and bulge in horizons
of corn, lakes of purple alfalfa,
a land drunk on spring promises,
half crazed with growth— I can no more
tell the secrets of its dark depths
than I can count the banners in a
farmer's eye at spring planting.

       ... James Hearst

She told Mother afterward, "Jim's eyes shone like two stars."

I thought of myself as a baby chick trying to peck its way out of the shell. This was another peck toward freedom. I knew that no matter how much I read or wrote or helped plan or achieved with my mind, what really counted was the work I could do. Perhaps this is true of all farms. It had always been true on the Hearst farm. I felt then that I might count for something.

The Farm and I

To Mother I said, "When I die, I want our hired men for pallbearers. They've boosted me on and off the tractors and in and out of the car enough times to be used to carrying me."

It had taken strength and ingenuity to conquer the tractor. Later, all four tractors had hand clutches and adjustable throttles. But, with that first machine, I had my hands full.

It was a 15-30 McCormick-Deering with long sharp lugs on steel drive wheels. It had no power take-off shaft. It had to be cranked to start and had no power unless the throttle was wide open.

The men at the Van Deest implement store were helpful. They welded an extra length on the gearshift lever, fastened a back to the seat, and tried to release the pressure of the clutch spring. When I got on the tractor, Chuck would strap my foot to the clutch pedal and the rest of me to the back of the seat. "If you ever get in trouble," Chuck advised me, "shut down the throttle and the engine will die."

The tractor had a hand lever to retard the spark so the man who cranked it would not have the engine kick back when he turned it over. Once, out of matches, Chuck tried to light a cigarette from the exhaust. While he was doing this, I retarded the spark and then opened it up suddenly. The engine backfired. Flame shot into the air and blew Chuck's cigarette all to pieces.

I had my problems. Once I turned too short and one of the lugs on the drive wheel caught the chain fastened to the end of the harrow. It took just an instant to pile the harrow on top of the tractor fender. "Good thing you stopped quick," Ed told me. "Another few feet and the drag would have been on top of you and good-bye Jim."

I sank into a wet spot in the field one afternoon and killed the engine. There I sat stewing in frustration. But the school bus went by and stopped. One of the high school boys, Kenny Nelson, ran across the field, cranked the tractor and helped me back the disk out of the mud. More than once George Petersen, Pete Ericksen's hired man, climbed the fence and started a stalled engine for me. We worked in fields just across the fence from each other. It got so that I was afraid to stop and use the pee can for fear some neighbor would call Mother on the phone and say, "Jim is stuck."

Sometimes I ran out of fuel. It always seemed to happen at the far

end of the field. When that happened, I just sat and waited until someone noticed. Soon the truck would come bounding across the field with
a can of fuel. Then I would sound off about someone sending me to the
field without a full fuel tank.

Finally Chuck tired of hearing me complain. "Listen, Jim," he
said. "You make it your business to see that the tank is full before you
go to the field. Then it will be up to you." Sometimes I forgot but since
it was my own fault, I quit bellyaching.

A few times, when work pressed, I asked Mother for a sandwich to
put in the toolbox and I stayed in the field all day. I would come home
triumphant but utterly pooped. I liked to be out in the fields with the
men and to be able to discuss field and crop conditions with the
neighbors.

I discovered my limitations. One end of an alfalfa field came
through the winter with a poor stand. Chuck said, "About ten acres,
let's plow it up and plant it to corn. It ought to raise a whacking big
crop."

There were no fences on either side of the plot to limit turning so I
made my first try at plowing. Chuck fastened the rope that let the
plows in and out of the ground where I could reach it easily. It went all
right. The tough sod kept the moldboards scouring, and I did not need
anyone to come and clean them off. It gave me a good feeling to plow
the whole piece without any help. "Now I'll disk it and level it so you
can plant it," I told Chuck.

I drove down to it the next day pulling the tandem disk. One of the
hired men rode on the fender to set the disk for me. Suddenly I was
aware of the peaks and valleys in the upturned sod. "She'll be rough,"
Ed said, cheerfully. "Be careful."

Rough was no name for it. Spring-plowed sod does not have time to
melt down and become mellow through the winter. The edges of the
furrows, being grass bound, stood up in ridges. "Better put it in low,"
Ed said. In low! I wished for a super low. The tractor climbed and
dropped, climbed and dropped. It was all I could do to hang onto the
steering wheel.

By the time I had finished the field I felt as though I had been put
through a cement mixer. "And only ten acres," I groaned. "Now I
must hit it crossways and level it down." The second time across did
not batter me as badly as the first time, but I was shaken up when I
finished. I shut off the motor and just sat there in a stupor.

I could not straighten the disk by myself and I didn't want to chew
up the field going to the house so I sat and waited. After a while Chuck
drove down in the car to help me. "Let me get in the car, Chuck. I'm
beat."

Chuck lifted me into the car. "She was kind of upsy-daisy, huh,"
Chuck said. When I did not answer, he asked, "You all right? You look
tired."

"I've just got to sit here for a while in something that doesn't move. Go ahead with the tractor. I'll come along pretty soon." Lord, I was weary.

I did not eat any supper. The next morning I could not get out of bed alone. For two days I sat around the house, my muscles sore and aching. The third day I could move without pain, and in the afternoon I went out and disked cornstalks. But a week went by before I fully recovered tone of muscle and spirit. It's a hard way to learn, but I never forgot that there may not be limits to my ambitions but there were limits to achieving them.

Along in April sometime Will Isley, one of our neighbors, came to see me. He cleared his throat, twisted his head in a characteristic gesture, and said, "We elected you secretary of the school board at the March meeting."

"You what?" I must have looked stunned.

"Why not? You can write, can't you—keep the minutes, write orders to the treasurer, keep track of the money we get from the supervisors. You have to post notices of the annual election, but Chuck can do that. You have to come to the annual meeting and keep the minutes like I said. You can't vote on board decisions but you don't have to keep still either."

I was both pleased and apprehensive. "Let me talk to Chuck about it."

"I've already talked to him. He says it's up to you. I brought the secretary's book and order blanks with me. You'll see your father used to be secretary. Might as well keep it in the family."

"I'd sure like to if I can, Will."

"Everybody should pull their weight in community affairs. We thought that this is one way you can help." He twisted his head again as he often did when pleased.

This opened a door for me. I was a recluse, afraid to come out of my shell in public. I had the idea that people shunned me. Because of this I no longer cared to keep in touch with my college friends. I refused to go to concerts and lectures. At times I avoided going to the big family gatherings. "I just have to sit," was my excuse.

But the real reason went deeper. My image of myself was badly damaged. I would not forget my past. My mind would remind me of my athletic ability, the dances I had attended, how I played pool with the housemen in the billiard parlor and knew a couple of bootleggers. And now I couldn't go to the bathroom in a strange place. Once I broke colts for my father, stacked straw on the threshing gang, pitched semipro ball, took charge of the farm when Father was away. Now I had to be carried up steps and lifted into cars. I owned an unruly bladder.

It wasn't that people were unkind. They were almost too kind. The barber came out of his shop to take my arm as I walked in with Chuck's help. If Chuck wasn't around, the mechanics from the implement stores would come to the house to consult me. Chuck always stood ready to help. The hired men too. Mother encouraged me. Louise, bless her heart, brought me armload after armload of books from the library. Uncle George often drove out to the farm to check on my condition. But that was partly the trouble. I did not want to be deferred to. I wanted the satisfaction of going my own way.

When waves of depression overwhelmed me, I withdrew into a swampy retreat where I was hard to reach. I would have periods of not speaking. Other times, if I spoke my words were hurtful, aimed at whoever was close by—Mother, Louise, Chuck. At those times I wished I could live in a cave and be a hermit.

My father reminded me of the selfishness of my behavior. I lay face down on my bed one Sunday afternoon drowning in misery, shaken by dry sobs. Father, home from Des Moines for the weekend, sat beside me. He put his hand on my shoulder. "Don't give way, Jim. We count on you to rise above your troubles. Your mother has all the burden she can carry. She looks to you to make life more cheerful by ignoring what you can't help."

I turned to face Father. "At times it seems more than I can stand."

Father nodded. "But it need not ruin your life or ours. Your example raises our spirits, holds the family together. Don't forget you have an obligation too."

My father's words not only sank in, they shocked me. They made me realize how much we all depended on each other. Never again did I show distress, or hint at suicide, or overdraw on the family's goodwill. My states of depression thereafter were my private business.

Slowly Chuck and I began to upgrade the farm. We bought woven wire and creosoted posts to replace dilapidated fences. We had the barn painted, planted a windbreak of pine and fir trees, set out an orchard of apple and plum trees, and planted a few grape vines. Chuck set out a hedge of honeysuckle bushes along the road so Mother could work in the garden in privacy. We moved the chicken house away from our house and built a three-car garage in its place with room for our car, Louise's car, and the farm truck.

We tried to find out how much money Father still owed his brothers and sisters and how much back interest was due. Even Dr. Ida, Mother's sister, had loaned Father money. "We will never get it all paid off," I said, astonished by the amount still owed.

"We can start with one debt at a time," Chuck said, somewhat shaken too.

"We're always running an overdraft at the bank."

Uncle Will, one of the bank's directors, had a suggestion. "Why don't you leave five or six hundred dollars in your account. Then you wouldn't have overdrafts."

I faced him with a downside grin. "Why, Uncle Will, when we have five hundred dollars we whack it on our bills just to keep our heads above water."

Something had to be done to increase the farm's income. The sale of corn, oats, and hay did not bring in enough money. Father, like Grandfather, maintained a herd of purebred Shorthorns. Father sold bulls to other breeders. He went to all the farm sales, knew who needed a bull, and knew how to sell one. Neither Chuck nor I had the talent nor the enthusiasm for the business.

"Hell, let's cut the bulls and feed them out as steers."

Chuck shook his head. "No, Dad wouldn't like it. This herd is part of his life. The purebred business is an art. To be a big wheel in the Shorthorn business you must either have a lot of money to buy quality or be an artist at crossing bloodlines."

I said, "All right, let's buy a few fancy bred cows and put a bit of gold leaf on our herd."

We attended a few Shorthorn sales. I told Mother, "It's like being in church. Before the sale a few old-timers, hats in hand, stand in front and recite the text of all the great Shorthorn families, the important bulls, the prize-winning bloodlines. We all sit there solemn as deacons."

We bought a few good cows from local breeders, all Scotch females, not just Scotch topped. Then the Allen Cattle Company from Colorado came to Des Moines for a dispersal sale. It was a chance at top-quality cattle.

The day of the sale was terrible—cold, windy, roads blocked with snow, a regular Iowa blizzard. In response to my inquiry, one of the fieldmen wired back, "Allen sells today."

The Hearst brothers crept behind a snowplow from Marshalltown to Ames. When we reached the sale pavilion in Des Moines, there were only a few men in overcoats huddled in the bleachers. "May be bargains for us today," I said.

A group of three men from the University of Minnesota bought the first bull for two thousand dollars. Chuck, pop-eyed at the price, said, "We may as well go home."

This was during the Depression. Two thousand dollars looked like a million to us.

But we finally bought a cow, of the Missie family, for three hundred dollars. She was sold as with calf, but the calf never appeared. The Allen Cattle Company refused to make restitution. That was the last sale we attended.

The new home pleased us. Two bathrooms, a porcelain sink with a drainboard in the kitchen, hardwood floors, and hot water under pressure. But the pressure came from a pump Chuck worked by hand in the basement. It made us all shrink when visitors let the water run to get a glass of cold water. We knew how much of Chuck's efforts went into that running water.

At last I could stand it no longer. "Damn it, let's buy a gas engine and a jack. We won't have electricity for a while yet." So we did.

A room on the first floor, just off the bathroom, served as a study and bedroom for me. At last I had a place of my own. Mother found a large cherrywood desk in Grandfather's house, one that Grandfather had had the Nauman Company in Waterloo build for him. It stood in front of the south windows. A walnut spool bed of Grandmother's occupied the east wall. A closet in the west wall left a narrow aisle to the bathroom. I hired a carpenter to build bookshelves on the north wall and I had a place for my books.

It was wonderful to have the big desk with drawers to put things in. One drawer I kept for the farm account books, day book, and ledger. One drawer held paper and envelopes. Another held letters and one held work sheets of poems and stories.

A living room across the front of the house opened out to a screened porch. The living room had a piano at one end and a fireplace at the other. Mother loved to sit in front of the fireplace in cold weather and read. For many of our friends such arrangements were commonplace. To us they were luxuries. The quality of our lives rose like yeast in bread dough. But misfortune was not done with us yet.

One November morning Mother stumbled downstairs, her clothes awry, hair half combed, and bewildered. She mumbled, "I can't use my right arm. I can hardly talk."

Uncle Will came tearing out. "You've had a stroke, Katharine. Either you go to bed and stay quiet or go to the hospital. You can't even get up to go to the bathroom for a few days."

A crisis indeed. Mother was our mainstay, our keeper of the house, the one we looked to for support. That she should be struck down was beyond reconciliation. The Hearst family no longer appeared in the Congregational Church on Sunday mornings. Too much was too much.

Now what, I wondered. Mother should not be stuck away upstairs. We had no hired girl to help. Louise spent every day in school except for weekends. Cornhusking was in full swing—by hand. That meant three extra men to feed. How would we manage?

Chuck and one of the men brought down Mother's bed from upstairs and set it up in the living room. Sliding doors gave her privacy. Father phoned Mother's sister, Viola, who was secretary to the State Board of Instruction. She asked for a ten-day leave and it was granted. So Aunt Vol pitched in. She cooked meals, made beds, and washed clothes. Mother directed her.

In the evening we all gathered around Mother's bed. She rapidly regained the use of her voice. "The blood clot absorbs slowly," Uncle Will said.

Mother asked Chuck, "Can you finish cornhusking before Vol must go back?" She worried about everyone but herself. I read to her in the afternoons. She liked the *Forsyte Saga* by John Galsworthy. I read and read and read her to sleep.

By the time the last ear of corn was husked and the men paid, Mother could move around by herself. Her right arm and hand remained limp but her voice returned to normal and her leg muscles regained their strength. Aunt Vol went back to Des Moines. The crisis eased off.

"Never again," I said to Chuck. "Never again will we feed and room cornhuskers. Money or no money, we're going to buy a corn-husking machine. I should be able to run it with the tractor."

By diligence and practice Mother learned to write with her left hand. She tried my typewriter but preferred to use her hand. The writing was legible but looked a little like the writing of a child.

It was not long before Mother was back in the kitchen helping prepare meals. Louise tried to be home in time to get dinner. I stood against the sink and wiped the dishes. I would sit in a straight chair and scramble eggs and mix up baking powder biscuits. I liked to cook. All the Hearst men can cook. Bob was an excellent cake maker. Chuck would set the table and carry out the dishes.

Then we had a stroke of good luck. As Mother said, "It is an ill wind. . . ." It was early winter, in the evening. A dilapidated car drove in the yard. One headlight shone on the snow. Both broken side windows were covered with cardboard. A thin, gray-faced young man came to the door. His jacket was ragged, his shoes laced with twine. "My wife is in the car," he said.

"For heaven's sake, bring her in," Mother said. "It's too cold out there."

He brought her in, a pretty young woman in a coat too thin for winter weather. The warm house made her shiver.

I looked at Chuck and we both thought, "We don't need more help."

The young man said, "We farmed in South Dakota. The drouth and Depression busted us. We sold out and paid our debts. I had a few jobs but nothing lasted. Our baby girl died last week. I have an uncle here in town. He said you might want help."

That is how Elsie and Art Jensen came to Maplehearst Farm. Elsie helped Mother, and Art worked outside. An advance in wages enabled them to buy warm clothes. I never knew how many tears Elsie shed for the lost baby. She was always cheerful and worked quickly with the skill of an experienced housewife. She was a good cook. Her cornmeal muffins with butter and honey made breakfast a meal to anticipate.

"We'll be fat as pigs if you keep this up," I told her.

One afternoon, when Art carried me to his car to take me to the hospital to see Father, I noticed a small rubber tube in the back of the car. "What's that for?" I asked.

"To siphon gas out of cars when we needed it and didn't have money to buy it," he said.

I said, "I've often thought if my family was hungry and couldn't afford to buy food, I would smash a bakery window and not feel guilty."

"When you're up against the buzz saw," Art said, "you will do most anything. We didn't have money to bury our baby girl so I borrowed from Uncle Hans."

We've been poor but not that poor, I thought. I wanted to say something reassuring to Art, but I just said, "I hope you're over the hump now."

When I told this to Chuck he said, "We've been just about as miserable. Remember the time the sheriff attached some of our land to pay the taxes?"

I never forgot that day. Uncle George took Mother and Father out to lunch so they wouldn't be humiliated by having papers served on them. We boys met the sheriff and accepted the notice. There are some things you never get over; they are like a sore that does not heal.

The next year contradicted the old saying: "Iowa is a place where it always rains before it is too late." Rains not only came too late, they hardly came at all. Clouds would form but no rain would fall. Abnormally high temperatures came in April. Grass and oats sprouted but made a poor stand. By corn planting time the earth was so dry it was a problem whether to set the planter deep enough to try to reach moisture and take a chance on smothering the seed or plant the usual depth and hope for rain.

During these hot days I hung a pail of water on the tractor fender. In it I soaked a bath towel which I hung around my neck. It was a primitive air conditioning system, but it worked.

Metal heated in the sun. The iron tractor seat would be so hot after dinner that I asked for a handful of grass or straw to sit on. Chuck taped the iron steering wheel so that the skin would not peel off my hands from the heat.

Wind piled up drifts of dust along the fence rows. It took years to eradicate the signs left by these banks of earth. Clouds of grasshoppers flew in with their trick of eating only the stems that connect the oat kernel to the stalk. Oat kernels littered the ground and there was no way to save them. Chinch bugs attacked the corn.

"Talk about the plagues in Egypt," Chuck said.

I marveled at the way the corn shoved down its roots in search of moisture. The crop showed promise at first. But the hot July winds cooked the tassels, turned them white, and no ears formed. It took one hundred and twenty acres of corn to fill our silo when normally ten acres would do it.

On a hot July morning I took Mother to town for groceries. The Buick had a hand gas feed and by riding both the clutch and brake with my feet I managed. But I felt insecure in the Main Street traffic. Automatic transmissions, when they came, were a godsend to me.

After letting Mother off I drove to the college to pick up Louise. I did not enter the grounds but pulled off to the side of the road and parked. I must not have shifted completely out of gear for, as I shut off the motor, the car lurched forward, ran down an embankment, and stopped in Jim Messier's back yard. Jim came running, jerked open the car door, lifted me out, and set me against a tree. He didn't hear me protest that I was all right.

Then Roy Porter stopped to see what he could do. Soon Al Matson came by with his livestock truck. Jim Messier backed my car up to the embankment, Al hooked a chain around the bumper, fastened the other end to his truck, and hauled the car back on to the road. It was late afternoon and people were coming home from town. I guessed half the neighborhood stopped to give aid and advice.

Jim and Roy made a saddle of their hands and carried me back to the car. I protested over and over that I was all right but Roy Porter stayed with me until Louise came, to assure her I was not hurt.

It embarrassed me, being lifted in and out of the car like that in front of everybody. I was mad at myself for letting the car get away from me, after all those years of driving a car!

I brought Mother home safely that hot July day. The night before, Chuck and the men had agreed to get out in the field at four-thirty to cultivate corn. Then they would stop at ten and keep the horses in the barn during the heat of the day. That summer the heat and equine encephalitis killed horses all over the Midwest. The rendering works was so busy gathering dead animals they would not answer their phone.

I stopped in the shade of a tree. Mother got out with her groceries in a basket. Chuck came running, "King and Kit are down in the corn-field."

The saying goes among farmers that once a horse is down from the heat, it is as good as dead. But I thought it an old wives' tale. "Chuck," I said, "you know how I keep cool with a wet towel? Let's haul the horses up beside the well house and run cold water on them."

Chuck ran to the shed, backed out the tractor, and hitched on the stoneboat. He and Ed and Bill clanked off to the cornfield.

I wondered, "How do you strip the harness off a horse that weighs almost a ton, move it away from the cultivator, and roll it on a stoneboat."

But pretty soon the tractor came pulling the stoneboat on which lay what looked like a dead horse. It was the iron gray Belgian, King. It made me sick to look at him.

In about twenty minutes the tractor roared back with Kit on the stoneboat. Chuck and Bill rolled her off beside King and Ed sprayed water on her too.

I had a way with horses. Even as a youngster Father let me handle three-year-old colts. I had the knack of bringing calm to an excited horse. I couldn't explain it, I could just do it.

Now began a time of waiting. The horses lay as if dead. The men took turns with the hose, soaking their bodies with cold well water.

Kit revived first. After an hour or so, she rolled over on her belly and snorted. She reached out with her front feet and hoisted herself erect. It took several lunges to get up on her hind legs. She stood there trembling, head down, eyes half closed.

Chuck and Ed, one on each side, walked her over to the shade of a big maple tree. Now it was King's turn. It was another half hour before he rolled from his side to his belly and lifted his head. He stuck out his front legs, made a lunge, and stood up. Chuck held his mane and led him across to the shade. A light wind funneled across the yard and helped cool down the horses. They stood there all afternoon. They walked to their stalls when evening came and nibbled at their feed. They worked no more that summer.

"We saved 'em," Chuck said. "The best team we have too."

At the supper table Mother asked, "Why don't you buy a small tractor with a two-row cultivator. Then you wouldn't need horses."

I knew this was the inevitable move. Machines were coming in and horses going out. The time had come to mechanize the farm. By spring all the horse stalls in the Hearst barn were empty. Chuck traded the last four horses for a tractor-cultivator, a combine, and a disk. I felt like a traitor when the horses climbed in the truck to be hauled away. For us, as for many farmers, an era had ended and a new kind of farm life begun.

I wondered how the change affected the older farmers. Perhaps they relaxed when the horses went away. All those chores ended now. No barns to clean out, stalls to bed down, bodies to curry, harness to repair, no corn and oats to carry and measure, no mangers to fill with hay, hooves to trim and shoe. How much easier to crank a tractor than to harness and hitch up six horses on a gang plow. The young farmers knew how to set the points on a spark plug but not how to fit a collar on a horse. The change was abrupt, extreme, and to me cruel.

An ancient companionship drifted into the past. A relationship between men and horses had existed for centuries. History names famous horses as well as men. Where the relationship was well established, there was trust and a sense of responsibility on both sides. A man could make friends of his horses. No one ever goes into the machine shed, slaps a tractor on the rump, and asks, "How are you this morning, old boy?" The machine age stinks up the air and crowds flesh and blood into oblivion.

But selling our workhorses was not the only sadness to touch our lives at this time. For the past few years Father had not been well. He still drove home from Des Moines on weekends, walked around the farm, talked to us about crops, weather, and the livestock. But he did not move with his usual vigor. Something had gone out of his stride.

Often on Sunday morning all three of us would get in the car and drive to the Thompson eighty, land Father owned with his sister, Aunt

Jennie. It lay a mile west of the farm, had no buildings, and was divided by a creek.

We always drove over to check the cattle, to see if there were any new calves, or cows in heat. It provided good pasture and our cows and calves spent the summer there. We usually took a block of salt and a block of mineral. Usually we took a rifle for a crack or two at a gopher or woodchuck. Once we saw a red fox trotting across a field. Father loosed a shot at it and that fox just floated through the air, its bushy tail stuck out behind like a rudder. It moved with such grace and speed that we were speechless.

But Father declined invitations to look at the cattle. "Bring them home after the first frost," he said. He went over the farm books with me but did not offer his usual criticisms and suggestions.

It alarmed and irritated me to have Father so resigned. I tried to rouse his interest. "Come on, Dad, shall we keep the Rosewood cow? She has a black nose and probably her calves will have it too."

But Father just said, "Use your own judgment."

After Thanksgiving Chuck said, "Let's come to some business arrangement about the farm. I work without any wages and no evidence of a partnership."

Father answered, "We ought to do something to give you and Jim and Louise some sign of ownership. And you ought to have a salary, Chuck. Let's think about it."

That is as far as it went. Father did not want to be bothered. Mother said, "You know your father takes pills for his heart." We had not known.

In February the headlines in the *Des Moines Register* said, "Charles Hearst Resigns after Thirteen Years President of the Iowa Farm Bureau."

Uncle George put Father in the hospital, saying he wanted to make some tests. But when Mother came home from the hospital two days later she said, with a catch in her voice, "I don't think Father will ever come home again. He's so sick."

She was right. He did not.

An End—A Beginning

EVEN IF I TRIED I could not give the date nor the occasion when I banished the dream of a miracle and accepted the hard fact of my condition. I came to accept the fact that my handicap was not a temporary one and that there was no surgeon able to knit the ends of my spinal cord together. I dropped the pretense I had clung to so desperately that some day I would walk away a sound man. This recognition battered my spirit but it helped me build a new life without a constant yearning for a never-never land. I sloughed off the skin of the past and grew a new one I could wear with assurance.

Words of Dr. Steindler wrote themselves large in my thoughts. Dr. Steindler had once said, "Not until we have better techniques will we be able to repair damage to the central nervous system. We may never have that skill."

These words were spoken to me by the world's greatest orthopedist. That the famous Dr. Arthur Steindler became head of the Orthopedic Department of the College of Medicine at the University of Iowa surprised more people than James Hearst. For the rest of my life I felt the influence of this great man.

"He helped me most," I told Mother, "when he dropped into my hospital room on Saturday afternoons and smoked a cigar. We talked about books, music, politics, humanity—everything but medicine. I learned from him. I learned to be ashamed of myself only if I did not live up to my ability. I basked in the warmth of a man who had great affection for people in need."

I noticed at the hospital that when a state patient, a person so poor he or she must have state aid, became critically ill in the night, Dr. Steindler left home and came to see him or her. If a private patient faced a similar crisis he often sent his first assistant.

Once, discussing professions, Dr. Steindler told me, "We won't need to worry, Jim. People will always need doctors and farmers, even the communists."

My decision to bear my physical condition without more fantasy started me on a new road. I needed to educate myself. After cornhusking ended and the machines were greased and stored for another year, my field work was finished. I kept the farm accounts, paid the bills,

71

and discussed plans and decisions with Chuck, but I had time of my own. I set myself a reading program. Somewhere I found a list of the one hundred books an educated man should have read. So I started the Jim Hearst Self-Improvement Society. One by one, Louise brought the books home from the library and, one by one, I absorbed them.

I told Mother, "I cannot understand philosophy unless I keep translating the abstractions into concrete examples. Makes slow going." But I ploughed my way through Plato, Aristotle, Kant, Thomas Aquinas, and Spinoza. No philosopher spoke to me as a friend until I read Alfred North Whitehead. Here was a man I thought I understood.

I formed the habit of concentrating on the books of one country. I began with the Scandinavians. I read Knut Hamsun, Ibsen, Undset, and Georg Brandes's *Main Currents in 19th Century Literature.* Then I read the French authors, English, German, Italian, and Spanish. I read a few Oriental books and was greatly impressed with the poems of the Indian, Tagore. I reread the Bible, took on the *Bhagavad-Gita* and the *Book of the Dead.* My appetite for books seemed to grow sharper as I tried to satisfy it. Poor Louise, lugging those tomes home and back again. She deserves gold stars in her crown.

Chuck and I built a radio set out of an empty oatmeal box wound with wire, a condenser, and vacuum tube. Mother listened on the earphones to the "Music Shop" from WOI in Ames and to Andy Woolfries reading books. Chuck used it for market reports. I listened to it when I tired of reading.

I began to write verse and stories on the typewriter. It was slow business. My cramped fingers did not always strike the right keys. But I banged away and took my lumps as the errors showed up on the pages. I have no idea why I wrote what I did. I threw it away. It never sounded the way I thought it should. But I kept on, that was the strange part. I kept turning out what I called "drivel."

My Aunt Mamie, Mary F. Hearst, taught in the English department at the college. She heard of my writing and asked me what poets I read. "Oh," I said, "you know, Longfellow, Emerson, Whittier, that crowd. Plus a few English poets—Keats, Shelley, Wordsworth."

I asked Aunt Mamie, "Are there any new American poets?"

She sent me a copy of the first Untermeyer anthology and I almost fell apart. "Why," I said, "some of this stuff is written just the way we talk. Some of it isn't even rhymed!"

Aunt Mamie sent me the poems of Whitman and Poe as examples of two trends in American literature. I was so ignorant about what she said that I wouldn't have known a trend if I met it in broad daylight. But I could tell the difference in the poetry. I liked Whitman but found Poe precious and arrogant. Free verse did not seem quite kosher to me, yet Whitman's long lines rolled away just like the psalms in the Bible.

I read over and over the poems by Robinson, Frost, Sandburg, Lindsay, and Masters. My English instructor at college had warned me away from such subjects as Beauty, Death, the Flag, Home, and Mother. He told me to write out my own experiences, to stick to what I knew. And here they were, prominent poets writing about ordinary things that happened to ordinary people.

I puzzled over this. Finally it came to me that the way they said it made it poetry. A new use of language, a new way of saying. I commenced to see with new eyes.

My experience with poetry had been limited to poems written in traditional meters. I was comfortable with Robinson and Frost, though Frost sometimes startled me with a casual line that just happened to rhyme with another. Sandburg and Masters seemed daring and not quite "poetic." But Aunt Mamie reminded me that Milton, one of the great prosodists of English poetry, wrote free verse. When did English poetry begin to use rhyme?

I thought, "Why, always." But then I wasn't so sure.

Prosody. What did she mean by prosody? So Louise brought home books from the library on the writing of poetry. I read everything from Sir Philip Sidney to Harriet Monroe. Then I read Ezra Pound and Amy Lowell on "Imagism." And I thought Pound was some kind of a nut.

All the discussion of verse forms and styles and patterns disheartened me. "I can never remember all this stuff. How do they know so much about it?" I wondered.

Poe's essay on how he wrote "The Raven" baffled me. "I don't believe it. No one can calculate how to write a poem." But I was afraid that maybe Poe did it just that way.

When Louise went to school and Chuck outdoors, I talked to Mother. "I wrote a poem for you once before I was old enough to go to school. It was about rain and it said, 'filled the ditches up so high/they nearly reached the sky.' I thought if the ends matched it was a poem."

"What did I say?" Mother asked.

"You said I was making my *S*'s the wrong way. In the eighth grade I rewrote stories in rhymed couplets, though I did not know what a rhymed couplet was."

The many forms of poetry irritated me—triolet, rondel, villanelle, sestina, sonnet, ballad. And then the line lengths—tetrameter, pentameter. "Who the hell cares?" I shouted in my mind. I was fearful I could never learn the basic techniques of poetry. But, tempted by the difficulty, I tried some of the forms I made fun of. It put me to it. I still complained, "Who cares if it is a Petrarchan sonnet or a Shakespearean sonnet if it is a good sonnet?"

But I knew who cared. I did. Once exposed to studies of verse forms and techniques, I could not let them alone. My discoveries infected me like a disease.

I protested to Chuck but he gave me little satisfaction. "Sure," he said, "everything has its shape and pattern. We build a straight fence to enclose a field. Who'd like a field where the fences are catty-wampus. There're so many acres in a field, so many square rods to an acre. What're you yelling about? You're just in new territory and you're upset because you don't know as much as you thought you did."

I knew my failing, my need to prove over and over again that I was a person of some account. It made me too sharp, too positive, too aggressive. It was as if I must always keep saying, "I'm here too." Sometimes it soured my relationship with Chuck when I insisted too vehemently for my own way. With friends, too, it happened. I was afraid of being overlooked. My sharp criticism made Louise cry one morning and I hated myself all that day. A couple of times I apologized to Chuck but he just said, "Forget it." I could not seem to stop being too assertive.

Timidly I put the books on prosody away. I turned back to the typewriter. I rolled in a clean sheet and said to myself. "Now to make the right black marks."

I typed several of my best pieces—not daring to call them poems— and sent them to Aunt Mamie for criticism. This pleased her but she confessed her inability to make suggestions. But she corrected my grammar and punctuation.

She sent one of my poems to a woman she knew who had won a poetry prize. The woman revised the poem, cut out words, improved the meter, crossed out lines, and wrote on the margin, "Avoid trite phrases, clichés, use original imagery."

At first I was offended, as if the woman looked down her nose at me for trying to write verse. Then I cooled off and considered what she had done. She had taken pains to *show* me, not just *tell* me. My ear had betrayed me. The meter was faulty. She had tightened the lines and turned statement into image.

"So that's how it is done," I thought. "I need more practice. Better I should count the stresses on my fingers until I can hear more clearly." She had given me elementary criticism but perhaps it was just what I needed.

I decided to write a sestina. But what was a sestina? Back I went to the books on prosody again. I shoved the typewriter aside and gripped a soft lead pencil between my cramped fingers. Thoughts rolled out better when I wrote longhand.

Each month Louise brought home a list of new books the library had received, usually ten or twelve pages. I used the backs of the pages for scratch paper. The rough surface took the soft pencil easily.

Aunt Mamie phoned that she had asked the local editor if he would print some of my work. He suggested a summary of articles I had read. So began a column called, "Things To Think About." If the *Cedar Falls Record* liked it, why not other newspapers? I tried to sell it to other papers without success. I felt a bit let down. I had never heard of syndicating work. But the pressure of having something ready for the printer each week and the experience of seeing my words in print taught me more about writing. The printed word looks different from the same word written longhand. Mistakes and awkward sentences loomed with fearful emphasis.

One Sunday afternoon the minister and his wife came to call. The minister mentioned the need for me to find some useful occupation.

"He does quite a bit of farm work now," Mother said.

"He can't keep that up," the minister answered. "It's too strenuous and there are too many things he cannot do."

Louise said, "He might become a writer."

The minister smiled a knowing smile. "No, I'm sorry, James, but writing takes skill and talent."

Mother asked, "What do you suggest?"

The minister waved white hands. "A course in watch repair, perhaps, or bookkeeping, or a course in leather work."

When they had gone, I asked, "What ails him?"

Louise said, "I'll bet he's a frustrated writer, never could quite pull it off."

Father had said, "I wouldn't pay any attention to what he said, Son."

"I won't," I said. "His kind of encouragement I don't need."

Every spare minute that winter I wrote and typed, wrote and typed, and sent the poems to Aunt Mamie. I did not know why I wrote. I seemed to be fascinated by what I was doing. The variety of word patterns seemed infinite and I wanted to devise some that would speak for me.

I was not prepared for it when it happened. One day Aunt Mamie came out to the farm all flustered. Breathless with excitement she confessed, "Perhaps I shouldn't have done it, James, but I sent some of your poems to *Good Housekeeping*. One of them was accepted and here is a check for thirty-five dollars."

My feelings boiled over. A mixture of resentment, because my aunt dared send off my poems without my knowledge, and a great wonder that a poem I had written would be published and paid for. I did not know what to say. The prospect of having a poem of mine in a national magazine overwhelmed me.

Mr. Goodwin, the editor, sent me a page of instructions on how to prepare a manuscript for submission. I memorized the rules: name and address in the upper left-hand corner, number of words in upper right-hand corner, title in capital letters, lines double-spaced, and return postage included.

I tried to settle down to work but for the next few days all I could think of was the poem *Good Housekeeping* had accepted. I knew I couldn't rewrite it, but I wanted to. I studied it to see why it was different from my other poems.

One of Louise's friends, Hazel Strayer, was head of the drama department at the college. She had written some poems and stories. When she discovered my interest in writing, she joined me. We became good friends. Many times she walked out to the farm to spend an

afternoon with me. After supper Louise or Chuck would take her back
to her apartment.

Hazel joined our family. She bullied, coaxed, and encouraged me.
She had spent several winter vacations in New York. She knew Carl
Van Doren, literary editor of *Century* magazine. She brought stories of
the new plays, new musicals, and new hit songs. She introduced me to
the plays of Eugene O'Neill and prophesied that some day he would be
America's foremost playwright.

Mother came home from town one afternoon and found Hazel sitting on my bed close to my desk. Mother threw up her hands in mock
horror, "Hazel Strayer, you look just like a gypsy—your scarlet dress,
coal black hair, long silver earrings."

Hazel asked, "Are you afraid, Katharine, that I might seduce
Jim?"

"I'm sure you could if you wanted to."

Hazel gave a little flirting gesture, "Who knows, I might want
to."

It bathed me in an emotional shower to have someone as nice as
Hazel speak so even in jest.

She was an excellent critic. She knew the work of contemporary
writers. She had heard lectures by Frost and Sandburg. She was familiar with the "Imagiste" movement powered by Ezra Pound and Amy
Lowell. She told me to quit trying to be Shelley, to let his "Skylark"
alone, to be James Hearst listening to a rooster crow. She took Aunt
Mamie's place as a sounding board against which I threw my poems.

When spring came, it brought us into the fields. I put writing aside.
After a day on the tractor I was too tired to do more than read the
paper and tumble into bed. On rainy days I worked on the farm books
and paid bills. On Sundays we all loafed, read the paper, wrote letters,
visited with friends and relatives.

Always the first week in the fields in the spring nearly killed me. I
grew soft sitting around the house all winter in spite of my daily exercises. The tractor shook and jarred me. The cold winds chilled me.
Wet spots in the fields threatened to bury the tractor. I could not keep
warm. I wore long underwear, a wool shirt, coveralls, and a sheepskin
coat. I was so bundled up I could scarcely move. I carried a can on the
tractor to relieve a full bladder, but with all my clothes on I had trouble
making contact. One of the hired men suggested that I tie a string to
my penis so I could pull it out.

Gradually muscles regained their tone, hands grew tough, and
cracks in my lips from the sun and exhaust healed.

But when fall came, and corn and beans were stored in crib and
bin, the season nailed tight the door on my outdoor activity. I opened
my books again and sailed the seas of words. I gave up reading poetry
anthologies as too much the shotgun approach. I studied individual

poets, essayists, and novelists. I liked the Irish writers. Yeats fascinated me even though I turned up my nose at what I called the hocus-pocus of Yeats's concern with magic. The early works—the Celtic twilight and fairy poems—did not stir me. But the later Yeats held me spellbound. I could not understand how Yeats used words so simply yet so loaded with meaning.

My real adventure was the discovery of John M. Synge. He insisted that men must learn to build houses before they build cathedrals. He said poetry must have its roots in the clay among the worms. He was the man for me. Although Synge was a dramatist and wrote only twenty-seven poems, he provided the home base I needed.

I wanted to write about the land and its people, about their experiences with love, death, birth, anguish, and joy. I wanted to express the relationship of farmers to the seasons. I wanted to express the appetites of earth, the roll of furrows, the push upward of green stalks. I would do this in the language of common usage. I had not yet read Wordsworth's "Preface to Lyrical Ballads," but I would have been reassured if I had. In later years I admitted that I never spelled it out as distinctly as this, but these feelings and thoughts were implicit in my dim sense of mission.

I sat at my desk and wrote. I sent a sonnet to *Harper's* magazine and one of the editors wrote me, "This poem almost made it."

Stirred by this encouragement I fired off poem after poem to the big four magazines—*Harper's, Century, Scribner's,* and the *Atlantic.* But they all came home rejected. It was many years later that *Harper's* bought a poem.

Instead of discouraging me, the rejection slips stimulated me to write more poems. For the first time I put myself on a schedule. Mornings I devoted to farm business—the everlasting accounts, bills, phone calls, and discussions with Chuck. I wrote a letter to Father once a week to let him know how we were and how the farm had behaved itself. Afternoons I saved for myself.

I remembered how a German neighbor, an immigrant, had been ridiculed during the war. Yet he had a son who was killed fighting as a soldier in the U.S. Army. How shamed the neighborhood had been. How they tried to atone for their tawdry actions. I wrote it out in a story called, ironically, "America for Americans" and sold it to the *American Legion Monthly* for fifty dollars. I tried the editor with three more somewhat patriotic stories but none of them quite made it.

Louise urged me to submit work to some of the small literary magazines. "They won't pay you much, if anything. But they'll give you a reputation." She brought home a copy of the *Midland,* published at Iowa City. The editor was John T. Frederick.

"Some good names among the contributors," I said. "Even I've heard of them."

I mailed a group of poems to the *Midland* and enclosed a timid note. A month went by and I heard nothing. I wondered if the poems ever arrived. But one day my return envelope appeared in the mail. I tore it open with nervous hands. Only two poems were enclosed with a note saying, "Dear Mr. Hearst, I like what you are doing. No one has ever written about the farm in such an honest way. I am keeping four of the poems and I hope you will let me see more of your work. Sincerely, John T. Frederick."

My spirits soared. "Mother," I called. "Come and read this."

"That's very nice," Mother said, after she read the note. "But don't forget to order the load of cottonseed meal that Charles wants."

I look back on this as my start in life as a writer. At last I had found someone who understood what I was trying to do. I began to think scornfully of Robert Frost as a farmer with a rocky slope farm, a flock of chickens, and one cow.

When I met Frost for the first time at our farm he was equally scornful. "Too much land in this farm," he said. "Mile-long corn rows. . . ." They roused his indignation.

After that first acceptance by the *Midland,* Frederick and I began a friendship that lasted until his death in 1976. He left the University of Iowa for Northwestern University and ended his academic career as chairman of the English department at Notre Dame University. I wrote him a note of congratulations saying, "Pretty good for a Presbyterian."

I found a friend in one of the college students. He was a young man of Danish ancestry named Viggo Justesen. He was interested in writing, especially in the new movements in literature. A free swinger in his mind, a rebel against authority, a thorn in the side of conservative professors, Viggo introduced me to the work of H. L. Mencken, first in the "Smart Set," then in the *American Mercury.* He brought me copies of the liberal magazines—the *Nation* and the *New Republic.*

I ate this new intellectual food with a hearty appetite. I subscribed to the *American Mercury* and received a copy containing the famous "Hat Rack" story. The Watch and Ward Society of Boston had Mencken arrested for publishing this story. It was a mild tale concerning a small town prostitute and it became a flaming issue of freedom of expression.

We chuckled over the testimony given in court. Watch and Ward asked Mencken, "Would you want your children to read this story?"

Mencken replied, "I am not publishing a magazine for children."

Viggo helped break the shell of my reluctance to appear in public. "What the hell do you care? Everyone has something the matter with them. On you it just shows more."

Together we worked up a carnival act. Viggo printed a sign that said, "READ HAT RACK FOR TWENTY-FIVE CENTS," stuck it on his car, and we drove down to College Hill and parked.

Viggo told the students, "Get in the car and read the story. Two bits." Since the magazine had been taken off the newstands by a court order, we had some customers.

Years before Sartre appeared with his "Existentialism," Viggo introduced me to the Danish mystic, Sören Kierkegaard. Since I could not read Danish and Kierkegaard had not yet been translated into English, Viggo and I spent days out in the car under the maples while he laboriously translated *The Seducer's Diary.*

Viggo was intensely interested in the political scene. I had just finished reading Veblen's *Theory of the Leisure Class* and I was full of undigested chunks of economic theory. We argued, wrangled over our evidence, and sharpened our wits on each other's assertions. The Hearsts had been, like many Midwest farmers, a conservative Republican family. But Chuck and I failed to see any help for the farmers in the Republican veneration for the protective tariff.

Now with Viggo to prod us, we became liberal Democrats and outspoken opponents of Republican commandments. The foundations of our house rocked slightly.

Viggo had already discharged a few shots at contemporary education practice. He had read about Rousseau educating his son, Emile, without benefit of schools. Viggo prepared to start a revolution in American education. "Blow out the cobwebs, get rid of formal academic junk. Open the students' minds by interesting them in learning. Don't stuff them with dull facts."

After his graduation Viggo went to Des Moines and taught civil government in a highly original way. The students loved him but the administrators frowned on him. However, the superintendent of schools, a man named Studebaker, said, "Let him go. Maybe he'll teach us something."

Viggo joined a group of young intellectuals that H. A. Wallace gathered around him. Every time a celebrity came to Des Moines, Chuck and I were invited to be present. There were lunches and dinners with Wallace presiding, the guest of honor beside him. One of the guests, George Russell (AE), an Irish poet, friend of Yeats, and editor of the *Irish Statesman,* had helped Sir Horace Plunkett found the Irish Cooperative movement. He entertained us by reciting poetry. He used a high singing voice and explained that this was the Irish way. "Blind Rafferty would have used a harp," he said.

After these sessions, some of the young men met and played poker, drank bootleg booze, and argued and discussed ideas with vehemence and sometimes acrimony.

I became acquainted with the young editors of the *Des Moines Register* and *Tribune,* especially Cliff Millen, Stuffy Walters, and Harlan Miller. MacKinlay Kantor and I became friends. Mac went on to become an important American novelist. Don Murphy from *Wallace's Farmer* was often there and men from the faculty of Drake University. I heard arguments I did not always understand and heard speakers attack each other with a candor and bluntness that surprised me. It was heady stuff and an education for a half-paralyzed young man from an Iowa farm.

I wondered at the patience and care Chuck showed me. He carried me to and from the car, helped me walk in my awkward fashion along halls in hotels and in strange houses. I hope he enjoyed those meetings with the Des Moines crowd. He always offered to drive me when the invitations came and he drank and played poker with the boys. At home we had sharp arguments about the farm business and stubborn differences of opinion. But Chuck stood ready to help me when I wanted to go to a meeting or a party. Chuck and Viggo hit it off well and we three often went places together.

There was always a strong bond between all the members of our family. Yet, as the eldest brother, I knew that when we were boys I had often acted the dictator to Bob and Chuck. I wished I could tell Chuck how much I owed him. But the Hearsts held back any expression of feeling. "No kissing and hugging in our family," I said. "A bunch of Scotch-Irish Calvinists."

Bob once said, "You won't get any compliments out of this family. You just do your best and shut up."

I continued to publish poems in the *Midland*. John Frederick encouraged me and offered me helpful criticism. He invited me to come to Iowa City and meet some of the students and faculty who were writers and interested in writing.

I hesitated and then gave way. I confessed to Frederick how handicapped I was. I wrote him frankly about my physical condition. He wrote in reply, suggesting that Chuck and I stay in a hotel and that he would bring the folks to meet us.

I had some reservations, but we went. And I enjoyed the visit. I found John Frederick a tall, thin, sensitive man who had published two novels. He too had grown up on a farm and he discussed farm problems with Chuck. Frank Luther Mott came to the hotel and had dinner with us. He was head of the journalism department and would soon join Frederick as coeditor of the *Midland*. I liked him and found his enthusiasm for writers and their work refreshing.

I asked Mother to invite the Fredericks to the farm and they came, John, Esther (his wife), and two small boys named John and James. They stayed the weekend and were easy and pleasant guests. Mother was amused when little James said, "Mother doesn't like to have the cat on the kitchen table because it gets hair in the butter."

The good friendship continued. John accepted one of my short stories for publication, a story called "Old Joe." It was based on a theme by Chekhov. I had just discovered this author and found in him the bread and butter of short fiction.

Frederick suggested that the time had come to spread my wings and try a wider flight. He wrote, "Try Harriet Monroe. She edits *Poetry*, a magazine that publishes the best work of the best poets."

I shrank from making the attempt. I knew the reputation of that magazine and I hesitated to knock on its door. I was reluctant to put my work forward. I was afraid if editors knew I was handicapped, they might publish me out of pity. (How little I knew editors!) And I was not sure of myself as a poet. Years later, in an interview, I said, "I don't think of myself as a poet but as a man who writes poetry. I think there is a distinction."

When I first taught the Romantic poets, I told the class of students, "Keats said the poet is nothing, it is the work that counts."

Then I added, "I can subscribe to that."

The winter after my meeting with the Fredericks, I signed in at the physiotherapy department at the University Hospitals in Iowa City. I knew my spinal cord could not be repaired, but I knew from experience that disciplined exercise, if persistent, brought good results. We had finished cornhusking and my outdoor work for the year had ended.

John Frederick often came to visit me in the evenings. On one occasion he said, "We're having a luncheon tomorrow at the Union for Harriet Monroe. I'd like to have you come."

I asked Dr. Steindler, who said, "Why not? Be sure to check out with your supervisor so she doesn't think you've been kidnapped."

My friend Pete Troyer, one of the orderlies, took me in his car and carried me up the steps into the Union's dining room. Surprised, but pleased, I found myself sitting next to Harriet Monroe.

I liked her. She was spunky and courageous. She told us how she fought the battle of poetry against the apathy of the reading public. She told us how she wrestled money from wealthy Chicago families to keep *Poetry* solvent and have money to pay contributors. "Poetry should be paid for like clothes and groceries," she said.

I remembered best her sharp glance at me and her crisp invitation, "Send me some poems. I want to see what you're doing."

I did send her some poems and she accepted a group of them. I could read proudly on the cover of *Poetry* the words, " 'Speaking of Iowa' by James Hearst."

She was a teacher as well as an editor and her tart, brief comments opened my eyes to some of the subtle techniques I was not yet aware of. For example, about one poem, she said, "The second stanza falls flat on the ear. Pick it up with a metaphor. Let the sky represent the earth as a mirror image."

I had a long and pleasant experience with *Poetry* magazine. Every editor but one used poems of mine until I was seventy-nine years old. For me it is always the Supreme Court where poetry is judged.

With new confidence in my work, I began to send more of it to other magazines. I received rejections, letters of commendation, and a few acceptances. My skin grew tough and I could brush off rejections without feeling the bite. I had almost enough poems for a book when Robert Frost came to town.

Frost came to lecture at the college and he wanted to see an Iowa farm. Dr. H. W. Reninger, head of the English department and a friend of mine, brought him out to Maplehearst Farm. Frost, stocky, brown haired, and energetic, roamed from barn to fields. He spied a small group of untrimmed, unsprayed apple trees. His face lit up and his voice filled with satisfaction as he said, "At least we can beat you with apples."

He wanted dinner at noon. He helped carry out the dishes and complimented Mother on doing her own work. He said, "That's the way to get it done right."

Someone had told him about my poems. Before he went back to town he said to me, "Get enough poems for a book and send the manuscript to me. I'll pass it on to my publisher."

It was a kindly meant and generous offer from one of America's leading poets. It was a helping hand, extended to a young farmer with more aspiration than achievement. But somehow it struck me the wrong way. I felt patronized and my own New England blood pulsed in protest.

I said, "Thank you, Mr. Frost, but if I'm going to make it I'll have to make it on my own."

Frost's eyes blazed, his eyebrows bristled, and his lip curled. He turned away abruptly. But when he said goodbye to Mother, he also said, "Maybe Jim is right. Maybe it is best to make it on your own."

When I was older I wondered if it would have made any difference to have had a New York publisher rather than a midwestern one. I have never regretted my decision.

Frost's words stirred me to think about publishing a book of poems.

Hard Road

"EITHER YOU GO AHEAD or you go back, you can't stand still." The message came in a plain envelope with no signature. I read it aloud.

Chuck added, "Or you just survive. A lot of people just survive."

Mother asked, "Who do you suppose sent it?"

"Some person, well meaning, who thinks life is lived by rules."

"Lots of people base their lives on old sayings like that," Chuck said. "It's easier to decide when you have an old rule like that to tell what's right and what's wrong. You don't get mixed up having to allow for human nature."

"Whoever wrote that will think I've taken the advice when he or she knows I've gone to Iowa City," I said.

The field work was finished. The corn was in the crib, soybeans in the bin, and fall plowing ended. I sat beside a half-filled suitcase. I was getting ready to go to Iowa City to Children's Hospital to work out in the physiotherapy department. I now had enough strength and muscle control to take advantage of a system of exercises. I heard that Children's Hospital had installed a heated pool and I wanted to try it.

A letter from Dr. Steindler's secretary gave me an appointment. Chuck said he would drive me down.

"It's a lot to ask to use the farm's money for hospital expenses," I admitted.

"Not if it'll do you any good," Chuck answered. "It's been eight years since you were there and you sure couldn't do many exercises then."

At the hospital, the packed waiting room looked familiar. The building smelled the way it always had—a mixture of odors from disinfectants and sweeping compound.

"Don't wait, Chuck," I said. "It will be five o'clock before I get to see Dr. Steindler."

"Will you be all right?" Chuck asked. He hesitated and then said, "I would like to be home for chores and it is a good two-hour drive."

"Sure, please go," I said, even though I hated to sit there alone in one of the wooden, creaky, high-backed wheelchairs.

It depressed me to check into the hospital. I was a stranger. Doctors and nurses hurried back and forth, called to each other, and joked as they passed. I longed for someone to step up and say hello and give me a welcome smile. Hospital waiting rooms are like a foreign country where the patients don't speak the proper language and proffer their disabilities in place of passports.

I looked at the people in the waiting room. A young mother tried to balance a baby that had both legs spread in a cast. A small boy whined against his mother. His braces of steel and leather snapped as he moved. An old man, eyes dim and sunken, clutched his crutches. A teenage girl, bright faced and nervous, chatted with an intern. She showed no injury or blemish until I saw the withered arm she kept hidden. We all come broken and lame but with hope, I thought.

The secretary motioned to me. I wheeled into the office. Dr. Steindler smiled and shook hands with me. "Do you remember me?" I asked.

Dr. Steindler sat down and leaned forward. "Of course, of course. You look greatly improved. I hear you are a writer, no?"

I smiled and shook my head. "I'm just in kindergarten."

"That's where we all start." He glanced at my letter, then at my history. "You want to try some exercises. Miss Woodcock is head of our physiotherapy department. We will ask her to set up a schedule for you." He called to his secretary, "Mrs. Hicks, please have an orderly take Mr. Hearst to his room."

"How does he do it?" I wondered. "Here it is, the end of the day, and he must be tired. Yet he's as pleasant and interested as if I were the only patient he had seen."

One of the staff men told me, "With the Chief, it is never the man with the arm or the girl with the hip, it is always Mr. Brown and Miss Smith, a human being in distress to be treated with respect."

An orderly wheeled me to my room, pushing the chair with one hand, carrying the suitcase with the other. "One of the girls will help you put away your clothes. Supper will be along in a few minutes. Need any other help?"

Just then a nurse in a white uniform, a black band on her cap showing she was a graduate of the university's school of nursing, rustled in the doorway. "What do you mean, Pete, by bringing an adult here? This is Boys' Ward."

The orderly patted her shoulder. "Now Miss Moore, not so hasty. The private rooms are all full. I was told to bring him to your isolation room." He swayed past her and went down the hall.

She smiled at me and said, "I'm Miss Moore, supervisor of Boys' Ward. My girls are all student nurses but we'll look after you. What help do you need now?"

I liked her face, snub nose, eyes set wide, and light brown hair. She appeared a bit over five feet tall with a nicely rounded body and a quick step.

"If I can have a low bed I can undress and dress myself. I can get in and out of the wheelchair alone. Could someone put my clothes in the dresser and my books on the bedside table?"

Just then the maid brought in my supper on a tray. "Oh, goodness," Miss Moore said. "Suppertime. I'll see you later."

After supper and after my suitcase was unpacked, I picked up one of my books and tried to read. I had brought Thomas Mann's *Magic Mountain* and Whitehead's *Science and the Modern World,* books I had planned to read and never got around to before. In later years I chuckled to remember how I always brought important books to the hospital but read mystery stories and westerns instead.

Miss Moore stuck her head in the door. "We'll have a low bed for you tomorrow. I'm going off duty now. There's a bell on your table. Ring it if you need anything. Good night."

A few minutes later a man in a white suit, a stethoscope in his pocket, came in. He was lean, tall, black-haired, and spoke with a casual drawl. "I'm Dr. Cowart, one of the staff. I want to examine you a bit. Can you get up there?" He motioned toward the bed.

"Yes, but I can't undress myself on a high bed."

Dr. Cowart called for a nurse to help and to bring a hospital gown. He jotted down details of the accident, went through the routine of hot and cold, sharp or dull, checked reflexes, and peered into my eyes.

I rebelled. "What the hell is this all for? Why don't you read my history. It's all there. I go through this every time I come down here."

Dr. Cowart beamed at me. "Orders on your chart and we Texans obey orders."

The next morning I said to a nurse, "Get the orderly to help me dress. I'm getting up."

The student nurse, in her striped uniform and white apron, scissors dangling from her waist and cap askew, shook her head earnestly. "Oh no, sir. I must take your temperature, pulse, and respiration. Do you have a bath this morning?"

"Bath!" I exploded.

Then Miss Moore came in. "Good morning."

"Look," I protested, "I'm not sick. I don't need all this routine stuff. I came down to work out in physiotherapy. For God's sake get me out of this bed."

"But we don't have any orders for you," she explained. "We must treat you as an incoming patient."

A flurry of footsteps in the hall, like an invading army, swept in Dr. Steindler and his staff. They were making morning rounds. "Mr. Hearst, you're still in bed. Taking a vacation, perhaps."

I protested, "But Dr. Steindler, they won't let me up."

Miss Moore broke in. "We don't have any orders for Mr. Hearst and the girls told him to stay in bed."

"No, no," quipped Dr. Steindler. "This man is here to work. Where is Miss Woodcock?"

A small, sandy-haired woman with a look of intense attention said, "Here I am."

Dr. Steindler waved his hand toward me. "This is Mr. Hearst. He has a fracture of the fifth cervical vertebrae with resulting paralysis. I want him in the pool in the mornings and in the gymnasium in the afternoons." He and his entourage swept on down the hall.

A few minutes later the tall orderly, who had helped me the night before, ambled in and said, "You're to get dressed and go down to physiotherapy." He picked up my T-shirt and shorts.

"Your name Pete?" I asked him.

"That's what they call me."

Later I discovered that his name was Alva Troyer, but everyone called him "Pete." He was the orderly on Men's Ward and held in high esteem by both staff and patients. He was a kind and sensitive man.

Pete wheeled me down the ramp to the lower floor. We turned into a steamy room filled with patients lying on hospital carts or sitting in wheelchairs. A pool occupied the center of the room. It had a two-foot cement railing around it and steps at each end leading down to the water.

In the pool, a woman in a bathing suit manipulated the shrunken legs of a child. The woman spoke gently to the child, urging the little girl to make an effort to move her legs. She spoke in a low musical voice. I noticed it at once. Too, I noticed her strong arms, her well-shaped figure, her flaxen hair.

She glanced up and said, "Put him in Woody's office, Pete."

"That's Miss Balkema, Antoinette Balkema, called 'Tony' by her friends. She's second in command."

Pete wheeled me out of the steam-filled room into a small office. "I'll leave you here. They'll call me when it's time for you to go back."

In about five minutes Miss Woodcock whisked into the office, alive with energy. "Ah, Mr. Hearst," she said, with her British accent. "Here you are. We want you in the pool in the mornings and in the gym in the afternoons. We'll plan some exercises for you. Now tell me, what can you do? Can you get up? Can you walk at all?"

I hoisted myself to my feet. "With crutches I can walk as far as I need to at home. I mean from room to room."

"You best use the wheelchair until we test you. These floors are slippery when they get wet."

She filled out some forms. "You'll need a bathing suit and tennis shoes. We want you to walk in the water where the buoyancy supports you. The pool maintains a temperature of ninety degrees, which will relax most of your spasticity."

"Can I send downtown for the suit and shoes?"

Miss Woodcock thought a moment. "Miss Balkema or I will pick them up this afternoon. Then you will be ready tomorrow morning. Put on your bathing suit and shoes in your room but bring your clothes down with you. After you come out of the pool, you take a shower and get dressed. Leave your suit and shoes here to dry. Someone will bring them to your room in the morning."

She looked at the form on her desk. "Here's a report on your muscle response. Let me see your hands." I held them out. "Can you open your fingers?"

"Only if I drop my wrists."

"Let's see if you can close your thumbs . . . now open them. . . . Hmm, you can contract but not extend. . . . Have you ever tried occupational therapy?"

I shook my head. "About the only special exercise my hands get is typing and grasping the steering wheel."

Miss Woodcock regarded me with a steady gaze. "You've done well. You have more strength than I would've thought. I suggest you go to occupational therapy this afternoon. You might enjoy it."

After lunch I asked Miss Moore to phone Pete and ask him to help me downstairs. When he came, Pete said, "Don't bother to have Geraldine phone. Wheel out by the ramp and I'll see you. Men's Ward is just down the hall."

I looked at the ramp. "Maybe I could go down that by myself, though I might slam into the wall making the turn."

Pete shook his head. "Better be safe than sorry."

He left me at the door of a room labeled "Occupational Therapy." A half dozen people sat around tables working with reeds, leather, and copper. A young lady came to meet me. "I'm Miss Thornton. Are you here for therapy?"

I passed her the slip Miss Woodcock had given me. "Oh, yes. Mrs. McDowell, who's in charge, is not here today. I'm a student-in-training."

When Miss Woodcock mentioned occupational therapy I had looked down my nose at the suggestion. For me it seemed contrived busywork. But I had the afternoon to kill and I was lonely and, who knew, I *might* enjoy it.

"We have some wet reeds," Miss Thornton said. "Why don't we try weaving a basket?" She smiled a bright smile.

"Oh, yes," I thought. "Why don't we." But I knew she was learning her job and she had to deal with people who might be even more indifferent and inept than I. And it would be good exercise for my hands. "Yes," I said. "That would be nice."

She showed me how to begin and then left me while she helped some poor soul mired in perplexity. A shadow fell across my work. I looked up and saw Dr. Cowart lounging in the doorway. "You like that?"

"It's fascinating," I said. "I'm intrigued by it."

He shrugged but did not smile. "That is what I'll end doing some day," he said, and moved on.

Through the hospital grapevine I later learned that Dr. Cowart had a severe alcohol problem.

I never went back to occupational therapy.

That evening after supper, Miss Balkema dropped in with the swimsuit and tennis shoes. "Hi," she said. "Here are your duds." She smiled, her whole person radiant. "Nine fifty," she said.

I wheeled over to the dresser, took my wallet from the top drawer, and counted out the money. I dropped the half dollar and it rolled under the bed. "I'm sorry. I have trouble handling coins."

Miss Balkema sat on the bed, scooped a long arm under it, and brought out the coin. "You have a low bed."

"It was here when I got back from occupational therapy. I can't dress and undress unless my feet are on the floor."

"Good for you. Keep your independence." Then she added, "Woody and I talked about you. We're awfully glad you're here. You'll give us a chance to see what progress can be made with someone in your condition. So many folk with your disability are either afraid to try or they give up."

I liked her. She was wholehearted, free-swinging, and a darn good looking gal. She acted so informal and friendly, as if we were old acquaintances. I hoped she would stay and talk.

She stood up. "I must go. See you in the morning. By the way, Woody may haunt you. She heard you have done some writing. Woody has the bug. You'll hear from her." I looked forward to seeing her in the morning.

The night supervisor stopped in, introduced herself, and winged away on silent feet. Probably sends the student nurses into conniptions when she makes a sudden appearance, I thought. I read awhile, then turned back the covers and went to bed.

The familiar hospital smell reminded me of Sartori Hospital and my life there . . . how many years ago? When I was lonely, memories of my betrayal of Prudence Hopkins returned to trouble me. My conscience never let me forget that tragedy and the sorry part I played— especially when I was alone, especially when I needed reassurance and affection. These worms in my mind kept me awake until I slept from exhaustion. It is a great privilege to be friends with yourself. I was not.

The next morning as I sat on the bed eating breakfast, Pete came in. He looked neat and dapper without his orderly gown. His voice had a rising inflection and was slightly hesitant but well modulated and low keyed. "Here," I said. "Can you eat this egg? Have some coffee too."

"I'll just use your lavatory and towel to wash my hands," he said. He neatly peeled the egg. I passed him the salt. "Thanks," he said. "I stopped to tell you, Hearst, that I won't take you to the pool this morning. There's a pool orderly named Ace Carter who takes all the chairs and carts downstairs."

I said, "As soon as I finish breakfast I'll put on my swimsuit and tennis shoes."

"No hurry," Pete said. "They take the kids first. I'll come down before lunch and help you shower and dress."

"Miss Calderwood will be on my back if I don't show up soon." He unfolded himself and started for the door. Then he stopped. "There is a new patient in one of the private rooms something like you. He has a broken back."

When Carter wheeled me to the ramp I saw a man, husky, broad-shouldered, and a few years younger than me, back his wheelchair down the ramp. He had strong-looking arms.

"I wonder if I could do that," I wondered. "My muscles are atrophied but I'm pretty strong."

"I wouldn't try it," Carter said, as if he read my mind.

The hot steamy pool room was crowded with carts and wheelchairs. Miss Balkema, in her swimsuit, again stood in the pool and manipulated arms and legs. I rolled up beside the man I had seen backing down the ramp.

"I'm James Hearst," I said.

"Art Sanders," the man said, reaching over to shake hands.

"Going swimming?" I asked.

"That's what they tell me."

I explained, "A dive into shallow water was my mistake."

He said, "I was on the University of Michigan's freshman football team. On the way home from a game the driver rolled the car. I had a broken back. The driver was killed."

"Can you stand at all?" I asked.

"With braces and crutches. Got no feeling below my waist," Art said.

I thought, "What a pair. He has strong arms and hands. I have sensation and my legs will support me."

Slowly the room emptied. I looked at my watch. It was ten-thirty. I heard Miss Balkema say, "Now will you two men come to the pool, please. Do you need help, Mr. Hearst?"

I saw Art take his legs in his hands and lift them over the wall. Then he slid down into the water. "I wish I could do that," I thought. Then aloud, "I'm afraid I'll need help."

I stood up, shook down my trousers, sat down, pulled them off, and tossed them on the chair with my other clothes. "I could sit on the wall and fall in backwards."

Miss Balkema climbed out of the water. I admired her figure. It was not sexy—just the splendid shape of a woman. She said, "Sit on the wall. Put your arm around my shoulders. Don't be afraid."

But I was, a little. I put my arms around her shoulders. She placed her hand under my knees and neatly flipped me over the edge.

I had forgotten how buoyant water is. My feet floated up while my head sank to the bottom. I was not alarmed. I twisted over, felt the wall with my hands, and pushed my head above water. I grinned at Miss Balkema. She smiled.

"I'm all right," I sputtered. I was amazed how easy it was to stand up. I walked along the wall. It was a great feeling. On later visits, to strengthen my legs, I walked and walked.

Miss Woodcock rushed in. "Nette," she demanded, "aren't you finished yet?"

Miss Balkema shook her head. To me she said, "Lie on your back and grasp the bar behind your head. I want to test you. Pull your legs together. Hmm . . . adductors strong. Now spread them." I wrestled and pulled and spread my legs a few inches. "Abductors weak. Flex your ankle . . . now your toes . . . straighten them. You do have some motion." She pushed my legs open and shut, then bent my ankles. "Flex, extend, flex, extend. There. Try walking while I work with Mr. Sanders."

I walked along the wall. The water came up to my armpits. I tried a few crawl strokes and floated on my back. All my muscles were relaxed and pliable. Then Pete showed up. "I'll help you out over here by the steps."

I grabbed the rail and started up the steps. As I left the water my body became heavy and limp. I gasped, "You'll have to help me." Pete lifted me under the arms until I stepped out on the floor. I sat in the chair and rolled over to the shower cubicle. Pete pulled the curtain and helped me pull off my suit and shoes.

"Leave your wet things here," Miss Balkema called. "We'll hang them on the line to dry."

I stepped into the shower. I clutched the grab rails. "I can make it," I told Pete. "Don't come in and get wet." I showered with hot and then cool water. I was weak as a kitten. An hour in the pool had sucked the power right out of my muscles. Pete helped me dress and we went upstairs to lunch.

I lay down after lunch. The warm water took the starch right out of me. I must have fallen asleep. I felt someone shake me and I opened my eyes to see Miss Moore. "Time for gym," she said. "Carter is waiting."

Miss Woodcock took over in the gym. She showed me a small room containing a set of parallel bars. At one end was a full-length mirror.

"I want you to walk back and forth," she said. "And watch yourself in the mirror. Pick up your feet, stand straight, make your legs work. Don't sway back and forth. Look at yourself in the mirror. Place each foot ahead of the other and don't wobble. Balance with as little support as possible."

She left and I began my exercises. It was hard work. At home I had been content to stand up with my crutches and take a few shambling steps. Now I tried to make the figure in the mirror take exact steps, stand up straight, pick up the feet, not drag the toes.

I began to sweat. I reached over and opened the window a crack.

Two sparrows were quarreling outside. I stood and watched them.

"No, no, Mr. Hearst. Looking out the window won't exercise your muscles." Miss Woodcock sailed into the room. What a lot of energy there was bundled in that slight body.

"Here," she said. "Put on these kneepads and crawl out into the gym. This exercise will strengthen your thigh and back muscles. Then I want you to climb steps. Can you put on the pads?"

I nodded. I sat down and buckled on the pads. Crawling! My second childhood. I slid off the chair and came to rest on all fours. I pulled one leg ahead, then the other. I was surprised that I could do it.

Twenty-eight years old and crawling like a child. But it took muscle to keep my back straight and advance each knee in turn. I kept my arms stiff to hold my nose off the floor. I was proud of myself.

I crawled into a corner of the gym and sat up. A class of boys and girls with scoliosis moved on hands and knees in rhythm with a lively march tune played on a phonograph. A sturdy blond-haired girl directed them.

Suddenly Miss Balkema stood beside me. "How did you get along? I'll bring your wheelchair and help you up so we can try the steps."

"You better have help getting me up."

"Oh, I don't think so." She placed her hands beneath my arms, gave a quick lift, and I was on my feet. I gasped. "How did you do that? At home it takes my brother a good heave and he's a strong man."

Miss Balkema smiled. "It's in knowing how. Now here are three steps. See if you can raise your foot on the first step. These are low steps. On the other side are higher ones."

I clutched the handrails, gritted my teeth and tried to raise my foot. I could feel the muscles trembling and I tried to control the correct ones. Up . . . up . . . up . . . and I got it on the step.

"Now lean forward, put your weight on it, raise yourself."

But I could not do it. My leg just wasn't strong enough. I was disappointed, as much for Miss Balkema as for myself. But she beamed at me. "A good start. We'll try again tomorrow."

I had little time now to be miserable. The pool, the gym, and the exercises took so much energy and concentration that I looked forward to the end of the day and a chance to collapse on the bed. I could feel improvement. I could exert more control over the wild spasticity of muscles. I lost weight rapidly but I gained confidence.

The weekend caught me unprepared. Nothing happened. There was no pool, no gym, no nothing. Dr. Steindler made rounds but only said, "Good morning," and hurried on.

Saturday night after I had gone to bed, I heard someone walk past whistling "Margie," a tune I had often danced to at fraternity dances. A wave of loneliness, mixed with helplessness, washed over me and I wanted to go home.

Even Pete did not come on duty to eat my breakfast egg and gossip about the day's affairs. The kindness, enthusiasm, and concern shown by the folk downstairs had nourished me all week. Now my own society seemed pretty thin gruel.

Sunday came and I scolded myself. "Why this moping around? Do something." I wheeled down the hall to Art Sanders room. It was a double room. An old man lay on the other bed. Art was sitting in a wheelchair reading. "Hello," he said, looking up. "Come in."

I moved in. "I'm looking for company. Today this place gives me the willies. You play chess?"

Art brightened. "I play at it."

"Come down to my room and we'll set up the board I brought with me. I don't even know any nurses except my supervisor. Pete looks after me."

Art said, "I'll tell Miss Calderwood where I'm going."

"Oh, hell," I said. "She can find you."

Art gave me a steady look. "I'll tell her. Where's your room?"

Nearly every evening Art and I played chess after supper. We were evenly matched. Art was more cautious than I. He moved only after a study of the position of the pieces. I was more impatient and quick to move.

I wrote to Mother, "I only win the games that Art loses."

Sometimes we played until midnight. No one seemed to mind. The night supervisor warned us to be quiet but she did not know what a quiet game chess is.

One night I threw in the towel. I told Art, "I've got to get more sleep. The exercise routine takes all the energy I've got."

This was true but I also had found another interest. Twice a week John Frederick came to see me. Often he brought his wife Esther. I looked forward to those evenings. Professor Frederick brought me books, talked about literature, discussed poems and stories.

One evening John said, "I want you to meet a young man just back from England. He was a Rhodes Scholar. He writes fine poems and his name is Paul Engle."

Not long after that, as I was setting up the chess board one evening, a young man peered into my room. He said, "I'm looking for James Hearst."

I said, "You've found him."

"I'm Paul Engle. John Frederick told me about you. He said you wrote poems and helped run a farm. I know about horses. My father ran a riding academy."

This began a friendship that has endured to the present time. Paul did not come often or regularly, but when he came he often brought graduate students who were interested in writing. I found my literary horizons expanding. These young men played for keeps in their assessment of current literary theories and trends. I heard the names of critics I did not know existed.

Then Craig Ellyson, a senior medical student, discovered me.

"Your uncle, Dr. McAlvin, told me you were here. My father's a doctor in Waterloo."

The next time Craig came he brought three other students with him. "We all graduated from Grinnell and we're a sort of a club." My social life suddenly became crowded. I scarcely knew what it was to have a quiet evening to myself.

I went home for Christmas and stayed a week. Father said, "You look thin. Are you all right?"

"I think so. An hour in that warm pool really takes it out of you. I work hard in the gym. They put me to it. Miss Balkema and Miss Woodcock are always urging me to do something I can't quite do."

"You sure move around easier," Chuck said. "Look at you standing without your crutches, just leaning against the door."

"I'm trying to walk up and down stairs and that's a struggle."

Holidays meant a great deal to the Hearsts. The relatives all gathered for Christmas and New Year's dinners. Mother and Louise made holiday cookies and candies. I burrowed into the comfort of home. Gifts did not matter. What mattered was just to be at home. That was enough.

Uncle George took me aside after the Christmas dinner and asked, "Does Dr. Steindler encourage you?"

I thought a moment. "Yes and no. Dr. Steindler is a great man and he made it plain to me that I shall find no easy road to improvement. It's up to me, how hard I'm willing to work."

I told Uncle George about Art Sanders. "Now I see what happens when the cord is completely severed. Art has no sensation, no muscle control below the waist. But as Dr. Steindler says, I am getting some messages past the lesion. The warm pool helps my bladder too. It's not so spasmodic."

The return to the hospital did not depress me. Usually a hospital visit even for only an X ray made me bite the bullet. But now I knew the people, knew what I was doing, and knew I was being helped. Miss Moore said she would hold my room for me. I liked that room, away from the main hall, away from the ward, with just the privacy I needed.

The warmth shown me at my return surprised me. Dr. Joe Milgram dropped in one night with a book wrapped in brown paper. He said, "I thought you might like to read this. It's a copy of *Ulysses* by James Joyce. I smuggled it through customs when I came back from Paris."

I tried to thank him but Dr. Milgram did not wait. "Don't ask me what it's about," he said as he shot out of the door.

The delights of forbidden fruit. I had heard of the book. Sylvia Beach had published it in the *Shakespeare and Company Press* in Paris.

It caused a great stir in literary circles and was not allowed to enter the United States on the grounds of obscenity.

After I finished it, and it took me several weeks, I wondered who had raised the stink. I though of Dubuque, where groups of citizens tried to censor books and films they had neither read nor seen. Why? I wondered. No one had forced them to read the books or see the movies. Censorship is funny business.

I plugged away at my exercises. Sometimes at the end of the day Miss Balkema would have me get up on one of the tables under the ultraviolet lamps. Sometimes she gave me a quick massage.

"How do they do it?" I asked myself. "Day after day they keep up their enthusiasm and cheerfulness and they work hard. They do work hard."

One night I saw Miss Woodcock and Miss Balkema walk down the hall after a day's work was done. They drooped—heads bowed, arms dangling. My god, they did look tired.

Miss Woodcock asked me to introduce her to Professor Frederick. She wanted to take a course in creative writing. I set a date with both of them, left them together in my room, and went down to visit Art Sanders.

On the way there, I used the big bathroom off Men's Ward. Someone always opened the door for me and I could stand up in the stalls. As I stood, I noticed, pasted on a wall, a book review I had written for the *Des Moines Register*. Underneath was printed in capital letters, "OUR JIMMY."

There came an evening when Miss Balkema appeared in her street clothes. She had left the nurses' home after supper and dropped in for a visit. She was more relaxed than when in her uniform. She walked with a free-swinging stride. I discovered that she was also a musician and sang in the choir of one of the local churches. She had studied in the university's school of music.

She read a lot, too, and knew about books. She stirred me in my feelings, made me conscious of her as a woman. I liked her very much. I asked her to come again. But after Prudence, well, I still had an open wound and was guarded in my feelings for women.

The days rolled by and the weeks. I worked every day as hard as I was able. Miss Balkema even had me in the pool on Saturday mornings. It made me a little self-conscious to be singled out for such a favor, but I took advantage of it.

About the middle of February, on a Saturday afternoon, Dr. Steindler stopped in my room and sat down. "I would like to smoke a cigar and visit for a few minutes," he said.

I was honored to have him visit. We talked about books, movies, and plays. Dr. Steindler said, "I almost became a writer, then I thought I would be an engineer."

His foreign accent delighted me. "You came here from Vienna," I said.

"Yes, that's where I studied medicine." He picked up a mystery story from my table, one of Raymond Chandler's stories. "Mystery stories," he mused. "How I hate them. They keep me up until three in the morning."

What a delightful visitor he was. Then he said, "Perhaps you have gone as far as you can go for the time being. You should take a vacation. As athletes say, you go a bit stale. We want you to come back."

I agreed. "It's time I went home. By the time I get the farm accounts in balance, income tax forms filled out, and the seed oats tested it will be time for spring work to begin."

"It's good for me. I like being out-of-doors. I feel useful when I finish working a field. But I had planned to be a doctor. Medicine runs in our family."

"We each do what we can," he said.

I appreciated the visit. I told Miss Balkema, "This is my last week. It's time I went home."

Miss Woodcock bustled into the room. "You're leaving us? We're pleased with your progress. We've enjoyed your acquaintance. You can make still more improvement with exercise."

I told Art Sanders good-bye and said, "If you're back here next winter we'll renew our chess games."

Another Mile

I RETURNED to the physiotherapy department of the orthopedic services at the University Hospitals for a third winter. I knew this would probably be the last time. I had reached a plateau of progress and further exercise seemed to gain no new ground. But I had become more independent than I ever dreamed I would be. I could walk from my study at home through the bathroom, out the kitchen door, down the back steps, along the woodhouse wall, and get in the car parked beside the cement platform where I got on and off the tractors. I could do this alone, without crutches. The steps had handrails. I could get out of the car alone, walk through the woodhouse, up the steps, through the kitchen and bathroom, and into my study all by myself.

I could stand up at my closet door, select the clothes I wanted to wear, put on and take off my heavy mackinaw—all by myself. I could sit down and get up from the john in the bathroom, stand at the lavatory and shave and wash my hands and face, walk back through the study and into the dining room with a chair back for support. I had never expected to achieve this much freedom.

I was grateful for the encouragement and direction the folk at Orthopedic Hospital had given me. I had worked like a dog but they had cheered me on and promised me victories.

I remembered the day Dr. Steindler left his office and came to the end of the hall to watch me climb stairs. I walked upstairs from the gym to the first floor. I held onto Pete's arm with one hand, the railing with the other, and stepped up one stair after another. Miss Woodcock and Miss Balkema followed in a kind of triumphal procession.

I stood on a familiar footing with the staff. Outside working hours, I called the women "Woody" and "Tony." They had a friend, Margaret Campbell, in charge of X ray in the big hospital. She spoke with a delightful Irish brogue. The three women often invited me to have tea with them.

Sometimes on weekends I went upstairs to the interns' quarters and played poker with the staff men. As often as I wanted it, whoever had the night duty would bring me an ounce of alcohol which I diluted with grape juice for a highball before supper. Prohibition was still in effect and I was careful as to who brought the booze. Besides it was not much fun to drink alone.

96

When there were no students in the amphitheater, Dr. Steindler and Dr. Milgram invited me to watch them operate. I sat on the front row and they lectured to me as if I were a medical student. Those orthopedic operations were often long sanguinary affairs. I wondered that a surgeon could stand on his feet for three hours, alert, retaining his skill under the pressure the surgery demanded. I have seen Dr. Steindler leave after the major work was complete and leave the assistants to "close up."

I had a mole on the point of my jaw which I often cut while shaving. Just after lunch, as I staunched the flow of blood, Dr. Miltner, first assistant to the Chief, happened by.

"You keep cutting that thing and you'll have a cancer on your face. Come down to the operating room right now and I'll take it off."

As we were talking, Shorty, a former captain of the Iowa football team, stopped by to try sell Leo Miltner some insurance. Just then a nurse from pediatrics brought in a child with abnormally bowed legs. "What do you do with those?" Shorty asked.

"Break the legs, reset them, put them in a cast so the girl will grow up with straight legs."

Dr. Miltner picked up an instrument shaped like a huge nutcracker and broke first one leg and then the other. The tiny bones made a soft crackling sound. The baby, under an anesthetic, hardly moved.

I heard a sigh and a thump. I looked toward the door and there lay Shorty, in a faint. "Let him lie there," said Dr. Miltner with a grin. "He'll come to. Tough, isn't he."

To me surgery was one way of correcting the body's ills. The techniques fascinated me. That girl would have been terribly embarrassed by her bowed legs. "I think I would have made a good doctor," I told myself.

When Dr. Steindler came in on Saturday afternoon to smoke a cigar, as he did most Saturday afternoons, he asked me, "What are you going to do, become a farmer?"

The question had surfaced in my mind many times. "It keeps me outdoors, the farm does, at least two-thirds of the year and makes me use my muscles. I continually wonder at the enormous energy of nature to bring to birth the many kinds of life. Each spring the farm shudders with birth pangs."

"Dr. Milgram says you write poetry, good poetry."

"I've published a few pieces. It's not a way to make a living, at least for me. Not a large demand for farm poems."

Dr. Steindler puffed his cigar. "Would you like to work in the laboratory here? You would be paid regular wages and you could eat your meals at the hospital."

I warmed with gratitude. "Thank you, Dr. Steindler. Let me think about it."

"We could arrange a room for you here." Then Dr. Steindler dismissed the subject. "The book you are reading, *The Magic Mountain*, I read it. It's too long. Cut out a third and I would like it better. Did you read Mann's *Buddenbrooks*? A better book." And Dr. Steindler discussed Thomas Mann.

A few weeks later, when John Frederick made one of his regular visits, he said, "I've resigned from the university here and I'm going to Northwestern at Evanston. And I'm going to take the *Midland* with me."

The news surprised me. "Better job?"

"Yes, all graduate work and one class a week at Notre Dame. I commute by train. There's no future for me here. The university is not as interested in the *Midland* as it is in its football team."

"You've uncovered some fine new writers," I said. "I remember last winter, when you asked me to read manuscripts for you, I found some remarkably fine poems. And the name Mark Van Doren didn't mean a thing to me either. Is he Carl's brother?"

"Could I persuade you to come to Evanston with me and be an associate editor? The building where my office is has an elevator. You could live with us. I would pay you a good salary."

"Well," I thought. "Two job offers in less than a month. Never rains but it pours, huh?" Aloud I said, "I appreciate the offer, John. But I'd need to talk to Chuck and Father first. They're entitled to my time and ability if they want it. I owe my family a heavy obligation."

A group of younger men on the faculty of the medical college met once a month to hear a paper read by one of the members. I had been invited to attend several of the meetings. I had made friends with Dr. William Mengert from the obstetrical and gynecological department. I heard Bill read a paper on the "Male Midwife."

The Mengerts invited me to Sunday dinner. Ida's sister Grace was there. I had known Grace some years before when she taught in the drama department at the Iowa State Teachers College in Cedar Falls.

Grace said, "Oh, come to Evanston. I'm going to teach at the J. Sterling Morton School next year and you can live with me. I could take you to the office in the morning and pick you up after school."

I bowed. "That's an extremely tempting offer."

But I knew people were not aware of the problems I faced. Bathroom facilities would need to be available to me. Most folk did not realize how difficult it was to live in a world not made for the physically handicapped. At home I had worked out ways to satisfy my needs. In the hospital, help was always at hand; there I lived free of any anxiety about my body care. When I wanted a bath, Pete took me downstairs to the shower room. The hospital made the days pleasant for me, free from concern about my handicap, with meals served in my room, a highball whenever I wanted it, and friends from the staff and university faculty to visit with.

I enjoyed this freedom from worry. Never again would life be so easy and stimulating for me. I look back on these days as a golden time of well-being.

I did work to the limit of my strength every day, putting in strenuous hours at the pool and gym. I walked around and around in the pool with no support but the water. The water level could be lowered to waist high and I could still walk. I could get in and out of the pool by myself. I could hoist myself up on the high table under the ultraviolet lamp.

I left Miss Moore and Boys' Ward and lived in a room for private patients. It was a double room but I was allowed to have it by myself. It had two beds, a high regular hospital bed and a low bed where I could dress myself. I took turns sleeping in the beds just to prove I could get in the high one by myself. Often the staff doctor on night call napped on the other bed.

I attended lectures and concerts at the university. One of the staff men took me to an afternoon baseball game.

"Where do you want to sit?" Dr. Waring asked me.

"Let's sit behind the catcher so we can see what the pitchers are doing. I used to throw some on our college team. Even pitched a little semipro ball."

The short flight of steps up the bleacher seats did not deter me. I climbed three times that many every day at the hospital. But when I stood up from the wheelchair with the crowd rushing past, my feet took root and stayed flat on the ground.

"All right," Tom Waring said. "We'll wheel over on the grass behind first base."

I was less humiliated than bewildered. What had caused me to freeze up? I told Dr. Steindler about it and he beamed at me in his friendly way. With a touch of irony in his voice he said, "Maybe you have a psychic block. Would you like to see someone from psychiatric?"

"Yes, I would." Psychiatric Hospital was right next door and I was curious about psychiatry.

Not long after that, when I returned from my daily workout in the gym, I found a stranger sitting on my bed. He stood up and shook hands when I entered.

"I am Dr. Langway from psychiatric. I hear you have a problem."

I told him what had happened. I went farther back and explained what a triumph it was for me to be able to climb steps.

Dr. Langway listened carefully, studied the burning end of his cigarette, and said, "I think you can work this out by yourself. You don't need anyone from our jungle to help you." With that he rose, shook my hand, and left. That ended my experience with psychiatrists.

When I visited the hospital the last time, after cornhusking was done, I had a queer experience that made me uncomfortable whenever I remembered it. It was Indian summer weather. The days spread soft, warm sunshine over people and fields. Pete asked me if I would like to attend an Amish church service the next Sunday. "I come from that neighborhood," he explained.

I had often wondered about these people, with their black suits, black shovel hats, beards, and no buttons on their clothes. They used horses instead of tractors and did much of the farm work by hand.

"They don't have a church," Pete explained. "They meet at someone's house, bring baskets of food, eat a communal meal. This kind of weather they'll meet outdoors. We can just sit in the car."

"Sure, I'd like to go. I've always been curious about the Amish. Will it be all right for us foreigners to show up?"

"They know me. Maybe they'll think I'm returning to the fold. Okay, next Sunday."

The weather held. Sunday bathed the earth in warm sunshine. Pete brought his car and we drove out into the country. Near Kalona, an Amish settlement, the cornstalks stood upright though the husks were empty. "Been picked by hand," I thought. "Machines break down the stalks."

When we arrived at the farm where the services were to be held, we found the yard crowded with horse-drawn vehicles—buggies, carriages, wagons. I admired the neatness and cleanness of yards and buildings. Everything looked well kept and painted. Gates hung straight, barn doors were solid, and corncribs were tight and filled with ears. The house, a large square building painted white, sat in the middle of a lawn that was neat as a pin. Men, women, and children sat on the lawn dressed in their somber clothes. Their faces set in stern expressions when they saw our car drive in.

"I don't think they want us," I said. "No welcome hand of fellowship."

"We better get out and sit on the grass," Pete said. "I'll help you walk over."

The people watched us and their expressions did not change. At a quiet word from one of the women, a boy went in the house and brought out a chair for me. One of the men stood up, faced the others, and the services began.

I tried to enter their worship, bowed my head when prayers were said, attempted to join the singing. Pete showed a half smile on an otherwise blank face. After the service no one spoke to us. A little girl brought me a plate of food. I saw mountains of food, baskets emptied on a rough plank table. But no one spoke to me. I sensed a chill in the atmosphere. I had never been so left out in my life.

We drove back in silence. At the hospital, Pete helped me into the wheelchair. I said, "You know, Pete, I don't think they liked us. I felt like a leper outside the gates."

"They didn't seem real friendly," Pete admitted. "But I didn't expect they would, at least to me. But I thought you might like to attend a meeting."

I was not through with the Amish. A few weeks later, as I moved down the hall, I heard sobbing. It came from my old room off Boys' Ward. Curious, I wheeled in and found a boy, about fourteen years old, in bed. His sobbing stopped when he saw me and his eyes showed fright. "Do you hurt?" I asked.

The boy shook his head but did not speak.

"Why do you cry then?" I asked as gently as I could.

Still no answer. I pushed down the hall to the supervisor's desk. Miss Moore was working on her charts. "Hello stranger," she said. "I thought you had forgotten us."

"Who's the lad in my old room who's so unhappy?"

"His name is Peter. He's one of the hook-and-eye Dutch. He's so lonesome he cries. But there isn't room for him in the ward, so we put him in the isolation room."

"Serious?"

"I don't think so. He's an old polio case. Dr. Steindler wants to reset the leg he broke."

"I'm going in and talk to him. I know just how he feels. Give me a book I can read to him."

Miss Moore motioned toward the bookcase. "Help yourself. You ought to know what's there."

"I seem too far away. It was easier when I lived here. Remember the boy who always wanted a chapter from the 'New Testament'?"

"The boys enjoyed having you read to them."

I studied the titles and picked out Stevenson's *Treasure Island*.

I introduced myself to Peter. "I'm going to read to you until suppertime. This is a book about pirates. Do you know what a pirate is?"

In a tremulous voice, heavy with accent, the boy said, "Ja, I know."

I read to him until the supper trays came. Then I laid the book on the table and said, "I'll come back and read to you tomorrow afternoon. Now cheer up, don't be afraid. The people here are kind."

I read to him every day. Peter's leg was reset and in a cast. "You'll go home in a few days," I told him.

I asked Dr. Milgram, Dr. Steindler's first assistant, "Joe, when will Peter go home?"

"In a few days if the X rays show the bone is knitting."

Conversation with Peter consisted of my questions and his short answers. But he grew used to me and lost some of his shyness. He looked forward to the reading each afternoon.

I told Miss Moore, "I don't know if he likes the story or just likes to have company. He's a lonesome kid."

I had one more chapter of *Treasure Island* to read before Peter went home. I came back after supper. "You get two readings today, so we can finish the book."

I had just begun to read when someone entered the room. I looked up and saw an Amish man. He wore the usual black suit, had a beard, and carried a broad-brimmed hat. Thickset, broad-shouldered, he owned a pleasant face. A youthful face with kind eyes.

"Fader!" cried Peter.

The man offered his hand. "I am Peter Dokken, young Peter's father."

I shook hands. I grasped a strong, work-worn hand. "You'll have to finish the book yourself, Peter. Take good care of your leg and keep out of mischief."

Mr. Dokken stopped me. "Thank you," he said in a deep voice. "for kindness to Peter. He is not much for being away from home."

"We got along fine, Peter and I. I know what it's like to be stuck in a hospital bed off by yourself."

"Wait," Peter's father held up his hand. "We were not kind to you when you came to our meeting. But you were a stranger and came in a car."

"I was guilty of bad manners. It was a religious meeting and I came out of curiosity. I'm sorry we disturbed you."

Mr. Dokken shook hands again. "You will be welcome if you care to join us another time."

I told Pete about this the next morning when he stopped for his egg and cup of coffee. Harry, the hospital carpenter, stopped in too.

I said, "He looked like a good man. He was friendly and thanked me. I imagine the Amish have to protect themselves against nosey people and some who are downright hostile."

"Yeah," Harry put in. "It's a free country. But just try being different."

He picked up his toolbox. "I got to go and fix the little Napoleon's garage door again. Every time he has a fight with his wife he backs out of the door without opening it. Then she calls me to come and fix it."

I raised my eyebrows. "Little Napoleon?"

Pete said, "Head of one of the departments over at General. A little man with a big stride."

I agreed with Dr. Steindler that I had gone about as far as I could go. By conscious, concentrated effort I could make my contracted hands and rebellious legs do some of the things I wanted them to do. But I could not repair the lines where the messages came through. Some messages never got through and never would. Even so, I had made great progress, more than I had hoped for. There was one situation I could not control. If I fell down I could not get up without help. I had to be careful about that.

But Miss Woodcock and Miss Balkema would not give up hope that I had more to gain. Miss Woodcock, good Catholic that she was, made a novena and slipped a couple of medals in my pocket.

"Just keep them with you," she begged. "Don't talk about it."

It amused me, but such friendship touched me too. From childhood I had believed there was magic in the world. Maybe there is.

Tony Balkema, who was more practical, subjected me to massage, diathermy, and electrical stimulation besides working me to the limit in pool and gym. She loved me and made no secret of her affection. I responded to her efforts by working my tail off. I liked her very much and regarded her dedication to helping mend broken bodies with awe and admiration. Our affection did not manifest itself in any outward way. It stayed a strong, secret, underground stream.

When I went home for the holidays or a weekend, I often brought someone from the hospital with me. Mother, Louise, and Chuck made them feel welcome. I hoped my family found pleasure in these guests from a different and highly specialized world.

One day Tony and I sat alone on our porch swing. She asked hesitantly, "What do your folks think of me coming home with you so often? I love you, Jim, but I'm too old for you. Does your mother think I'm a predator?"

I pressed her hand and shook my head, though such frank avowals made me a trifle uneasy. In our family we were not as open and direct about our feelings and I wasn't used to it. "I will say, Tony, that my family is full of gratitude for all you have done for me. As for being older, what are years among friends?"

"I'd do anything for you, Jim. Just anything."

I wished I could find words to tell her of my affection and admiration for her and not let our emotions overwhelm us. I was still shy of an involvement from which I could not extricate myself. Yet all the time I was acutely aware of the debt I owed her. And I did like her very much.

In those days a nursing school operated under rules as strict as a military post. One of the student nurses asked me one evening, as she went off duty, if my father was the Farm Bureau man. I assured her he was. She said her father was a farmer and worked in the Farm Bureau in the county where she lived. Her name, she said, was Lee Haines. She stood in the doorway relaxed, her cap in hand, white apron rumpled, hair slightly tumbled. A good-looking woman tired out from her day's work.

Suddenly a shrill voice rent the air. An older woman, thin, quivering, cheeks flushed with anger, and dressed in a white uniform, yelled at the girl, "How dare you loiter in a patient's room when you're off duty? Half-dressed like a slut! Now go!" She pointed her finger toward the door. The girl, already drooping from a long day of work and classes, slunk away. Her persecutor followed her.

Shocked at first, I burned with my own anger. The next day, the first supervisor I saw was my friend Geraldine Moore. I told her what happened. "I'm going to see Dr. Steindler about this and find out who's in charge of the nursing school. That girl and I were simply getting acquainted because her father knows mine. I won't have her insulted like that. Not in my room."

Miss Moore listened and then said, "That was Flora Weber, superintendent in charge of student nurses here at Children's Hospital. She runs the place like an army camp."

"I'll army camp her. I want to see Dr. Steindler."

The word got back, as I hoped it would, and in about ten minutes the angry superintendent entered my room, her lips bent in a thin smile. "I'm Miss Weber," she said. "You don't understand, Mr. Hearst. These girls must be taught discipline. They know they're not to visit with men patients. I'm sorry it happened."

She did not placate me. "I was in the army, I know about discipline. I asked that girl to stay a few minutes and tell me about her family. Our fathers are acquainted."

"But she knows better, Mr. Hearst."

I got my dander up. "Look here, it was not her fault. I asked her to stay. Do I bring this up at Dr. Steindler's office or not?"

She wilted a bit. "Very well, nothing more will be said or done about it." She frowned her way out.

I told Chuck about it. "You'd have thought I was raping the girl or she was raping me. Made me mad as hell. I guess I don't know how they run nursing schools."

I never saw the girl again. She was shifted to another service. But one of her classmates told me, "Lee made out all right."

About the middle of March the accident happened. I had stayed two extra weeks because it was my last visit in the physiotherapy department. I hated to leave. My work there had changed me. That included not only a bodily improvement but a rehabilitation of my mental and, yes, my spiritual attitudes.

I had outgrown my feeling of being an outcast. I no longer shrank from the reality of my condition. Other people had handicaps and were crippled, but overcame them. I had only to visit some of my acquaintances in Men's Ward to realize how lucky I was. I knew the world of the hospital is not the same as the world outside. But I could survive that one too.

The accident was my own fault. I was fooling around in the gym one morning early, before the instructors brought in the polio and scoliosis patients. I examined the various pieces of apparatus that I had seen dozens of time before. I paused in front of a square seat with iron panels sticking out at right angles to it. The panels had straps attached.

"What's this, Tony?" I called.

Miss Balkema said, "We seat the patient and strap the legs to these supports. Then with a lever we can move the supports out and in. We can stretch the adductors that way. Or have the patient lean forward and stretch the hamstrings."

"Let me sit in the thing and see if I can stretch my hamstrings. Maybe then I wouldn't pouch out so much when I stand up."

Miss Balkema showed little enthusiasm. "It's your weak abdominal muscles that fail to hold you straight. Your hamstrings have nothing to do with it."

By this time I had risen from the wheelchair, turned, and seated myself on the apparatus. "Help me strap my legs to these supports. We'll strap down my knees so they won't bend when I lean forward."

Miss Balkema said nothing, showing her disapproval by her silence. She fastened the straps.

"Now shove me forward," I insisted. I leaned out over my outstretched legs. I could feel the pull on the tendons behind my knees. "This ought to stretch 'em. Push harder, Tony, 'til my nose touches my toes."

She pushed. A loud pop answered her. I toppled forward. "I can't straighten up. I busted something."

For just an instant she stood still, shocked, stricken. Then she caught me by the shoulders and pulled me back to a sitting position. She held me against her. She called to a young instructor assembling the scoliosis class. "Sylvia, quick, run upstairs and tell Pete to bring down the cart. Mr. Hearst has been hurt."

She turned to me and wailed. "Oh, why did you have to be so foolish. Why couldn't we let well enough alone." She held me firmly against her. "Do you hurt?"

"No," I said. "But I can't sit up."

Pete whisked through the doors pushing a cart. "Sylvia, help us lift him on the cart."

The three of them laid me on the cart. "What's the matter?" Pete asked. "Hearst been cutting up?"

"Oh, I don't know." Tony spread a light blanket over me. "He must have fractured something. Take him right over to X ray. I'll give you a slip. I'll call Miss Calderwood and tell her where you've gone."

As I was wheeled through the tunnel toward General Hospital, I said, "It was my own fault. I pushed too hard."

Pete said, "I'll have to leave you and get back to Men's Ward or Miss Calderwood will scalp me. When the pictures are taken, X ray will send you back."

Margaret Campbell looked up as we wheeled into the X-ray office. "For goodness sake, what are you doing here?" She stared down at me.

"Here's his slip," Pete said. Then to me, "See you later."

"Emergency," Miss Campbell said. "Whatever have you been doing? We'll get you in right away. Nette must be frantic." Her rich Irish brogue always pleased me.

After the pictures were taken Miss Campbell approached me. "You have a fracture of the sacrum. It's the flat bone at the end of your spine. The doctor will call Dr. Steindler and send over the pictures. I'll have an orderly take you back. Oh, Jim, what in the world were you doing? I tell you, Nette will be so upset."

Back in my room and up on the high hospital bed, Pete and one of the nurses undressed me and slipped me into a hospital gown. In a few minutes Dr. Milgram entered, followed by a nurse wheeling a medical supply cart. Dr. Milgram rolled up his sleeves. "I'm going to strap your back. In fact, I'm going to give you an adhesive tape corset to hold the bones in place."

I frowned. "Is it a bad break, Joe?"

"A hairline fracture, but when the shock wears off you'll be uncomfortable for a few days."

"How long will I be laid up?"

"Depends on how fast it heals. Four weeks, six weeks."

Dr. Steindler came down wearing a worried look. "What are you trying to do?" he asked with gentle irony. "Break up our equipment?"

After supper Dr. Milgram stopped in. "You want company?"

Joe Milgram had been good for me. He was at home in many fields of culture. Born and raised in Brooklyn, he was familiar with the New York scene—the books, music, galleries, and theater. He helped educate me in the arts. He was stimulating and enthusiastic and I enjoyed having him visit me.

Three days later my temperature rose. A urinalysis showed pus in the urine. Pete loaded me on a cart and took me over to General to the genitourinary department. After a few questions, Dr. Harry Lee, first assistant to the chief, Dr. Alcock, moved me onto the treatment table and massaged my prostate. The pus just boiled out. "There, my boy, is why you have trouble with your bladder. With that much infection I'm surprised you have any control at all."

Each morning I was wheeled over to the G.U. services to have my prostate massaged. "Maybe we can get rid of the infection but it's an old one. You've had it a long time."

"Why did it flare up now and not before?"

"I don't know unless that break in your back stirred things up. Like a fire, once it starts . . . whooooosh!"

Tony came every day to bring flowers, books, a box of cookies. It hurt me to see her so concerned. After all, the accident had been my own fault.

She always came after supper. She once came in and put her arms around me. I reached out and dimmed the reading lamp. She wore a loose gown, her hair soft and falling around her face. She pressed her cheek against mine and murmured, "I wouldn't hurt you for anything."

I kissed her and explored the low V in the neck of her gown. In the darkened room I responded with more than friendly gestures.

Someone knocked. The door opened and there stood Father. He knew Tony because she had been home with me several times. He spoke kindly to her and she gathered herself together and fled. It was one of the few times I was embarrassed before my father.

"You don't write to your mother. I drove down to see how you are."

I told Chuck about it afterward. "He was awfully decent and friendly to her. Didn't act surprised. I'll bet I looked as if I had my hand in the cookie jar."

As if warned, from that evening on I kept my emotions under wraps when Tony and I were together. Over and over I told her, "Quit feeling guilty. You tried to discourage me. I should have left the stupid machine alone."

I gave no thought to anything but my own carelessness. Then one day a man came to my room after lunch. "Mr. Hearst?" he asked. I nodded.

"I'm Harold Sockert from Meany, McCrary, and Sockert. We're a law firm in Iowa City."

He spoke in a cultured voice. He was a well-dressed, dapper man with a dark, smooth-shaven face. He offered me a card and sat down.

"I believe you had an accident," he began.

"Yes, years ago."

"No, I mean recently, here in the hospital. A low back fracture I understand. In cases like this there is always the question of the liability of the hospital."

"Not this time," I told him. "It was my own damn fault."

"Let's not be hasty," Mr. Sockert looked at some notes. "Someone should have denied you permission to use that machine. You have suffered a severe injury which will cause you pain and discomfort and deprive you of your normal activity. For this the hospital must accept responsibility."

"No," I said. "I couldn't wait to get my mitts on that machine."

"On your behalf then," went on Mr. Sockert, "we are prepared to file a suit for damages. We will do this without cost to you and risk taking a percent of the amount the court awards you."

The man's message finally penetrated my thick skull. "You mean sue the hospital?"

Mr. Sockert smiled. "It won't cost the hospital anything. Hospitals carry liability insurance to protect themselves against just such contingencies."

I raised up on my elbows, my voice thick with anger. "Beat it," I said. "Out of my room. Out. Out."

Mr. Sockert leisurely returned his notes to his briefcase, picked up his hat, and walked out without another word.

I told Joe Milgram about my visitor that evening. "Why, the son of a bitch wanted me to sue the hospital."

Joe shrugged. "He knows his business. He probably could get you a fat settlement. The hospital wouldn't fight it. The insurance company would settle out of court. Why didn't you go ahead?"

"You horrify me, Joe. No one could have been treated better here than I've been. You folk are my friends. Look how much improvement I've made since I started to come here. Sue the hospital? You must be nuts."

Joe patted my shoulder. "I must go and change the dressing on Mr. Sorensen's leg. You're a nice boy, Jim, and I like you. I wish more of the world had your Iowa innocence."

"Go to hell," I said. "And hurry back."

I dozed off after supper and did not turn on my light. I heard someone at the door and roused quickly. A young woman in a scarlet dress stood in the doorway. "I am Carmelita Calderwood, your supervisor, and I thought it was time we became acquainted."

I was now fully awake. "Come in. You and I *have* met before."

Her gray eyes opened in surprise.

"You went to East High in Waterloo. After a basketball game we went to a party. One of the Rath girls was there and Glade Butterfield's girl, Jean. I came late, after I showered and dressed."

She smiled. "I remember those names if not the occasion. Would you have a minute to talk about books?"

If I had had extrasensory perception, I would have felt the thrust of the future right then. But alas, I did not. Here was a bright young woman whose gray eyes and blue-black hair woke interest in me. "Sure," I said. "Please come in. I have opinions on everything. What have you been reading?"

Joe Milgram stuck his head in the door, saw I had a visitor, and vanished. Our conversation leaped fences as we pursued our quarry. Miss Calderwood looked at her watch. "Ten o'clock. I've no business keeping you up so late. I must say good night."

"We can continue this talk tomorrow night if you can spare the time," I hinted.

She said, "I think so, if you don't mind me in uniform."

I wanted to see her again. "Of course not. Do come."

I lay awake a long time.

Promise of Love

"HAVE YOU THOUGHT about coming to Evanston?" John Frederick asked me. He still paid me a weekly visit, coming into the room with an armful of books and his briefcase. Sometimes his thin shoulders drooped, as if he had had a long day. Now that I was bedfast I looked forward to his visits and the books he brought to me.

Miss Woodcock had enrolled with him as a special student and they often discussed her work in my room. Whether she knew it or not, Miss Woodcock was preparing herself to write her famous book, *Scoliosis.*

"This cracked back of mine takes up most of my attention," I confessed. "As soon as I'm up and about again I'll let you know. I want to be sure this accident hasn't set me back."

Dr. Steindler did not mention the laboratory job again, but Joe Milgram told me, "If you want that place, the Chief will arrange it for you."

My fractured back healed nicely and did not worry me. I was caught in a web of attraction for Carmelita Calderwood. She intrigued me with her knowledge of books and her lightning flashes of revelation about the problems of writing. I was sure she was a writer herself, though she had not said so.

It hurt my pride to discover that she had read books I had never even heard of. The bawdy poems of Aretino, for example. Who in hell was Aretino? I was too proud to ask.

She said she liked to play chess and she brought her board and pieces so we could play. The first thing she did was to pull the "fool's checkmate" on me. It made me look silly.

An undertow of feeling began to carry us into uncharted waters where we either had to sink or swim. Our lives moved closer together. It didn't seem evident to me until one day Joe Milgram said, "Carmelita, when you die will me your skeleton. It'd be such a trim little set of bones."

Almost before I realized it I reared up in resentment and said brusquely, "The hell with you, Joe."

Joe just smiled and left us to our chess game. "You mustn't mind Joe," Carmelita said. "He likes to shock people." Then to change the subject she asked, "How did you begin to write book reviews for the *Des Moines Register?*"

I smoothed my ruffled feathers. Of course Carmelita and Joe had known each other and worked together long before I appeared. But I resented their playful innuendos. I did not want to share her with anyone.

"I did some work for *Wallace's Farmer* and when the managing editor, Donald R. Murphy, became editor of the book page he asked me to review some books. No pay but I got to keep the books. Some very nice ones too."

"Do you like doing it?"

"Yes, I like doing it. Murphy gives us a free hand. If a book stinks, we can say so. If it's a good book we praise it. Just our opinions, of course. We irritate some readers when we really stick pins in these gooey, semireligious novels that feed people on hot air."

"Who is 'we'?"

"A group of young men that Wallace and Murphy gathered around them. A whole bunch of smart young guys."

"Your move," she said.

"I'm going home for the weekend," I said. "Come with me. I have to come back to have the infection treated and Dr. Steindler wants to examine my back before I leave for good."

Friday afternoon Chuck came for me. Don McCavick rode with him for company. Don taught in the same school that Louise did and was a friend of ours. Carmelita asked if she could ride with us as far as Cedar Rapids. She had a free weekend and wanted to visit her aunt who lived in Marion.

On the way I begged, "Oh, come on home with us. I want you to meet my mother. You can always visit your aunt."

Don said, "Let's kidnap her. We're having a party tonight and she can meet some of our friends."

Carmelita may have been too tired to argue or she may have wanted to meet my family. She said, "All right, but I don't feel in a party mood. I'm tired."

She closed her eyes but made no protest when we drove past Marion where her aunt lived and pushed on toward Waterloo. When we reached home, Don carried in her bag and Chuck helped me into the house. The evening was well along. Louise had invited some of her friends and the house was lively with people. Most of the folk gathered around the dining room table where food and drink had been set out. Someone played "I'm Forever Blowing Bubbles" softly on the piano.

I introduced Carmelita to Mother, then to Louise. After that Louise took over.

Mother said, "I'm glad you came, Carmelita. We heard from Uncle George how well you took care of Jim."

"Come upstairs and I'll show you your room," Louise said.

When Louise came down she said, "She'll be down in a minute." Then to me, "She's nice, isn't she."

When Carmelita joined the party the other women regarded her with more curiosity than friendliness but the men gave her a hearty welcome. She was tired and I think she was glad when the guests went home. She kissed me good night and followed Mother and Louise upstairs. It pleased me that Mother and Louise took her in as if they knew that someday she would be part of our family.

My back healed and I left the hospital. But the infection in my prostate did not heal. "Stay off the tractor," Dr. Lee warned me. "Don't bang that prostate on a tractor seat."

Uncle George drove out twice a week to massage it and said, "This *Bacillus aerogenes* is the devil to get rid of."

Every day I got in the car, drove out to my parallel bars under the trees, and walked back and forth. Then I got in the car, drove back to the house, stepped out on the cement block Chuck had made for me, walked up the back steps to kitchen, and on through the bathroom to my study. It gave me great satisfaction to do this by myself.

I did stay off the tractor. I kept the farm books and told Chuck, "I'm going to pay the wages of one hired man from my share of the farm income until I can work again."

One Sunday, when Father came home, I asked for a family conference. I described the offers I had had from John Frederick and Dr. Steindler. "I must let them know. What do you think?"

Father asked, "Wouldn't you like to stay here and go into partnership with Chuck?"

I looked at my brother. "How about it, Chuck. Can we get along together?"

Chuck shrugged. "We have so far. I think you ought to stay here anyway, Jim, where you can work outdoors."

I agreed. "I would rather stay here. I have no great yen to go to Evanston. The hospital job doesn't offer me any future. Unless I took classes at the medical school I'd just be a lab assistant all my life."

Mother spoke up. "Of course you'll stay here. This is our home and our farm and you boys should stay here. What would happen if Mr. Frederick stopped publishing the *Midland?*"

"I've thought of that," I said. "But John would look out for me. He would find me another job."

Late in the summer I went to Iowa City again. I signed in at General Hospital and went to the urology service. "I can't get rid of my bugs," I told Dr. Lee, "and I'm pretty uncomfortable."

"I better have the Chief look at you," Dr. Lee said.

The next morning Dr. Alcock and trailing staff crowded my room. A short, hard-eyed man with a stern voice, he leaned over the foot of my bed. "I read the history and laboratory reports. I think we better go in there and drain the abcess."

"That mean surgery?" I asked him.

"We go in through the belly and excise the infected part of the prostate."

In a weak attempt at humor I said, "Don't take off any more than you need to. I may have use for that prostate."

No humor for Dr. Alcock. He pounded the bed with his fist and bellowed, "Goddamnit, don't try to tell me my business. If I make a mistake and touch that sphincter, my name will be mud with your four uncles up in northeast Iowa."

Surprised, I shut my mouth and let him glower. Later I told Dr. Lee, "First time I knew I had status because of my uncles. What was that sphincter business all about?"

Dr. Lee looked wise. "Just this, my boy. If he goes in there and bruises that sphincter muscle you would no longer be able to hold your water. It's tricky business."

I did not feel at home with these men. I missed the friendly, cultured atmosphere of the orthopedic clinic. "These guys are a little too ham-handed for me," I thought.

When I went into the operating room, just before the anesthetist slapped the mask over my face, I saw Dr. Alcock come in, masked, gloved, and gowned. I said sarcastically, "Good luck, Doc."

Harry Lee growled in my ear, "Don't get smart."

The next morning, hurting a little, groggy from the anesthetic and sedation, I stared unbelieving at the door where Carmelita appeared. She washed my face and hands, kissed me on the forehead, and said, "I'll see you later." Then she was gone.

Tears seeped from my eyes. I wondered how she had time to eat breakfast, walk all the way over to General, look after me, and get back in time to go on duty at seven.

At noon she came again and fed me my lunch. I felt pretty lousy but I whispered, "You don't have time. How do you manage?" She smiled and was gone. I knew how she managed. She went without lunch.

In the afternoon, Uncle George flew into Iowa City. He talked first to Dr. Alcock and then came to see me. "You feel all right?" he asked. "The surgery came off all right according to Dr. Alcock. There was an abcess and he drained it. He's a grim little cuss."

"Behind his back the boys call him the 'Little Napoleon.' "

"Are you getting good care? Want me to raise hell with anybody?"

I explained how Carmelita came over from the orthopedic service to look after me. "Here she is now."

She came in dressed in street clothes. "These are my hours off duty. I just came over to see if you're behaving yourself."

I introduced her to Uncle George. He put his arm around her and said, "God bless you, my dear."

She said, "I must go now—errands downtown. I'll feed you your supper. Tomorrow you can be a big boy and go it on your own. Oh, yes, Pete said he would drop in when he gets off duty. I'm glad I met you, Dr. George."

"Who's Pete?"

"Orderly at orthopedics who looked after me when I was there. We went through a lot together."

Uncle George raised his hand in mock salute. "You really rate when an orderly from another service comes to visit you."

"After three winters over there I practically belong to the orthopedic department."

Just before Uncle George rose to go, in came Dr. Steindler and his staff. He bent over me, "Well, well, how are you?" He shook hands with Uncle George, "Nice to see you again, Dr. Hearst." He smiled at me with a kind of impish smile, "You get along all right with the Plumber?" And they all swept out to finish making rounds.

Joe Milgram came back. "I'll be over tonight."

"Hold it, Joe. I want you to meet my uncle. Dr. Hearst, Dr. Milgram." They shook hands and Joe left.

Uncle George stood up. "Dr. Steindler is a fine man, isn't he. Why is he over here?

"There are orthopedic patients over here. The private rooms are a bit fancier. He makes afternoon rounds when he operates in the morning. Joe Milgram is his first man."

"I must go. Bite Livingston flew me down here. I said I'd meet him at the airport at four o'clock."

After Carmelita had fed me my supper and Pete had stopped to say hello, Joe brought a couple of books and chatted briefly. Then I settled down to sleep.

But sleep did not come. The night nurse said, "There is a p.r.n. order for you for a sedative."

I shook my head, "No, I'll wait a while."

P.r.n., whenever I want one. Maybe the Little Napoleon had more humanity than I gave him credit for.

Like watching a film run backward I drifted through memories. Two years ago brother Chuck caught his hand in the cornpicker. He could have lost his whole arm. The hired man, with a maul, broke the rollers apart that held Chuck's hand. What a nasty mess it was—broken bones of the fingers sticking through the flesh, blood dripping, Chuck with a stricken look on his face.

The hired man drove him to the hospital where Uncle Will set the bones and sewed up the torn flesh. But he did not want to tackle the tendon that straightens the little finger. It had been severed and the finger dropped.

I had discussed it with Dr. Steindler and Chuck had come to Iowa

City and had the tendon connected. It was Chuck who told me that our supervisor, Miss Calderwood, came from Waterloo and knew some of our friends.

I sighed. Chuck's fingers would always be stiff but at least he could open and close his hand.

Memories kept drifting by.

A memory surfaced of an incident that I wanted to forget. Once it plagued me with embarrassment, now it seemed more amusing but my half smile was still tinged with chagrin. It happened this way.

When Chuck and I had our yards full of cattle, we fed about twenty thousand bushels of corn more than we raised. We bought corn from farmers and elevators within a radius of twenty miles of the farm. To keep our expenses as low as possible, we used to hedge our purchases on the Chicago commodity market.

The business went something like this: usually the lowest prices for corn come at harvest time. So in November we would buy fifteen or twenty thousand bushels of corn futures on the commodity market, March or May futures, sometimes half one month and half the other. We had our price locked in that we would have to pay. Then, as we bought the actual corn, we sold an equal number of bushels on the futures market. It worked fairly well for us, though the local prices do not always keep in step with the futures market.

But one day I had an attack of gambling fever and bought two contracts of March oats on the futures market. This was just after corn-husking and before I made my journey to Children's Hospital for more intensive exercise.

I forgot all about it.

The winter rolled along and I spent my days in the pool and gymnasium. One afternoon Dr. Steindler's secretary came to the gym with a telegram for me. I was practicing stair climbing. I sat down on the stairs and wiped my face and opened the telegram. It was from Lamson Brothers and Company, grain and commodity brokers. It read, "Two carloads of oats on track at Peoria, Illinois. Wire shipping instructions."

I nearly fell through the floor. My god, I had forgotten to sell those damn futures before they came due. How could I have forgotten them? When Pete saw the telegram he said gravely, "I think we could clear out a couple of private rooms and store the oats in there."

It cost me close to five hundred dollars in commissions, demurrage fees, and unloading charges to get those oats off my back. The commodities market lost a customer right there. If I couldn't keep track of a risky speculation like buying grain futures, it was better to stay with buying popcorn.

This did not end it. Word spread through the hospital that Hearst had bought two carloads of oats. I took a lot of flak. Pete would saunter in before breakfast and ask, "How's the oat market today?"

Tom Waring, one of the staff men, stuck his head in the door and said, "There's a big demand for oatmeal these days over at pediatrics."

I was too stunned by my stupidity to make any smart replies. Finally, I did post a notice on my door, "Sold out of oats, both wild and tame variety."

The event was soon forgotten by everyone but me. My face turned red for months whenever I thought of it.

When my back healed enough so I could go home for keeps, Father drove down to get me. I told him how anxious the department was because Dr. Steindler had been invited to go somewhere else at an increased salary.

Father called Dr. Steindler on my phone and then went to his office to talk to him. In those days Father swung a lot of weight with the governor and Board of Regents. I do not know what was said, but Dr. Steindler decided to stay.

Carmelita was never far out of my thoughts. She had once sent her roommate, Meryl Norton, to see me. Meryl had a soft voice and big brown eyes. She was taking courses at the university and working part time. She was so easy to talk to—friendly, intelligent, interested in books. I told Carmelita it was risky to send such a nice girl to see me. Carmelita had laughed and said if Meryl would have me I couldn't do better.

I returned from my memory trip and snuggled under the bedclothes. When the nurse came to see if my drainage tube was open and working I said, "Tell the desk I'll take that Nembutal now."

When I came home from surgery I lay around, read, wrote letters, tried some poems. But my energy lacked staying power and I drifted along indolent, half angry with myself. I tried a few half days in the field, but the heat and work drained me.

Chuck advised me to wait until I got my strength back. I helped Mother with the dishes. Sometimes I helped with the cooking. On ironing day, I ironed the flat pieces. I wasn't up to ironing shirts and blouses.

Every day I wrote something. I had a stubborn belief in the efficacy of discipline and made myself sit at the typewriter each morning. Everything I wrote went into the wastebasket.

I tried to ignore symptoms that began to reoccur. I told myself that I imagined them. Finally I had to admit that the infection had not been cured.

I told Uncle George, "All that Urotropin I've swallowed, the surgery, drinking lots of fluids, staying away from liquor and women as they insisted. . . ." I was grim-lipped.

Uncle George sympathized with me. "Try the Mayo Clinic at Rochester. The men there are doing research every day and see clinical material from all over the world. I'll make an appointment for you. I think you should go."

Ten days later Chuck drove me to Rochester and I entered Methodist Hospital.

Dr. Cabot was head of the urology section—they are called "sections" at the Mayo Clinic rather than "services" or "departments." Dr. Cabot told me, "I never could see why the Lord put such an important gland beside a main sewage ditch."

Dr. Cabot, rather small, tough, wiry, tanned, arms and legs slightly bowed, looked like a polo player and spoke with a Boston accent. He referred me to Dr. Anson Clark. "Let Anson take a whack at this. He's doing a lot of research on the G.U. tract. Tell Anson what Shorty Alcock did to you at Iowa City. It'll be in your history but you tell him."

That is how we met, Anson and I, and began a friendship that lasted until his death. His suggestions and encouragements buoyed my spirits during some of my darkest days. He told me there is nothing like a spot of trouble with your genitourinary system to bring on depression and not to be surprised when I got down in the mouth.

When Carmelita was ill, Anson would phone her from Dallas. He cheered her with his wit and humor. He never failed to raise her spirits, to make her laugh. He joked with her. "Try bourbon without ice the way the English do so you can taste the whiskey. Tell Jim I love you as much as he does." She always felt better after a call from Anson.

When Dr. Clark asked to examine me, he called the hospital and an orderly wheeled me through the tunnel to the clinic building. We went up in the elevator and into the big waiting room. I heard names called and people rose and entered the offices. Dr. Clark's big Irish orderly loomed up beside me and boomed out, "William Randolph Hearst." He wheeled me into the office.

Embarrassed I said to him, "Maybe I can do something for you sometime."

The big Irishman patted me on the head and said, "I wish you could, me boyo." Then he lifted me onto the treatment table.

"We have an apparatus called a cystoscope," Dr. Clark explained. "It has a light and a mirror at the end and a loop of very fine wire which can be electrically heated to cauterize a wound or sore. I pass it through your penis and take a look in there and see what has happened."

I looked horrified at the gleaming metal tube. "There isn't room in my penis for all that."

Dr. Clark assured me. "It fits all sizes."

"So does the electric chair," I muttered.

Dr. Clark excised a piece of prostate with his fine hot wire to make the abcess drain better. He put me on a high-acid diet—no sugar, no salt—gave me several shots of salvarsan and sent me home.

I followed the diet. Mother baked the soggy muffins and I drank the acid medicine. But nothing helped. The infection became cyclic. I would be miserable for a few days, then the symptoms would disappear and for days, sometimes weeks, I would be fairly comfortable.

I wrote every day all winter and published a few poems and two stories. "When spring comes," I told Chuck, "I'll be ready for field work."

Many times I wondered why my family placed so much value on hard work. No matter how many poems or articles on farming I published, there was not the same approval as when I went out and nearly killed myself working in the fields.

"Strange where the emphasis is," I thought. "Mother read to us, taught us to love books, played the piano so we could all sing together. Perhaps too much work and worry numbed her pleasure in books and music. The Hearsts are specialists in hard work. No, not true either. It was Aunt Mamie who encouraged me with my writing and helped me sell my first poem."

Then I turned on myself. "Who do I think I am to pass judgment on the family? All the money spent on my medical expenses, all the support and care I've received. It must be hard to bear with me sometimes."

Carmelita spent Christmas in Iowa City with her mother. But she came to the Hearsts for New Year's. The family was all at home. Louise invited a few of her friends. Chuck invited a girl he was dating. In the evening I mixed a hot drink spiked with a little alcohol. Mother and Father joined in singing "Auld Lang Syne" at midnight. It was a good party, not noisy. No one drank too much, but we were all jolly.

On New Year's Day, Carmelita said, "I want to talk to you, Jim, privately." So we sat in my study and she said, "I've resigned my job at the hospital. I'm going back to school. John T. Frederick is leaving Iowa University to go to Northwestern."

I broke in, "I know, he asked me to go with him."

"I'm going to Northwestern to enroll in some writing classes with him. I want to take some other courses too. I feel awfully uneducated when I talk to you."

I could not believe what I heard. "Are you crazy? I never had but two years of college and then I was mostly interested in girls and baseball."

"Ah," said Carmelita, "but you educated yourself. Now don't contradict me. You've read and studied and thought and written and taught yourself."

"Baloney! When do you quit?"

"At the end of the school year, last of May, after I've taught my last class in the nursing school."

"Damn. I won't see you so often if you go to Northwestern."

"No 'if' about it. I'm going. No, we won't meet so often. But I want to make something of myself and not just settle down in a rut."

I said, "I'll be back in Iowa City in a couple of months. I have an appointment with Dr. Alcock on this crummy infection. I kind of dread it. He'll bawl the hell out of me for going to the Mayo Clinic. But he had the first crack at it. Maybe he should have another chance. Uncle George thinks so. Oh, well . . ."

I was right, Dr. Alcock sneered. He brought me a book to read written by a patient who scorched the Mayo Clinic with bitter words. "Sent you back to me, huh. Didn't want to tackle it themselves."

"Oh go jump in the lake," I thought.

Dr. Alcock performed a cystoscopic examination and again whittled off another piece of my prostate so the abcess would drain. I was in bed when the ambulance cart went by my door and stopped in the next room. I saw a flurry of doctors go by. One of the nurses told me, "It's Miss Calderwood's mother. She had an accident."

I looked out the window. Fog and mist dimmed the chilly March night. After awhile Carmelita came in. She dropped into a chair, her face weary with anxiety. "A car struck her as she crossed the street coming home from Mass."

"Bad?" I asked.

"She can't survive it." Then she stood up. "Jim, have them plug in a phone for you. I'll tell the special nurse to let you know if there's any change. Then you call me at the Nurses' Home. I've got to get some rest or I can't go on duty in the morning."

Three nights later when Carmelita walked into my room I saw that she was worn out. She said, "I think it'll be tonight."

I was sitting up cross-legged, leaning against the head of my bed, a book in my lap. Carmelita took off her cap, threw herself across the end of my bed, and fell asleep.

The night supervisor halted in the doorway and her eyes popped. A nurse asleep on a patient's bed! Her tight mouth all but said, "I'll report this."

I frowned at her, put my finger to my lips, shook my head, and whispered, "Shhhh."

But I thought, "You beat it and not a crack out of you either."

Carmelita slept about half an hour. Then she roused and sat up. I said, "I'll sit up and wait. Go home and go to bed. I'll call you."

Without a word she kissed me and left. One of the night nurses came in with a hypodermic needle all cocked and primed. "Dr. Alcock left an order for a sedative for you."

"I'll take it later."

"But the order is on your chart. I have to give it to you."

She was a student nurse and I did not want to get her in trouble. Maybe the night supervisor had put her up to it. I rolled up my sleeve.

It was a struggle. My head would nod and I would snort and come to. I slapped my face and exercised my arms. My head would nod again and my eyes close. But I kept awake. The night nurse peered in at me several times. "Little bright eyes," I said to her.

About midnight the special nurse came in. She looked weary. "Please call Miss Calderwood. Her mother is failing rapidly."

I called the hospital exchange and said, "Miss Calderwood at Westlawn. An emergency."

She came on the phone quickly and sounded tired but not sleepy.

"Better come," I said.

The funeral took place in Marion three days later. It was a wild and woolly March day. Meryl Norton drove the thirty miles with her head out the side window of her car, the windshield covered with ice. Only a few people attended. Meryl told me, "Almost all her relatives live in Ireland. Just her aunt here and her stepfather, poor old man."

For the first time I learned that Carmelita's father had been an engineer on the Northwestern Railroad. After a university football game some celebrating students derailed the locomotive and her father was killed. She was one year old.

I went home. The next weekend Carmelita came to see me. My father put his arms around her and kissed her. It startled me. Father so rarely showed emotion. But it touched me too. I thought he was saying, "We're glad you took such good care of Jim. Join our family."

I said to Carmelita. "Couldn't you sue the student who ran into your mother?" To clinch the argument I added, "The cop said she had the lights."

"No, at times Mother would be a little disoriented. I couldn't have that brought out in court."

When the spring semester ended, Carmelita went to Evanston. I went to the fields. Some kind of a chapter had ended.

A few weeks passed and Dr. Clark from the Mayo Clinic called me. "I have a new drug, still experimental. It belongs to the sulfa group. I want you to try it."

I said, "Maybe it'll do me in."

Anson chuckled, "Not if you've survived this far."

And that drug did it. From then on I had control of the infection. There were some side effects, not pleasant, but I ignored them in my relief of being free of my trouble.

There may be seasons in a person's life that take a turn for the better. We had another pleasant surprise.

Joe Milgram had visited the Hearst farm many times in the past few years. He was always a welcome guest. Mother said he was like one of the family. Joe made things easy. He helped Mother with the food and the dishes, made his own bed, regaled Mother with stories of his childhood in Brooklyn. He was an excellent storyteller.

He called me on the phone. "Altabelle Williard and I are going to be married. The wedding will take place in Dr. Steindler's backyard. I want you to be my best man."

I stammered, "But, but, but Joe."

"No buts about it. Your brother can stand beside you to support you and hand you the ring you hand to me. A Jewish wedding isn't much different from your Congregational weddings. If your brother or you drop the ring, pick it up. This is a wedding among friends, not a state occasion."

He wasn't finished. "We want your sister Louise to come and Carmelita is coming too. The men of the wedding party will wear blue serge coats and white flannel trousers. Think you can manage that?"

"This will be quite a shebang," I told Mother. "They say Dr. Steindler has a beautiful backyard."

Mother said, "I've heard that men at a Jewish wedding wear a hat. Be sure to tell me."

For the first time in our lives Chuck and I went to a tailor and were measured for blue serge jackets. We already had white flannel slacks. They were the style in those days.

Chuck said, "I almost feel indecent wearing a tailor-made coat. We aren't a family for such luxuries. But I think I can stand it."

The day of the wedding turned out to be warm and sunny. We three Hearsts drove to Iowa City, picked up Carmelita at Westlawn, and stopped at the Mengerts. Ida and Bill gave us a prewedding fortification of sherry and biscuits. Then we wound up the hill to Dr. Steindler's house and parked the car. I leaned on Chuck's arm and, with a hand on Louise's elbow, walked into the backyard.

It was lovely. Surrounded by tall shrubs, lilacs, and honeysuckle, the lawn was clipped and green with flowers in bloom all around the border. In one corner, a slender arch of boughs had been erected. Chairs, benches, and cushions were spread everywhere. The entire orthopedic staff was there and some strangers who I guessed must be Joe's relatives. Dr. and Mrs. Steindler welcomed us with warm friendliness.

Joe Milgram, a bit strange without a white coat and a stethoscope, wore his air of importance with distinction. Altabelle looked like Altabelle, only more radiant.

"Two doctors," I thought. "Both orthopedists, what Joe said were called bonesetters in the old days."

The Reverend Rabbi Mannheimer from Des Moines performed the ceremony. It seemed little different to me from other weddings except that the bride and groom drank the wine of joy and sorrow and smashed the wine glasses. I stood during the entire ceremony and Chuck and I managed the ring without fault.

Then it was over and servants brought out food and drink. Dr. and Mrs. Steindler moved graciously among the guests. Carmelita and I knew all the staff and Louise and Chuck soon found friends. Louise said she had the time of her life.

I went to Louise and Chuck and asked, "Why don't we invite Altabelle and Joe to come home with us. They're going on to Wyoming to-morrow to see Altabelle's mother. I'm a little plastered," I admitted. "Do you think it would be all right?"

"Who isn't," Louise said. "What a beautiful wedding."

"Sure," Chuck said. "Go ahead and ask them."

"Delighted," Joe answered. "Go ahead and we'll follow you."

So the bride and groom went home with the Hearsts. As they tip-toed upstairs, after seeing me safely in bed, Mother called out, "Did Joe wear a hat?"

I could hear them laughing. Mother slipped on a housecoat and met them at the head of the stairs.

Joe whispered, "No, Katharine. He did not."

A Sale and a Book

WINTER DAYS found me at my typewriter. Some feeling of determination or stubbornness or sense of discipline kept me at it. I quit my column in the local paper. I wrote book reviews for the *Des Moines Register* and the *Chicago Sun*. Through the prodding of Don Murphy, managing editor, I wrote a few articles for *Wallace's Farmer*. Occasionally I would fire off an angry article on the plight of the farmer.

The first draft of everything I wrote was written in longhand with a soft lead pencil on scratch paper. Then I rewrote it on the typewriter. It made for slow work. But I could not use the typewriter and compose my thoughts at the same time. The machine got in my way.

I did seem fated to write poetry. I worked only in traditional forms, though I had never heard Frost's dictum about free verse being like playing tennis without a net. I just felt more secure with rhyme and meter. Once in awhile a piece would begin with a free verse impetus and I was just smart enough to know that once a poem starts it must say what it wants to say. But I had almost no judgment about my own work. I could not tell a bad poem from a good one.

I made it a private business and rarely mentioned what I was doing. I kept the hurt of rejection slips to myself. But I plugged away. I told Mother in a shy burst of confidence, "I'm like an old horse. I have to keep working even though I haven't much to show for it."

Carmelita wrote me lively letters. She seemed to enjoy thoroughly her emancipation from hospital routine and the freedom of being a student again. She wrote a short story in Frederick's class that John said could be published. She said graduate work stimulated her and she sent me her love.

Once she wrote that she needed money. She had been without food for a week.

I wrote back angrily, "Why in hell do you do such stupid things? You want to get sick? I've told you and told you to call on us when you need help."

She wrote in answer, "I wanted to know how it would be to go hungry. I need the experience for a story I'm writing. Thank you for the check, my dear, I'll repay you next month."

I snorted. "She wants the experience of being hungry! Honestly, women."

One day D. R. Murphy of *Wallace's Farmer* called me from Des Moines. "There's an editor here from the *Nation* who wants a series of articles on the farm situation. Care to take it on?"

"Sure," I answered. "Have him get in touch with me."

The editor called and introduced himself as the son of a Canadian minister who wrote novels under the name of Ralph Conner.

"Yes," I said, "I know his work *Black Rock.*"

He sounded pleased. "You know his work? Good. Now here is what I want." And he explained.

I voiced a suspicion, "Must these articles follow the *Nation* line?"

"I didn't know we had one."

"I mean putting things in pigeonholes—labor is good, bankers are bad, industry exploits, farmers bellyache. Like that."

The man laughed. "You have a free hand. Frieda Kirschwey will take it just as you write it—if she takes it. Do it the way you want to but keep it tight and give evidence for your generalizations."

During the rest of the winter I turned out four articles for the *Nation*. I laid out the farm problem as explicitly as I could and tried to write with more light than heat, though now and then my feelings surfaced.

When field work started I had no more time for articles. I was amused one day by the reaction of one of our local businessmen to the articles. He warned me, "I'd be careful about that *Nation* stuff. It's a pretty radical magazine."

Now and then I went back to crutches for moving around the house. But the rubber tips would sometimes slip on the polished hardwood floors. After one bad fall I said, "The hell with it!" I never used crutches again. I could balance myself with the furniture and, if they were there, an arm from Chuck or Louise.

Chuck had built railings on both sides of the steps leading from the kitchen platform to the woodhouse floor. Once there, I grabbed a two-by-six and swung myself into a narrow aisle that led to a door cut into the west wall. Once through the door I stood on a cement block with a solid pipe railing.

Here the tractor was backed up so I could be helped onto the seat. Or the car was driven up so I could get into it by myself. I could put on my coveralls, all but the last hitch over the shoulders which Mother helped me with.

The ability to do this no longer impressed me. Even after a hard day's work, face black with dust thrown up by the tractor drive wheels (except for two white circles where goggles protected my eyes) and so tired I could scarcely talk, I walked through the woodhouse, up the stairs, and into the bathroom. The man who told God he would be satisfied if he could turn over in bed and feed himself had other things on his mind.

The winter of 1936 has its own page in weather history. Never had Iowa experienced so many consecutive days of below zero temperatures. It was minus ten or twenty or thirty day after day. The drifts on the main roads were so deep that the snowplows cut fences and made new roads across the fields.

On days when the wind blew the snow, the snowplow man would have the telephone operator call all the neighbors on Twenty-seventh Street and say he would open the road to town at one o'clock. He would wait at the city limits for three hours while people did their shopping and then plow the road back home. By the end of February the worst was over.

But not for us. Father drove home from Des Moines on one of the quiet days and could not get out of the car by himself. He complained of being cold, his legs and ankles were badly swollen, his breathing shallow. Chuck faced his chair in front of a hot air register. Mother fed him his supper.

"His heart and kidneys are not functioning well." Uncle George said. "He is a very sick man."

And so he was, too sick to live. He died on the eighth of March. I wrote a poem called "March Mourning" which appeared in *Wallace's Farmer*. It was the only poem the magazine ever published.

I remembered with irony the statement by Mark Twain that if you can get through March you can get through the rest of the year.

Simple services were held in the old Congregational church on Sixth Street, the church with the beautiful stained-glass windows. Grandfather Hearst helped haul the stones that built it. The center of the church was packed with men from the Midwest who came to pay tribute to a man who spent the last years of his life trying to improve the quality of farm living. I looked at their quiet eyes, intelligent faces, solid farmerish appearance and also saw men from Omaha and Chicago livestock commission houses. I wished my father could know they were there. H. A. Wallace did not come; he was too busy being Secretary of Agriculture. He sent a note of condolence in his place.

Spring rain, warm sun, waves of green grass, time to turn out the cows and calves to pasture. About half the cows had not yet calved. Their heavy bodies swayed as they walked. The herd bull, Milky Way Supreme from the Milky Way Farms in Tennessee, stood in his stall and bellowed.

Chuck scratched his back. "In a few months, old boy. But not now." He was a good enough bull with typical Shorthorn conformation—short wide muzzle and head, well-muscled hind end, and square body. But the calves he threw were nothing extra. Good blocky calves, well colored, but with no special quality.

I sat in the car and watched the cows mow off the grass. "It must taste good after a winter of dry hay," I thought. The calves bucked and cavorted, excited by their freedom and the warm sun.

I said to Chuck, "We ought to sell this herd. It doesn't make us any money. We aren't the salesmen Father was."

Chuck leaned on the fender. "I'm just not that interested in purebred stock either," he said. "We ought to cut the bulls and feed them out as steers. I'm not going to run around to farm sales and try to sell herd bulls."

We both knew the herd had been in the family a long time. Grandfather brought out from Ohio one of the sons of the famous herd sire, Whitehall Sultan.

"We couldn't sell the herd while Father was alive but now that he's gone we can do it."

I stared at Chuck, "I don't see how he stood it, being president of the Iowa Farm Bureau. All during the twenties, when farmers were losing their farms, they kept coming to him for help. What could he do?"

Chuck scrubbed the fender with his hand. "Everybody was stock market crazy and farmers were slowly sinking into a sea of debt. Remember when wheat dropped to forty-three cents a bushel? And we bought a thousand bushels of corn, delivered and shoveled off, for one hundred forty dollars. Dad helped get the land banks and production credit agencies going, but they couldn't do the whole job."

"Chuck, let's have a dispersal sale. We've both thought about it. Maybe we could take in enough to finish paying off Uncle George and Uncle Will."

"How do we go about it?"

"I'll talk to Jack Halsey. He's a fieldman for *Wallace's Farmer*. He can tell us what to do."

We planned the sale for the fall. Jack Halsey said, "After the summer work is out of the way and before cornhusking starts. When farmers have time to go to a sale."

We talked it over. We had some good foundation stock and it might bring buyers from a distance. We leased the sales ring at the Waterloo Dairy Cattle Congress grounds and Jack Halsey engaged an auctioneer. He said he would be in the ring to help take the bids.

The day before the sale we trucked the whole herd, cows, calves, and herd bull, to the barns near the show ring. Al Matson, who did the trucking, said to me, "This is how we'll work it. Chuck and the hired men will be busy in the ring bringing in and taking out the animals. You sit on one side of the ring and I'll sit on the other. If you think the bid is too low, rub your chin with your right hand and I'll raise it. Maybe that'll bring up the other fellow's bid."

I stared at him. "Well, I will be a son of a gun. Is this the way sales are run?"

"Sure," Al said. "Especially purebred sales where some stingy farmer thinks he can buy pedigreed stock at beef cattle prices. We've got to guard against that.''

The day of the sale turned out to be a comfortable September day, windless and sunny. The sale started at one o'clock. Chuck drove the car into the sale ring and carried me halfway up the bleachers. Austin Schulz, a neighbor and a purebred Shorthorn man, came and sat beside me. He said, "I'm not buying. I just came to the see the fireworks. Who've you got bidding for you?

I looked at him in surprise. "You know about that racket too?''

"It's no racket, just a way of getting a fair price. Some of these galoots would steal your stuff if they could.''

The auctioneer, Clair Mason, knew the cattle and the pedigrees and put on a good show. Jack Halsey worked the ring and exhorted the last dollar from the buyers.

There was a good turnout of customers, mostly farmers. I did see an order buyer from the Rath Packing Company leaning over the railing. The buyers thumbed through the catalogs and checked off the numbers that interested them. Chuck, with Ed and Bill, shuttled the cattle in and out of the ring.

A Webster City firm had printed the catalogs. I looked through mine and thought about what a tedious job it must be to proofread pages with an animal's family listed and their numbers. Some of them traced back to Scotland. There was a picture of the herd bull on the cover, but that was the only illustration. We were small potatoes compared to the big Shorthorn herds like the one on the Helfred Farms near Des Moines.

Al and I played our little game and pushed bids as high as we thought they would go. We kept the Rath Packing man from buying anything for beef. But we did get caught on a heifer and a bull calf.

"Load 'em up and truck them out to the farm," I told Al when the sale was over.

"I can't. I've already sold them to the man who made the last bid.''

I had never thought of that, of keeping track of who made the last bid. I said, "You do beat the Dutch, Al. Can we give you a few dollars for your help with the bidding?''

"You cannot. You boys have given me lots of business and I expect you to give me more.''

The empty yards and barns gave the farm a deserted appearance, as if the people had all moved away. I saw Chuck walk through the cow barn and close all the stanchions. He carried the stick with the snap on the end that we used to lead the bull to water. I had a feeling that he was wondering what Father would have said. It takes years of care and experiment to build up a good herd. And this herd had been in the family for three generations.

The sale closed and locked the door on the Maplehearst Shorthorns. I sensed a change in our farming. It was a move from what sentimental editors called a "way of life" to farming as a business.

Grandfather never concerned himself with financial reports or cash flow or bank credit. Father kept a running account of his expenses. Land prices steadily increased and my grandfather's net worth grew without any attention from him. And, except for staples such as salt, sugar, and flour, Grandfather and his family lived off the produce of the farm. Chickens laid eggs, cows gave milk, the garden and fruit bushes and trees furnished food for canning and preserving. The smokehouse hung with cured meat. Also, the windmill pumped water and the woodpile furnished fuel for the stoves.

Now the farm had to pay its way. Bookkeeping, accounts, income tax forms, charge accounts, and bank credit all became part of our concern. The luxury—if it could be called that—of being independent of the world outside the farm had disappeared. A different way of farming had begun. I wonder which balance sheet, if one could be drawn at the end of the year, gave the most satisfaction.

"Now what are we going to do?" I asked Chuck.

"Just what we talked about. Start feeding out calves and yearlings for the beef market."

We had sense enough to begin our new operation in a small way. We bought four yearling steers from Harry Jorgensen. Later we would buy out the whole calf crop of a Texas rancher.

That summer Louise married and moved to Seattle. Oh, how I missed her. She had brought so much life into the house from the academic world. I was ashamed to think how seldom I thanked her for the books she carried home from the library. I thought of the manuscripts she had mailed for me, stamps and paper she bought, errands she had run. During the Depression she contributed her monthly check to the farm account. I would miss her but I was glad she would now have her own home.

Her wedding was on a hot August day. The sun blazed down, the temperature shot up. The hearts of ice cream, packed in dry ice, slipped and slithered on the plates. Uncle Gregg's popped off his plate in an arc and landed in a flower pot.

"Why are people invited to weddings?" he demanded irritably. "It's a contract between two people. Why should anyone else show up?" Someone brought him another ice cream heart and he sat down and ate it.

I agreed with him. Whose business was it anyway? Uncle George followed Louise around holding a buzzing fan against her back. He tried to cool her and dry the perspiration on her dress.

One rainy day just before corn harvest began, I sorted out my manuscripts and selected enough for a small book.

"I'd like to get it published," I said at the dinner table. "But how do I go about it?"

"Try some of the publishers who wrote and asked if you had a novel started," said Chuck. "Every time you publish a poem in *Poetry* some publisher wants to know if you have a novel."

"I could do that," I agreed.

Mother said, "Farrar & Rinehart have written to you several times. Didn't Mr. Farrar publish one of your poems when he was editor of the *Bookman*."

"Good idea," I said. I wrapped the manuscript, put it in an old stationery box, and mailed it.

I waited, impatient, nervous. Weeks went by and hope and despair alternately raised and lowered my spirits. The day came when the manuscript was returned. A letter, signed by John Farrar, praised the poems but said the book would not have much sale. "I am sorry to return the manuscript and I wish you luck with it elsewhere."

Chuck said, "I'll bet he's written that sentence hundreds of times. It smells stereotyped."

"Why don't you write to Mr. Frederick?" Mother asked. "He knows about publishers."

"Why didn't I think of him in the first place," I said. "I'll drop him a note."

But to prove good luck had not forgotten me, before John Frederick had time to answer, I had a letter from the Prairie Press asking to see the manuscript.

"Who is Carroll Coleman and what is the Prairie Press?" I asked. I wrote John Frederick another letter.

John's answer said, "Coleman prints the most beautiful books being published in the United States. I'd let him have the manuscript if I were you and see what he thinks of it."

Away went the manuscript on a second trip, but this time it did not come back. Instead I received a contract—a publisher's contract. I tried not to seem excited, but I would haul out that contract and look at it just to prove I was not dreaming. So many copies to be printed, so much royalty, so many free copies to the author, so much time for proofreading. Did I want a dedication? Did I want an introduction?

I signed the contracts. What about a dedication? At once I thought of Mother. She had taught me to read before I went to school and shaped my taste for good literature. But what about Aunt Mamie, who encouraged me and got my first poem published? I remembered my doctor uncles and the obligation I owed them. No, I would have to think of something else.

My friend, Ferner Nuhn, home from New York and Washington, came to see me. Ferner was a writer. He had published several stories in Mencken's *American Mercury*. He was married to Ruth Suckow, the novelist famous for her stories of the Midwest.

I asked, "Ferner, have I the guts to ask Ruth to write an introduction to my book?"

Ferner squinted and rubbed his face. "Oh, I think so. I think she would be pleased. She was afraid you would ask her for a testimonial."

I had never thought of that. I didn't know much about publishing books. Ferner explained. "Review copies will be sent around and quotations from favorable reviews will be used to advertise your next book. Check the book jackets of most any book and notice the favorable testimonials."

"I'm sort of ignorant," I confessed. "I may have noticed those quotations and paid no attention to them."

Alone at my desk one afternoon I stuck a sheet of paper in the typewriter and began:

> DEDICATION—The Greeks said that agriculture is the mother of the arts. The objective creation that man achieves, he achieves with seed and land and labor, one eye always on the weather. The fruit of this union is so beautiful, so concrete, and so satisfying that the personal arts expressed in picture, song, and book seem faint by comparison. A book is only a kind of record, life is rooted in the earth. And it is to the people who understand this that this book is dedicated.

The short introduction by Ruth Suckow revealed a rich appreciation of what the poems tried to say. I called the book *Country Men.* It was published in 1937.

It was named one of the most beautiful books of the year by the Institute of Graphic Arts. The eastern reviewers mentioned this. The midwestern reviewers mentioned the poems.

One of them wrote, "This is no rocky hillside, one cow, flock of chickens farmer, but a man who knows black topsoil that will produce one hundred bushels of corn to the acre, whose farmyards are filled with hogs, cattle and sheep, a neighbor who wears his overalls with a difference and sees how people live, how they strive, fail, hate, and love."

I autographed all the copies of the first edition. Soon it was sold out. The Prairie Press issued a second edition. It was sold out. A third printing was made and it went the way of the others. Copies of them bring premium prices these days.

John Frederick said in his column in the *Chicago Daily News,* "When a book of poetry sells out three editions, it belies the belief that there is no market for poetry."

Mother said, "I hope Mr. Farrar reads that."

For several years Chuck had belonged to the local Rotary Club. Now I was invited to join. Uncle Will had been one of the charter members and president. Uncle George was a member. The meetings were held in the Black Hawk Hotel. I could walk in the back way if Chuck held my arm. I accepted the invitation.

Someone twitted me about joining the Rotary Club. It was a time when Mencken was hammering at all service clubs. He accused them of "boosterism" and ignorance of anything but pious platitudes.

I reacted with irritation. "Why not?" I demanded. "These men are my friends and this is one way I can meet them in a social way and not always at the business counter." Then I added with an edge to my voice, "I belong to the Farm Bureau too. You want to make something of that?"

The local Rotary Club gave me a copy of *Country Men* signed by all the members of the club. I was deeply touched. I still have it. It is a prized possession.

The slow rhythms of the farm flowed on. The publication of a book of poems did not interrupt them. As an old farmer said, "The time to plant corn is at corn-planting time." Steers and hogs must be fed even on Sunday. The sun shone as warmly, sweat ran as easily, the dust from the combine settled on my skin and itched whether I was the author of a book of poems or not. The hired men did not mention it. Mother continued to grow her flowers. The dogs hung out their tongues on hot days just the same.

I worked diligently at my poetry. I never expected to come down from the mountain with engraved tablets of stone, but I hoped to give meaning to the events and experiences of our lives. My wastebasket kept the secret of many revisions, many false starts, hours of effort.

"Some poems are born bad," I said. "Better let them die. No use to wear out your heart trying to save them."

The summer had a sweet-sour flavor to it. At the end of the spring semester, Carmelita came out and worked at Sartori Hospital. She needed to earn money for the next year and to be with me. She spent her weekends at the farm. She went to Mass every Sunday morning, but she could drive our car so it caused no problem.

Whenever I thought of it I grinned at the memory of the first time Carmelita visited the farm. One of my father's favorite expressions when something upset him was, "To hell with the Pope." It was just something he said instead of swearing. I always appreciated that there was no religious or racial prejudice shown in our family talk. We grew up never hearing that blacks, Indians, Jews, or Catholics are "not as good as we are."

One Sunday morning, Father spilled coffee on the tablecloth and muttered softly, "To hell with the Pope!" Then he remembered that Carmelita, sitting next to him, was a Catholic. He blushed and started to apologize. Carmelita placed her hand on his and said, "I won't tell him if you won't." Everyone laughed and Father felt better.

The sour part of the summer came when Carmelita talked to me about a position she had been offered.

"Do you know who Basil O'Conner is?" she asked me.

I shook my head, "No friend of mine."

"He is, or was, President Roosevelt's law partner. He now is the director for the Foundation for Infantile Paralysis. The foundation headquarters are in New York. I've been asked to be the clinical consultant for the foundation."

"Good god!" I said. Waves of feeling washed over me. An undertow dragged me down. I should have been proud of her, but all I could think of was, "I'll never get her back again."

I took myself in hand and tried to realize what the offer meant to Carmelita professionally. I made myself say, "Shall I get out the band and red carpet?"

She put her arms around me. "Don't overdo it, Jim. I know what you're thinking. Well, don't. I won't disappear."

"New York is a fer piece and you might fall for one of them there city slickers."

"Stop it." She frowned. "Jim, it is a once-in-a-lifetime offer. I'll have an office, a secretary, and a huge salary. I plan and organize polio centers around the country, see that they are properly staffed, and oversee the medical side of the foundation's work." She paused and drew a design on my desk with her forefinger. "I wonder why me?"

"Probably because of your work at the Steindler Clinic," I said. "It's one of the best known in the country. You've been a teacher, an administrative official, and you have written some articles. You're made for the job."

She sat on my bed and folded her hands. "Who do you suppose recommended me?"

I shoved back from my desk. "When do you leave?"

"September first. Jim don't sound so lugubrious. I'll be back."

I wished I could be sure of that. It seemed to me I was forever facing an uncertain future. I had a chronic bellyache of anxiety.

"It may be I'll have time off at Christmas. I can come and see you then. I'm my own boss about time and duty."

New York challenged and stimulated her. She wrote me about her new friends, co-workers, about plays she had seen, galleries visited, symphonies heard. "The damn town has bewitched her," I grumbled.

The Hearst family had always had close ties with the Iowa State Teachers College. Even when it was a normal school, my family had an interest in it. My mother had been the first secretary the president of the school had. My Aunt Mamie taught in the English department. All my uncles and aunts had been students for at least a term or two. Some even graduated. Louise taught earth science in the college. Chuck lacked three months of a B.A. I had gone to school there for two years.

Someone in the family had been a teacher or student there almost continuously since the institution began.

The family had friends among the faculty. Grandfather and Professor Bartlett, head of the English department, were friends. I remembered when we were kids how Professor Merrill, head of the music department, leaned over a panel in the hoghouse, and said, "A pig's eye is beautiful."

This drove us to hysterics. A pig's eye beautiful! It amused us for days. Even Father smiled.

Today I do not think it so funny. Beauty is where you find it. Why not in a pig's eye?

The present head of the English department and I were friends. He was H. W. Reninger, Ph.D., from the University of Michigan. He used to walk out to the farm on Sunday mornings and eat breakfast with us. He enjoyed the three-and-a-half mile walk. "It clears the cobwebs out of my brains. I catch too many academic flies in those webs."

One pleasant fall day when I was running the cornpicker, I turned the tractor, machine, and wagon around the end of the row and there stood Bill Reninger. I shut off the motor and we greeted each other.

"We have some students interested in writing," Bill said. "Would you come down and talk to the class once a week for the fall term? I'll put you on the payroll."

I took off my cap, stood up on the tractor platform, and stretched. "I didn't take any education courses, Bill, and I don't know enough about teaching to wad a shotgun."

Bill said sharply, "I didn't ask you to teach. I asked you to talk to the students. I'll have the class at my house. There's only one step. Chuck and I can help you in."

"What would I say to the students?" I wondered. I was tempted to try it and I was afraid to. I was a farmer. Writing poetry was my secret vice.

"Try it," Bill urged. "The students want you to come."

I still hesitated. Bill said, "If you don't make anything of your handicap, the students won't, if that's what's troubling you. They don't care if you're pink with purple spots if you can tell them anything about writing."

That decided me. "I'll wash my neck, put on a clean shirt, and give it a whirl. When?"

"My house, Monday evening, seven o'clock."

I later told Mother. "There sat ten students, men and women, waiting for me, looking bright-eyed and bushy-tailed. Bill said it was a two-hour class and left."

"How did it go?"

"In fifteen minutes I had told them all I knew about writing and there we sat staring at each other."

Mother asked, "What did you do?"

"A gal who works on the *Waterloo Courier* took over and asked some questions and we finished out the two hours."

I had never thought of a teaching career, but that session at Dr. Reninger's home opened the door to the teaching profession for me. I went through that door and did not close it for thirty-four years.

Once a student asked me what I thought was the secret of teaching. I raised my eyebrows and grinned at him. I said, "The secret of teaching is this: I can tell you all I know in fifteen minutes but I've learned to make it last for a whole semester."

There were days when I almost believed that.

Carmelita

EVERYONE EXPECTED the war to come and so it came. President Roosevelt would have liked more time to prepare for it, but the Japanese forced his hand at Pearl Harbor. The usual mishmash of directives and counterdirectives boiled out of Washington. But gradually disorder emerged from chaos, and disorder became a workable routine. Ration stamps for meat, sugar, gasoline, and heating oil were issued and a lively black market appeared.

The Hearst brothers, foreseeing the war, had bought an extra set of tires for the cars and tractors. One of the first things the War Department did was to call in all new tires.

"Sure, we'll turn them in," Chuck said. "I'll be damned if we're going to get caught sneaking a few tires. I phoned the oil co-op about gas and they said the word is that farmers will get enough. But let's use our ration stamps and buy gas for the cars in town. I don't want folks saying that we filled the cars from our farm gas pump."

"Amen," I said, "though I'll bet some of the boys slip a few gallons in the car from the farm allotment."

"Maybe so. There are always chiselers."

As the war rolled along we put our backs into the work of turning out all the food we could. The slogan faced us on billboards all over the country: "Food Will Win The War." Those of us old enough to remember the First World War had had a bellyful of slogans, and all this publicity seemed like mindless posturing on the part of the public relations boys in Washington.

But we knew very well that armies must be fed and that displaced and captive populations might be forced to a crust of bread and glass of water diet without our help. So we did what we could. I don't know if Chuck ever felt cheated because he could not join the armed services; he never said. I am sure he felt, as we all did, that no effort on our part was too great to make when our country needed help. In spite of our spoken protests about certain government policies, the pulse of patriotism beats strongly in most of us.

I asked Chuck, "Do you ever feel you should have volunteered for the army or navy or marines?"

He just grunted and said, "We've got all we can do right here. Floyd and Carl have families, I ought to be taken before they are."

We left it at that. Chuck insisted that we buy all the war bonds we could and we borrowed money to pay for some of them. One interesting experience happened to me. Sigrid Undset came to the college to talk about Norwegian literature but mainly to give us an insight into the plight of her country under German occupation. She came out to the farm to see us.

This famous Norwegian writer carried an air of authority and greatness with her. She was short and rather stockily built, grayish hair cut short and strong-looking expressive hands.

She had a strong accent but her English was very good. She told us of the bravery of the Norwegian farmers, how they tried to sabotage the efforts of the German officials to seize their crops. She told us how the farmers would hide their livestock back in the mountains, how they concealed their harvests of grain and vegetables in caves and sometimes by shipping it out at night in small boats to Allied countries.

She asked me, "Would you broadcast by international radio some short talks to the Norwegian farmers, word from one farmer in a free country to a farmer under the whip of a conqueror? Tell the Norwegian farmers that you commend them for their courage and urge them to continue in their efforts to resist the Germans."

I was glad to do it. Perhaps the fact that we lived in a Danish community and in my younger days all of our hired men and hired girls were Danish gave me a special feeling of empathy with Scandinavians.

In my first broadcast I said, "The radiance of your courage has warmed the hearts of free people everywhere. We farmers are bred to resistance."

In another talk I said, "As long as there are farmers to keep and cultivate the seeds of Norwegian culture and folkways, I know the spirit of Norway will never be conquered." Brave words easily said by someone sitting at ease in a free country. But somehow I took pleasure in these talks as if an encouraging word at the right time might help strengthen a man's resolve to resist the invader. I was glad I made the talks.

The government started a huge vacuum sweeper called the draft to suck up young, able-bodied men for military duty. "I've often thought," I said, "if governments would take the middle-aged men first, wars wouldn't last long."

Chuck added, "You forget about getting killed or being crippled for life when you're young."

"Let's go to the draft board and see where we stand. There's you, Chuck, Carl, and Floyd, all eligible. If any of you go, we'll need to pull in our horns a bit. I can run the tractor for field work but I can't feed the pigs and steers or do the chores."

But we could forget our worries. The draft board turned thumbs down on army service for any of us. The chairman told Chuck privately, "You four men, you, your brother, and your two men, produce and harvest double the amount of foodstuff of any other four men in the county. We want to keep you right on the farm."

When Chuck told me, I said, "I suppose food is as important as munitions, especially if we have to help feed the Allied armies. Some of the fields in Europe have been overrun by the German armies. Belgium and France won't grow much food for the Allies."

Summer brought labor problems. The shortage of temporary help showed its teeth. But aid came from an unexpected quarter. George Gates, from the English department at the college, told me, "Some of us would like to help out in the war effort. John Horns and John Dietrich in the art department want to help too. We were all born and raised on farms. We might be a little soft at first."

I almost threw my arms around him. "Welcome words. The hell of it is, George, we have to do custom work too for some of the neighbors. We have a baler and a combine and we're supposed to help out. To buy a new machine you have to go before the county committee, get down on your knees, swear on a stack of Bibles that you can't farm without the machine. Then all you get is a permit to buy. And if no implement dealer has a machine, you're up the crick."

George said, "I don't know about running a combine but I can sure shovel oats, stack bales, drive wagons."

The men were soft at first. But they pitched in with whole-hearted effort and gradually their muscles toughened and they could endure the hot sun. They came out after their classes were finished and worked until dark.

The pick-up baler required two men to ride it. One man shoved the wires through and handled the bale dividers. The man on the other side tied off the wires. It was a dirty job. Every time the plunger packed hay into the bale, dust flew out of the sides into the men's faces. Goggles protected their eyes, but they breathed dust until it almost choked them.

The work piled up. We let our own fields wait while we accommodated the neighbors. Daylight savings time was a pain in the neck. Some mornings the dew did not dry off until eleven o'clock. "Waste the morning and work half the night," Chuck grumbled.

We tried to work in teams so that no one had to work all day and half the night. Words might be scanty through cracked lips and from black sweaty faces, but tempers did not flare and no one complained. Harald Holst from the music department came out and loaded bales one afternoon when we were shorthanded.

Imagine standing on a swaying wagon drawn behind the baler, grabbing the bales as they came up the chute at the rate of four a minute, and stacking them four rows high on the wagon. Harald wouldn't quit. He worked all afternoon. It nearly killed him. He was so tired he walked, his sister-in-law said, "like a man with gonorrhea."

When a crop is ripe it must be harvested. I remember one of the longest days. It was hot with the sun beating down and not much air stirring. Chuck and the combine started on a neighbor's field. George Gates went with him to haul away the oats in our truck.

I drove the tractor hitched to the baler. John Deitrich fed the wires and swung the bale dividers. John Horns tied off. Floyd and Carl loaded the bales and stacked them in the barn. By four-thirty we had finished our field of alfalfa.

I said, "Let's rest a few minutes and have a beer. Then we bale hay for Norman Wolff. We promised he'd be next and the forecast is for rain."

"I have an evening class," John Horns said. "But I can skip it."

I shook my head. "We'll manage. Floyd and Carl have the rest of the hay to stack and then the chores to do. You don't shovel off corn for five hundred steers in ten minutes." I thought a minute. "I can get my cousin, Jack Hearst, to tie off. Norman will have his own help to load and unload the wagons."

Dietrich said, "I can stay."

We rattled down the road in high gear, tractor, baler, two wagons. We pulled into Wolff's yard at five P.M. At ten o'clock, working with the lights on, we finished. We left the machinery in Norman's yard and I rode home in Dietrich's car. I was so tired that Johnny had to carry me into the house. The next morning it was raining. "Thank god," I said.

The next year, through our friend Al Matson, who now owned a Case implement store, we managed to buy a big New Holland self-tie baler. We had the permit, but how Al wangled the baler we never knew. We did not ask and he did not tell us. He just said, "A carload of Venezuelan twine is part of the deal."

The twine was pretty sleazy stuff, but we were glad to have the baler. As Chuck said, "No more sore eyes and chest pains from the goddamn dust."

The war raged on. In the Pacific, the Americans turned back the Japanese, island by island. Names like the Solomons, Midway, and Guam appeared in the news. The losses of men and supplies seemed endless, but the enemy lost its grip on the gains made in the first devastating rush.

In Europe, Hitler made the mistake of opening a second front against the Russians. At first his armies, like Napoleon's, found Russia easy to enter. But when the heroes of Stalingrad held out day after day, the Germans were beaten.

I said, "I don't suppose the Russians will ever know how anxiously we watched the seige of Stalingrad. We could hardly believe it when the Germans gave up."

At the beginning of the fall term in the third year of the war, Dr. Reninger asked me if I could handle another class.

"No, Bill," I said. "I have all I can do to handle one class and help on the farm."

"As soon as my commission comes through I'm leaving to take charge of a navy V-12 program at a Missouri college."

I looked surprised. "I'll be darned. You sure kept that quiet."

"I suppose you know we're getting a company of WAVES here at the college. We house and feed them. Their own officers act as instructors."

"No!" I said. "What next?"

"I'll tell you what next. We're getting a company from the air force and we must find instructors for them."

I nodded. "I see why you wanted me to take another class. The staff will be spread a bit thin, won't it."

The WAVES arrived and settled in. They marched to classes in formation, these serious-faced young women swinging along in their blue uniforms. The air force men came but did not march in formation. This addition to the student body gave a bulge to campus activity.

The officers in charge entered the social life of the community. The admiral in charge of the WAVES had been retired for reasons of health but had been called back into service to act as a shepherd for these young women.

Before he left, Bill Reninger and his wife Betty invited two WAVES, Chuck, and me to breakfast. One of the WAVES, a blond-haired widow from Texas, took a fancy to Chuck. This began a quiet courtship. Gladys never forgave Dr. Reninger for being the one to introduce her to Chuck. Which proves the old saying: gratitude does not follow a favor bestowed.

I waited for Carmelita to resign and join me. She put me off. She liked her work and felt committed to the war against infantile paralysis. She wrote of working with Mrs. Roosevelt and Helen Hayes. The foundation people did not want her to leave. She loved me, but would another year or two matter?

I wrote to her. "My dear, I'm forty-three. We have wasted ten years of our lives not living together. Now I think we should keep our promises."

I liked that last bit, "keep our promises." Maybe that would stir her up.

It did. Right back I received an air mail special. "Don't talk to me about 'keeping promises.' Who said, 'Let's wait until we are more financially secure before we marry? You aren't fair, Jim, and you mustn't expect me to jump when you whistle."

I said, "Chuck, we better buy a house on College Hill. You and Gladys will want the farm home. If I'm near the campus, I can have my classes at the house. All those damn college buildings have steps going either up or down the minute you open a door. Mother can live with me or have an apartment."

Mother said, "I'll not live with my children. I want a place of my own."

Bravely said, I thought. But does she mean it?

Mother had aged in the past few years. Since her stroke her right arm and hand had never recovered their former strength. But her spirit was not dimmed. "If Carmelita won't come, Mother and I can live together."

John Horns told me about a house for sale. He, Chuck, and I went to look at it. The owner, a salesman for U.S. Steel, wanted to move. It was a fine house with stone front, blue roof, fireplace, two bedrooms and bath upstairs, two bedrooms and bath downstairs, and just two steps up from the double garage into the house. It had a good location in "faculty row," just six blocks from the college. But twelve thousand dollars made us hesitate. Most houses in town sold between six and eight thousand dollars.

I wrote Carmelita the details. She wired back at once. "Don't buy it. Too expensive."

In my next letter I wrote, "Too late, we bought it. How soon can you come?"

Chuck said to me, "You can drive back and forth to the farm in the Packard. It has an automatic clutch. You have your driver's license. We have Gladys's car."

I wrote Carmelita a do-or-die letter. My cupboard of patience was bare. "I need you," I wrote, "and I need you now. Later will be too late." Not much love in that letter.

She came. She saw the house and liked it. Chuck and Gladys were living in it. Carmelita stayed at the farm with Mother and me.

She said, "Listen, Jim, and don't get your feathers ruffled. I'm an old maid. I'm an only child. I'm selfish about my own life. My job in New York only made me more so. I had a lovely apartment, easy transportation, an excellent secretary, and enough money to do as I pleased. And I made some good friends too."

She might have added, but didn't, "And I have the ability to do my job and hold my own with the high-powered foundation people."

We drove out to the field. I was going to take Carl's place on the tractor and Carmelita would take Carl back to the barn. I wore a puzzled expression. What was she leading up to?

She continued. "I'll live with you but I won't marry you until I see if I can adjust to being a housewife."

I hit below the belt. "I suppose you won't marry a Protestant."

She flared right back. "That's not so and you know it. You aren't listening to me, Jim. I'm saying some very personal things and you won't listen."

That is the only time religion came into question. Our arguments, quarrels, disagreements came about because, as she said, "I'm Irish, you're part Irish. They say if an Irishman was left alone on a desert island he would fight his right hand with his left."

I did not care if Carmelita was a Catholic or a Muslim or a Shinto. In our home I never heard any religious prejudice. Religion was regarded as a matter of personal belief and whatever was right for a person was his or her own business.

Though a member of the Congregational church, I hung around the outskirts of what Emerson and Thoreau said. I shunned orthodox Calvinism, even denominationalism. A kind of live and let live attitude underlay my convictions. I used to quote, "There are many roads to Rome." And I was pleased when one of my friends said, "Denominations are God's kindergartens."

I heard the tractor pounding down the row toward us. I opened the car door. Chagrined, I said, "As Bejamin Franklin said, 'Half a loaf is better. . . .' "

She kissed me and finished it. "Than no loaf at all." She took my hand. "Let's see if we can stand by each other, Jim. We love each other but is that enough for a marriage? We'll see."

Moving day was a day to forget. I had called Takin Moving and Storage a month before to nail down a day when Gladys would be free of WAVE duty. I explained the situation—two houses full of furniture, the town house to come to the country, the country house to move to town, and Mother's furniture to her apartment.

Two men with a small truck showed up about noon. When they discovered the situation they yelled for help and burned up the wire to the office. I made the wire even hotter when I told the manager about our appointment made weeks ago.

He weaseled. There was another job that should have taken only an hour but had taken all morning. About the middle of the afternoon two semis and four more men showed up.

Night came and beds were still being taken down, dressers moved downstairs, rugs rolled up, and dishes packed. We got Mother moved and settled.

Two beds were set up in the town house and Carmelita and I slept there. For breakfast we had an apple and bread without butter. Two of the movers arrived after breakfast. They apologized. "Even though it's Sunday, we couldn't leave you in this mess."

In a few hours they had carpets down, furniture in place, and had brought stove and refrigerator from the warehouse where Henry and Fannie Harris had stored them. This was wartime. There were no stoves or refrigerators for sale. We were glad to borrow them from the Harris's. Henry was in the navy and Fannie had gone to her home.

I said to Carmelita, "I wonder what the navy does with someone like Henry Harris. A gifted pianist, he's played with most of the big symphony orchestras. I can't see him swabbing down decks."

Brock and Bessie Fagan lived right across the street. They sent over hot stew for dinner. Brock was a member of the English department. He had been my freshman English teacher, but we were still friends.

I organized the study. Grandfather's big cherrywood desk filled one side. On it I placed my typewriter and dictionary. I unwrapped the desk pen my father had given me. The farm books were in one desk drawer, my other books on the shelves of the small room. "I'm pretty well fixed," I said.

"I think I'll sleep upstairs in one of the bedrooms so folks won't think we're living in sin."

I exploded. "Oh, for god's sake, Carmelita. We've already 'sinned,' as you call it. Besides folks would think the worst even if you slept in a tent in the backyard. Why so prim?"

"Because I am prim, James Hearst, and at my age I don't change easily. Give me time to get used to this kind of life."

In spite of chiselers and black markets, the American public showed spirit in its dedication to the war effort. Rooms were shut off and thermostats were turned down to save heating oil. People limited their use of gasoline and drove cars as little as they could. Good citizens kept their purchases within the range of their ration stamps. Nearly everyone had a relative in the armed services. Like a crowd of people leaning forward, the country responded to its duty.

I drove out to the farm each morning. I tried to arrive home between six and six-thirty so Carmelita would know when to prepare dinner. I managed the car by using the automatic clutch and riding the brake pedal. Once a patrolman stopped me for having no tail light. He asked for my driver's license. I said, "I left it at home."

"Now isn't that just too bad," he said, with heavy sarcasm. "What's your name?" When I told him he said, "I know you. I gave you your driver's license. Get the light fixed."

I had a platform built along the garage wall that was level with the entryway. "Dog run," Carmelita called it. A railing extended from the garage through the entryway to the living room door. I could get out of the car, balance by touching car and wall, turn in the door, grasp the railing, and climb up one step to the door behind which my wheelchair waited. I could do this myself, though I liked to have Carmelita come out to meet me and supply a steadying hand if I should go off balance.

In a letter, Dr. Steindler had written, "I suggest you use a wheelchair now. You cannot afford to fall and break an arm or leg."

It seemed to me we had just settled down when a call came for Carmelita to go to Chicago and talk to workers in the field about the care of polio patients. The epidemic was bad in the Midwest. "I must go," she told me, "when the foundation calls me."

She persuaded one of the DeNeui girls to look after me. But I complained, "I thought you had resigned."

"I must go when I am needed. If I can do anything to help with this awful polio epidemic I'll do it. You would want me to."

But I disliked being left alone. Come right down to it, I disliked the way we lived. I wanted to be married. Was I so conventional or just insecure? Did I think Carmelita would leave me if we were not married? I knew better than that. Still, I was unhappy.

Once, in a sarcastic voice, I asked, "How do I introduce you? My roomer, companion, housemate?"

"Your friends all know me. Stop gnawing on that bone."

When she returned from Chicago she said, "I don't like leaving you alone, but sometimes I'll have to. The DeNeui girls get your meals and look after the house but you're alone from breakfast until dinner. I don't like it. Why don't we ask Harald Holst if he would like to live here? He can have a bedroom and bath upstairs. I'll move into the other downstairs bedroom. Don't say it, I know your bedroom is large enough for two."

"Good idea," I said. "Harald is sort of a shirttail cousin of mine."

It pleased Harald. "The only thing," he said, "I'm often out nights to attend performances in the music department for student and faculty recitals."

"We'll give you a key," I said. "Could you be around sometimes when Carmelita is away?"

It was company having Harald in the house. He ate Sunday breakfasts with us. Then he and I would do the dishes. Often Harald's friend, Jane Birkhead from the music department, joined us. I began to see more faculty folk and fewer farm friends. I lived in town now.

Dry, warm fall weather matured the corn early. We began the corn harvest the middle of October. I put on my coveralls each morning, drove to the farm, was lifted on the tractor and started down the row with the cornpicker. The papers called it a bumper crop year. The yellow ears flowed out of the elevator in a steady stream. Every twenty minutes I filled a wagon. When a chain came off or the elevator clogged, I would wait impatiently until Floyd or Carl or whoever brought the empty wagon gave me help.

Chuck started to combine beans. He needed a man to haul the beans away from the combine so we hired Herman Mixdorf, who had worked for us before. He was on vacation from his job in the John Deere factory.

"Let's go while we can," Chuck said. "You know it's hell on wheels when the rains start."

I remembered a year when it was so wet we had to use two tractors to pull the cornpicker and wagon. The field behind us looked as if a giant sow had been rooting in it.

On Monday afternoons I left the field early to get home, cleaned up, and supper eaten before the students arrived for a seven o'clock class. I used Sunday as the day to read and criticize their stories and poems.

But the canker of my discontent still festered. One Sunday afternoon I issued an ultimatum. "All right, sweetheart," I said. "For two months now we've let you feel your way toward an adjustment to our living together. Now it's time to decide. Either you can do it and we get married or we give it up."

It startled me to hear myself speak so positively. But frustration, anxiety, fear of being thought unable to man my station in life, it all poured out.

To my surprise and relief, Carmelita meekly agreed.

"Women," I thought. "Women, for cripes sake."

Aloud I said, "Get in touch with Father Mauer and see when we can set a date."

"Oh, but you have to have instruction first."

"I . . . what?"

"You must have several weeks of instruction about the Bible before we can be married by a priest."

"Well, if that. . . . Well . . . to hell with the Pope! Oh, I'm sorry, I didn't mean that. Okay, instruction it is then. But you better warn the priest that I have an Aunt Jenny."

Carmelita actually grinned. "I wouldn't be a bit surprised if you knew more of the Bible than the priest. Some of the priests don't know much except to say Mass."

But Father White was a bright young man. A broad-shouldered athlete who coached at St. Pat's and refereed basketball games in the Cedar Falls-Waterloo area. After the first two sessions he gave up. "Your Aunt Jenny really drilled you. You know all you need to know. Now about that East-West Waterloo game tonight."

Father White said, "You can't be married in the church, you know. You can in the chapel."

"How about right here?" I asked.

"I wish Meryl Norton could come," Carmelita said. "She's my best friend. But we need a Catholic witness."

"You want it private, so do I. We'll ask Chuck and Gladys, and I have a cousin in Grundy Center who's Catholic, Josephine Thielen. We'll ask her."

It was a warm November day. As I shaved that morning I sang, "Don't Fence Me In."

Carmelita sang, "So they sailed away and were married next day by a turkey who lived on the hill."

The sun shone in the west windows. Father White performed the ceremony. We all drank a toast with champagne. Carmelita cut and served the wedding cake. Harald came in and was invited to join us. He said, "I thought something was in the wind. I'll kiss the bride, Jim, and congratulations."

When we were alone again I said smugly, "Now you can move your bed in with mine."

"All in good time, sir. All in good time."

The war ended as all wars must. The terrible havoc caused by the newly created atomic bomb destroyed Japan's will to continue. On the European front the giant scissors—the Allies one blade, the Russians the other—had cut the German armies to pieces. The killing had stopped. But the unbelievable torture and suffering in the concentration camps came to light. It seemed the twilight of civilization.

Campuses across the country throbbed with returned veterans. I found my class alive with sober-faced young men in worn flying jackets who had things they could write about but not tell. The other students found themselves in competition with young women and men who tried to catch up on the years they had lost. I welcomed the excitement. "Get some of these dead-heads off their butts," I told Carmelita. "Let them work for their grades."

Just the faintest cloud smudged the horizon at our home. It was scarcely a hint, a sign so slight no one noticed it.

Carmelita was called to South Carolina. She was asked to make over an abandoned army barracks into a hospital for polio patients. The governor ordered convicts from the penitentiary to be her labor force. She was gone two weeks. She wrote to me as if the situation had a humorous side; it was she bossing convicts and their guards as if she were the governor himself. But her letters sounded tired. When she came home, she looked white and tired. "I feel as though I'll never get rested again."

On the first Thanksgiving of our married life, Carmelita decided to have the family dinner. That morning, as I rolled up to the fireplace to lay the fire, I suffered an emotional shock. For dinner there would be Mother, Chuck and Gladys, and a few friends from the faculty. Where were the thirty members of the family who had once filled the house for holiday dinners? For a few minutes I lived with ghosts. The four uncle doctors were dead, Father was gone, the aunt who was an M.D. was dead, Aunt Mamie was dead, and Aunt Jenny was too frail to venture out. Sarah, Uncle George's widow, and her two children would be with her family. The cousins had grown and scattered to Chicago, Pennsylvania, California.

I remembered a sentimental line from one of Villon's poems, "Where are the snows of yesteryear?" I piled logs on the kindling. I shivered to think how empty the world of Hearst had become. I went to the kitchen and told Carmelita to lie down and take a nap. She had been up since five-thirty to stuff the turkey and put it in the oven. No stuffing the bird the night before for a nurse. "Do you want to die of food poisoning?"

I said, "I'll set up the card tables and get out the liquor. Lie down and rest a few minutes." My feeling of emptiness did not go away.

After dinner Chuck and I excused ourselves to go out to the farm and drive the steers out of the cornstalks. We had to move them out of the field, across the road, and into the feed yard. The steers gleaned the fields after harvest. This year there were plenty of dropped ears. Too much corn too soon would make them sick. We let them stay in the fields a few hours each day until they had cleaned up most of the corn and began to eat stalks and husks.

All the guests decided that they wanted to go too. I stood up at the door and faced them. "No," I said firmly. "Strangers might spook them. It's hard enough as it is. Norma and Carl will help and we have the dogs."

I drove. I used the car as a "horse" and drove through the cornstalks to round up the cattle. On the way back to the house Chuck said, "Weren't you a little rough with your guests?"

"You know, Chuck, the college is a different world. A lot of the faculty would think that driving the steers out of the cornfield was a kind of pastoral picnic. They have no idea how quick a bunch of western-raised yearlings can stampede and scatter all over the place. Besides I needed to get away for a while from all the academic talk."

"How do you feel, Jim? Did all that cornpicking do you in?"

"I feel pretty good. My bladder kicks up once in a while. Then I have a bad time. I miss Uncle George. Jesus, how I do miss him."

"Who does look after you?"

"Jim Henderson is our local doctor. But when I feel real bad I call Anson Clark at the Mayo Clinic. He always perks me up. He's a good friend."

Chuck asked, "How do you think Mother seems?"

"Better since she went to live in the Western Home. She was too lonely in her apartment."

"She said she never wanted to live in a retirement home but she didn't want to live with either of us."

"She has twenty-four-hour nursing service, good meals, and Dr. Henderson looks after her. She has her own furniture and a phone. She just wishes the place was called the Manor House instead of the Western Home. Be more stylish." Then I added hesitantly, "Mother could never play second fiddle to her daughter-in-law. I don't blame her."

Chuck said, "We've got to do something about Aunt Jenny. She mustn't live alone much longer. She's too frail."

We drove back to our house in a thoughtful mood. We saw each other at work every day but Chuck and I seldom were alone together to talk about family matters. I was glad for the chance.

Carmelita lacked rapport with an automobile. She said the car took delight in making a fool of her. One afternoon a friend asked her, begged her, to go on special duty for his wife at the hospital. The request irritated her. She felt she should not be asked. "Why, I haven't been in a hospital as a nurse for years. I don't even know the modern techniques."

But she went to the basement, dug a uniform out of her trunk, ate her supper, and went out to the garage. I heard the motor rev up as she bore down on the accelerator. Then the car shot out of the driveway and I heard a bump. Then screaming tires, then silence. "What the hell?" I wondered.

Across the street I could see car lights and moving figures. After awhile the car drove off.

Brock Fagan came in the side door with an ax in his hand. "She hit the telephone pole and jammed it between the fender and bumper. She couldn't back up or go ahead. I chopped her loose."

"I couldn't figure out what had happened."

"She's all right. I heard the tires screaming. I knew it was Carmelita. You remember she backed into J. Foy Cross's car a few months ago. Cross never left his car opposite your driveway again." Brock chuckled.

One cold winter morning, twenty below, Carmelita got ready for church. She always went to early Mass. Then when she came home we had breakfast together. It gave me a chance to sleep late if I wanted to. Usually I had the table set, the coffee perked, and the scrambled eggs ready by the time she got home. She came into the bedroom, booted, coated, and gloved and pulled the bed covers off my face.

"The damn car won't start."

"Call a taxi," I said. "You can't get a garage to send out help on Sunday morning."

After she had gone I got up, dressed, shaved, and came out into the living room. Harald sat there reading the paper. I said, "I'm going out and give the car a try. I should make it alone all right. If I yell for help, will you come?"

I stepped out, the air stung my nostrils and made my eyes water. I carefully stepped down the step, held tight to the railing, edged around the corner, moved along the platform, opened the car door, and sat down.

It was cold! Everything I touched, seat, steering wheel, hand gas feed. "She probably flooded it. I won't pump the accelerator." The starter moaned and whined. Slowly it turned over the motor. It coughed a couple of times, then suddenly caught, and I was in business. I let it run awhile to warm up. Then I decided to drive down to the church and pick up my wife.

There was no parking space. The Catholics, Methodists, and Baptists were all on the same street and the place was lined with cars. I double-parked, motor running, heater beginning to warm up. Among the crowd of people coming out of St. Pat's I spotted Carmelita. I honked the horn and caught her eye. She climbed in and we drove home to breakfast.

I told Harald, "She was mad at me all day because I got the car started and she couldn't."

A few weeks before Christmas Dr. Henderson called me. "Your mother fell and broke her hip. I've taken her to the hospital." Carmelita jumped into the car and went to the hospital.

When she came back she said, "Your mother is quite uncomfortable. She wants to go home, I mean the farm home. She thinks if she could go there she would be all right. I felt so sorry for her. Do you want to see her?"

I shook my head. "Not now. She might not want to see me. Mother is awfully proud. She'd hate to have me see her helpless and uncomfortable."

"Jim," Carmelita said. "I don't want to sound like a prophet of doom. But don't be surprised if your mother does not recover. Broken hips and old people often mean pneumonia. Katharine couldn't stand that."

A few weeks after Christmas, Katharine Schell Hearst died. My last tie with the older generation vanished. My family, except for Aunt Jenny, had gone. In spite of my love for Carmelita, I felt terribly lonely.

Gathering Clouds

THE SHRILL CRIES of the present so often drown out the low tones of memory. No one remembered how exhausted Carmelita felt after setting up a hospital in the army barracks in South Carolina. She forgot it herself.

She told me, "I like keeping house. I never thought I would. There's something exciting about cooking. I never make anything as splendiferous as the pictures shown with the recipes. But we like it, don't we?"

I encouraged her by praising everything she made. But I did not need to exaggerate. She *was* a good cook. A woman came in once a week to clean the house. But I had one gripe—things moved too fast.

I rose promptly in the morning, dressed, shaved, stood at the stove, and fried the eggs and bacon while Carmelita perked the coffee, set the table, and made the toast. We ate quickly. I hurried to the bathroom to do my chores there, took the morning paper with me to glance at the headlines. I pulled on my coveralls, Carmelita fixed my lunch, I gave her a hasty kiss and was on my way to the farm.

Our peaceful time came at dinner. I took off my farm clothes in the bathroom, washed off the dust and chaff, put on a clean shirt, and wheeled into the dining room to the table. Often we had a bourbon highball while we exchanged the news of the day. Evenings we read or went to a party or a movie.

"Damn it," I complained. "We don't have enough time in bed together." On Sunday mornings when I could stay in bed, Carmelita rose early and went to Mass. This was her commitment and I respected it. I envied the dedication she had to her faith.

Most of the day Sunday I spent going over papers for my class. I wrote a few paragraphs of criticism for each student. I tried to be both critical and encouraging and it took time. I told my boss, Dr. Reninger, "Gosh, Bill, these young people are awfully sensitive. They're shy about exposing what they write. In one of my first classes I discussed a paper the way I would write a book review and the poor girl burst into tears. Scared me. I learned to be more gentle."

Dr. Reninger did the office work for me. He enrolled the students, limited the class size, opened the class to only juniors and seniors. He excused me from staff meetings and committee assignments. He attended the first meeting of each class and introduced me to the students.

Finally he said, "You run your own show. I'm not going to come to your classes. Still touchy about being in a wheelchair?"

I had to confess, "You know, Bill, the students pay no attention to it. I'm just the teacher they hope will tell them something about their work to give them a boost."

"I shouldn't try to give you advice," Bill said, "but I will. Just face the fact that you're in a wheelchair and forget it."

I distrusted my ability to give final grades. It seemed such a subjective decision. And after thirty-four years of teaching, I never faced final grades with confidence.

In a creative writing class there were no final examinations. I tried to assess the value of each student's achievement by the work done during the term. But I always asked myself, "Who gets the 'A'? The gifted student who writes with distinction and has little struggle with the assignments or the student without much ability who works like a dog and makes a lot of progress?" I never resolved my dilemma.

Carmelita set out the chairs each Monday night and for the last class of the term she served chocolate and cookies. "I ought to split my check with you," I said. "You do half the work."

It came as a shock that teaching college students is not as simple as I had expected. My class was not a required course. But I experienced a few problems.

One young man, before four-letter words so liberally sprinkled our language and books, brought in a story loaded with them. I had the students read their work aloud to permit class discussion. I argued that discrimination and criticism helped produce good creative work. But this story irritated me. I passed it by during class. After the class was dismissed the writer wanted an explanation.

I said, "This may be the way people actually talk in the situation you've described, but are we trying to reproduce life or treat it imaginatively? Are you a camera or a painter?"

"But my character must talk like that to seem real," the student explained.

"If you were in my place, responsible to the college for what goes on in class, and if, in that class, you had girls who had been brought up in strict Catholic, Lutheran, or Baptist homes, and a student brought in a story such as yours to be read aloud, what would you do?"

Jim Albrecht grinned. "I'd say, 'hell no.' But it's up to you, not me, to say I can't read it."

I considered the problem. "All right, you go ahead and read it. I won't limit freedom of expression. I don't believe in censorship. I can stand it to be fired."

But he never read the story.

Another student, who has since become a famous announcer for NBC, asked belligerently, "Will I get my money's worth in this class?"

The question startled me, nettled me. I had never thought of the class in that way. But the question was relevant. "How do I know," I snapped. "You get out of a class what you put into it. If you want to write, then stay. If you just want to talk about writing, go knock on some other door."

The last day of class I asked, "Did you get your money's worth, Tom?"

He nodded. "Yeah, I guess so. Yeah, it was a good deal."

Carmelita and I decided to give a New Year's party. The war had ended, ration stamps had disappeared, liquor could be bought at the state liquor stores, the temper of the times had cooled down. "Let's have our friends in and be cheerful for a change," Carmelita said.

The party shook loose the tight discipline of wartime controls. Everyone got a little drunk. Someone brought a guitar and the singing went on and on. The pleasure of friends in each other's company verged on the pathetic. Carmelita had more help than she could use. The guests seemed eager to make the party a success. They fell in each other's arms not from drink, but from the relief of being free from wartime restrictions. After we sang "Auld Lang Syne" and everybody kissed everybody else, Carmelita disappeared. We found her later when the women guests came to get their coats. There, burrowed underneath, was Carmelita fast asleep.

When the last guest had gone I said, "Leave everything. We'll clean up tomorrow."

"It's tomorrow now," yawned Carmelita. "I'm done in."

A feather of apprehension reminded me that Carmelita had not recovered her energy and strength since she had returned from South Carolina. The work, worry, and pressure had exhausted her reserves. She tired easily now and often refused the gauntlet when challenged by an occasion. I heard, or imagined I heard, faint tones of distress in her voice. But I had my own ills and bad moments to contend with and I dismissed my apprehension as a bad dream.

For a Christmas present Carmelita had given me a copy of the *Prairie Schooner Anthology*. She had a story in it.

I was pleased, pretended amazement. Carmelita said, "You goose, you knew when it was published. Loren Eisley was the editor. I wrote the story in John Frederick's class."

"But," I protested, "I didn't know it had been selected for the anthology. You're in good company, too. Here's a story by Eudora Welty."

"We'll be known as the writing Hearsts. You have another book of poems on the way."

"As soon as the Alan Swallow Press publishes it." I pointed my finger at her. "Write more stories. Isolate yourself every morning for a few hours. Make it a habit."

"Yes, Professor. Thanks for the advice. I'm now trying to write a full-length mystery story."

My eyes bulged. "I'm a son of a gun. Is that what all those sheets of yellow paper are doing in your study?"

"I'm on chapter four. I'm going to call it *The Bonesetters' Brawl*."

"Where did you get the title?"

"Each spring the orthopedic department gives a whing-ding of a party and it's called 'The Bonesetters' Brawl.' "

"A mystery," I said. "Well, we've read enough of them. Once a student asked me if I ever read anything but serious literature."

"What did you say?"

"I told him I bet I had read more mystery stories than the whole class together. I said they beat Nembutal. A week later one of the young men brought me a copy of the *Book of Mormon* with the inscription, 'Mr. Hearst, this beats Nembutal too.' "

"Well, does it?"

"I haven't had any sleepless nights since then."

I drove out to the farm every day, even in winter. I had problems to solve, business to discuss, invoices and tractor sheets to pick up. Chuck and I spent some time each day together. We planned the work and checked over the livestock. When income tax came around I collected my data and swore and sweat and squirmed to satisfy Uncle Sam. It was the job I disliked most.

Proof sheets from my book of poems arrived and I worked on them. I didn't ask Carmelita what progress she was making with her mystery story. One day she asked me to write a description for her and a couple of pages of men's dialogues. I assumed she was forging ahead. The days slid by on greased tracks. I kept turning the calendar pages.

I did not visit the Mayo Clinic that year. My bladder behaved itself most of the time. Dr. Clark sent me a prescription for a new antibiotic. He wrote, "These pills really work, I wish we had had them years ago."

Anson asked me, "How's your sex life?"

I told him, "What I need is time. One of us is always going or coming someplace."

Late that winter, Bill Reninger and I gave a party. We did it to prove our contention that women worked so hard getting ready for a party that they were too tired to enjoy it. We said a party need not take all that much preparation.

Bill concocted an invitation which read, in effect, "Jim and I will furnish the house, heat, light, and liquor. You bring whatever nourishment you usually take at bedtime. Bring nothing that must be cleaned up afterward. Paper plates and napkins may be burned in the fireplace. Each guest will be given a job to help clean up the house after the party. Bring your wife or best girl or both."

It was a great success. Guests emptied ashtrays, washed glasses, ran the vacuum, set the table for breakfast. Bill and I refused to let our wives have any part in the preparation. Carmelita said, "I never saw the house so clean. I couldn't believe it."

"See?" Bill and I said together.

For a few days Carmelita did not feel well. "I'm going to stop having a drink each night before dinner. Maybe I'll feel better."

I fell a few times. Once the towel rack in the bathroom pulled loose. Our next door neighbor, Leo Priest, installed a new one that he said "would hold an elephant." Leo worked as an engineer at the John Deere experimental farm. He was one of those men who could do anything with his hands and do it well. He took us under his wing—did small carpenter jobs, rewired the kitchen, fixed a leak in the plumbing.

"What would we do without Leo Priest?" Carmelita asked.

When I fell, Carmelita tried to help me up. Once she piled volumes of an encyclopedia under me until I sat high enough to push up with my legs. But if he was home, she called Leo. My falls always happened at the end of the day when I was tired. I was lucky. I always managed to grasp something to break the force of the fall. But once down I was helpless. So when I was alone in the house I was very careful.

"It's time to tell you," Carmelita said, "that the last time I was in New York a representative of Mosby and Company asked if I would consider writing a textbook on orthopedic nursing."

"What did you tell him?"

"I said I'd think about it. In today's mail I have a letter from the chief editor repeating the offer."

I stiffened. "Who are Mosby and Company?"

"One of the two publishing firms who handle most of the medical texts. That's all that they publish, just medical texts."

Maybe I had a slight touch of jealousy. "And I thought I married a gal who wanted to be a housewife."

"No, you didn't. You married me." Her words arched their backs like angry cats. "Do I complain because you want to farm, teach, and write poems?"

I raised my hands in a mock defense. "But you're more lenient than I am." Than half to myself I added, "I thought after those polio trips were finished we'd just rest easy and act housebroke."

"But you don't know it all yet. A doctor would write the medical half and I'd write the nursing half. I'd need to organize the book with him so that in clinical situations we wouldn't overlap. I'd need to spend at least a week in New York collecting data from my files there."

"Well, Jesus H. K. Rist, you leave my bed and board again? You don't love me any more? I'm no good in bed?"

Carmelita planted herself, feet apart, hands on her hips. "Don't be a jackass. Every time we meet a problem you retreat into your little boy act. Now stop it. I know you hate to have someone from outside get your meals and take care of the house. I know you're afraid something might happen to you when you're alone. I'm just telling you about the offer. If you don't want me to do it, I won't."

"Of course I wouldn't say no if you want to do it. But I do have a kind of chronic insecurity about being left alone. Who'd work with you?"

"Mosby suggested Dr. Funston. Do you know him?"

I brightened. "Funston? Sure, he was Dr. Steindler's first man when I went to Iowa City back in 1922. Where is he now?"

"Professor of orthopedics at the University of Virginia. He came from Virginia."

"Nice guy as I remember him. Be easy to work with."

Carmelita perched on the arm of my wheelchair. "I don't know him. He was before my time. This book would be a feather in my cap, professionally speaking. It would bring in some money too. Mosby sells to a lot of medical schools and medical texts are expensive. The royalties would be, to quote from the letter, 'substantial.' "

"What about your mystery story?"

"It's finished except for retyping. Another problem is, would I have the energy to work on a textbook with all its drawings, diagrams, and illustrations? Some days I feel like just sitting. I get some funny G.U. symptoms too. Maybe just menopausal, 'change of life,' as the old ladies say."

I protested. "You mustn't have G.U. symptoms. That's my specialty."

"It worries me a little but I'll probably get over it."

A bit ashamed, I used my old nickname for her. "I'd be proud of you, Callaghan. Go ahead and write the book. Tell Mosby yes. I can manage with Irene and the DeNeui girls."

Carmelita signed the contract and received an advance on her royalties of $2,500. This impressed me. I couldn't get over it. "Why you haven't even written a word yet. This beats poetry, even ten dollars a line from the *Ladies Home Journal*."

She spent a week in Virginia. I suffered a hollow feeling in the guts when she got on the plane. Chuck had driven out to the airport and he carried Carmelita's bag to the office. Then he and I went directly to the farm.

When I came home that night, Irene Davis was waiting for me. She had been a high school classmate. She had married, her husband had left her, and now she worked to support herself and her son. I could never remember her married name.

She came out to the car and watched me slide across the front seat, slowly stand up, and shuffle into the house. "Let me know when you need help," she said. By the time I washed and slipped on a clean sweat shirt, she had dinner on the table.

In the morning, Harald and I ate breakfast together. I fried the eggs and bacon. Harald made the coffee and toast and set the table. After breakfast one of the DeNeui girls came, cleaned, fixed my lunch, and watched while I got in the car. I tried to be careful but I did not have the same feeling of security I had when Carmelita was with me.

She wired me the date of her return. I drove out to the airport and watched the passengers unload. When I saw the trim gray caracul coat appear, a great warmth flowed through me.

She looked around the house, hugged me, and sighed. "It's good to be home again." She looked out the windows at the backyard. "Let me unpack and I'll tell you about my trip."

I banged around in the kitchen and started the coffee pot. She came out of the bedroom. "You didn't go to the farm?"

I looked at her. I couldn't look hard enough. I pretended to be tough and scowled, "On the day of your homecoming? Not on your life. Now give, what's Funston like?"

"Short, plump. Well, you know what he looks like. Hair gray now, very much the southern gentleman. But he knows his field. The department is small compared to Steindler's but up-to-date and very professional."

"What did you decide?"

"We mapped out our respective fields of work—what the doctor should do, what the nurse should do. He's agreeable and cooperative. We settled boundary lines with no trouble."

I said "Mail here for you. A letter from Simon & Schuster. What do they want? They aren't publishing your book."

Carmelita tore open the envelope. Her voice rose in excitement. "My gosh, Jim, they'll accept my mystery story if I make a few revisions." She passed the letter to me.

"Revisions . . . mostly minor, wouldn't you say?"

"Yes, but I can't work on it now. This orthopedic book comes first. Just think of the work it will be."

She consulted her notes. "We need an artist who knows the requirements of medical books—how to show a Stryker frame, brace for scoliosis, cast for a club foot, different kinds of traction. These drawings must be done accurately. Then I need pictures of actual people—patients in various stages of treatment."

She closed her eyes and frowned. "I'll write to Simon & Schuster that I can't sign a contract yet." She folded the letter and put it back in the envelope. "Isn't it funny that the first publisher I sent it to would pick it up. As the saying goes, 'It never rains but it pours.' "

I asked, "How do you feel?"

She made a face. "I had a couple of bad days in Virginia. Dr. Funston thinks I should go through a clinic. But I'm all right now. Just tired. I hate traveling."

Carmelita spent the next few weeks organizing her part of the book. "We do it by chapters. When I finish a chapter I'll send it to Dr. Funston and he'll send his to me. I'm a little out of date on some procedures but I can pick up the information I need in New York."

The old hollow feeling hit me. She would be away again. More Irene Davis, more DeNeui girls, more care not to slip or lose my balance. It is hard to be careful when you can't anticipate what will cause your downfall.

"Grit your teeth," I told myself, "and take your chances. Nothing is guaranteed in this world."

Carmelita went to New York and stayed for ten days. She wrote to me, "This will be my last trip. I am getting all the data I need. I called the Powers Model Agency to send over a couple of models. We need pictures of normal feet and pelvises. I sent the models back, we couldn't use them. Their feet are misshapen and deformed from wearing the wrong kind of shoes. They were just impossible. I finally took pictures of my former secretary. She has nice normal feet.

"Mosby and Company found an artist for us. He has been an illustrator for medical textbooks so we shouldn't have any trouble with him. I miss you very much. Don't worry. I will soon be home."

I went out to the farm every day. With Carmelita gone the evenings stretched out interminably. I wandered around the house unable to settle down to read. I fiddled with our shortwave radio, picking up the London newscasts as I had during the war. One day it rained. No cornpicking. I stayed at home and caught up on my bookwork. I tried a few poems on the theme of loneliness but threw them in the wastebasket. "Maudlin stuff," I muttered.

Chuck and I owned a series of Boston bulldogs. They were all named "Boojum." We picked the name from Lewis Carroll's "The Voyage of the Snark." The name seemed to fit them. They raced around on their short legs and tried to follow the collies everywhere. This time of year, during cornpicking, I drove directly to the field in the morning. Whoever had already started the machines would boost me up on the tractor and drive the car to the house. The dogs always came to the field to chase rabbits and scare up pheasants.

One night as I reached home and sighted on the ribbon hanging in the garage to bring me close to the platform, I opened the car door and out jumped Boojum, all smiles and wiggles.

"You little bastard. How did you get here?" I demanded. She had jumped in the car and hidden under the front seat. Pleased with herself, she danced around me as if to show what a friend she was. I let her out just before I went to bed and when she came back she jumped up in my lap and licked my face. She found a place under the bookshelves where it was warm and free of drafts. In the morning Irene Davis fed and petted her. Boojum wiggled out of her skin. She leaped in the car when I was ready to leave and lay down on the front seat. "Company for a lonely man," I said.

Boojum pulled that trick several times. Carmelita thought it was cute. I wondered how she got in the car without being seen. Carmelita said, "It's almost dark when you leave the farm. While the door is open and someone lifts you in, she could sneak in."

"Pretty slick," I thought. Chuck said that at the farm on cold nights Boojum would lie under the kitchen stove until bedtime. When he let her out she would race to the woodhouse door and bark furiously. The collie would leap out of his barrel to see what the fuss was about and Boojum would slip into his warm barrel. Night after night she did this and the collie never realized he was being bamboozled.

When Carmelita returned, I followed her around almost as if I were a Boojum. The house wasn't empty anymore. But she looked white and drawn. "It was a hard trip," she said.

"Can you imagine how difficult it is to get a good photographer? We wanted just clean, clear pictures to show anatomical changes. But no, the photographer wants to pretty it up, work in some lousy background. Even in the hospital where we wanted some pictures taken, darned if they didn't want to make the picture 'art' as they called it. Well, phooey on art."

Shortly after her return, Carmelita told me, "I saw Dr. Henderson this afternoon. He thinks I ought to see a urologist and suggested Dr. Harold Entz of Waterloo."

I shuddered. "Why do I get these premonitions of doom each time Carmelita goes away or has a pain?" But I tried to speak calmly, "What does he think is your trouble?"

"Some kind of bladder infection. But he wants me to see a specialist."

I called Dr. Henderson. "Jim," I said, "what ails Carmelita?"

Dr. Henderson reassured me. "She has an infection somewhere in her G.U. system. I'd rather not fool with it. I think Dr. Entz is the man for her."

She stayed overnight in St. Francis hospital in Waterloo and came home the next day. "Dr. Entz did a cystoscopic examination. He didn't find much—some irritation of the bladder wall. Gave me some pills. Said it should clear up soon."

Carmelita spent every spare moment on her textbook. Letters and manuscripts passed back and forth between her and Dr. Funston. Negatives of pictures and proofs of drawings fattened her files. One day I came home to find her seated in the middle of the living room, surrounded by twenty-six piles of proof. "Don't disturb anything," she said. "I'm doing the index."

"Doing the index" took up more time than I expected. For more than a week I wheeled carefully around alphabetically piled pages. I said, "You must have written like crazy to have the proof sheets back so soon. You've been at it less than six months."

"I roughed out several chapters while I was in New York. I've thought about a book like this for a long time. And when you have the data and know your field the actual writing isn't hard. It's the things like checking references and quotations and supplying footnotes that take time. I had to write for permission to use some of the data. Dr. Steindler generously let me use some pictures from his files."

"Different from publishing a book of poems," I said.

"Different from writing a mystery story too," added Carmelita. "A book like this must be dependable in its statements, absolutely accurate in its data. Literally it might be the difference between life and death if we make a mistake."

When the page proofs came, I read the text for typographical errors. I was fascinated by the drawings of orthopedic apparatus and prostheses. "The artist sure knew his stuff, didn't he," I said as I admired the drawing of a level and pulley arrangement for suspending multiple fractures.

Carmelita and Dr. Funston made the last exchange of proofs and notes and the manuscript was ready for the printer. But Carmelita was in the hospital again. She lay white and sick in a bed in St. Francis Hospital. I drove home from the hayfield and cleaned up and grabbed a sandwich. I remember a neighbor, Lyle Baum, stopped with her two young sons in a baby carriage and asked if she or Russ could help me. Chuck and Gladys took me over to see Carmelita. Dr. Entz's pills had not cleared up the infection.

"I'm sure there's an opening from the lower bowel into the bladder," Carmelita whispered to me one evening. "There are signs of feces in the urine. But Dr. Entz won't listen. He says it's a ridiculous notion."

"You better come home," I said, heavy with foreboding. "You aren't getting better here."

"Come and get me tomorrow," she said. "I want to go home."

I called Dr. Henderson. "Hell, Jim, she gets weaker all the time. She says she has a lesion in the bladder wall. Entz sent a psychiatrist to see her. Is he off his nut? She knows her symptoms."

That night I called Dr. Entz at his home. I spoke with the harshness of desperation. "Sign out Mrs. Hearst in the morning. You aren't helping her."

Dr. Entz argued. "She thinks she has a fistula in the lower bowel with an adhesion to the bladder. Cystoscopic examination doesn't show it. I had a psychiatrist try to improve her mental outlook."

I could scarcely control myself. "She doesn't need a psychiatrist. She knows what she has. I'm bringing her home." To myself I said, "Oh, you son of a bitch."

She came home. Gladys brought her. She seemed so weak and frail I wanted to cry. But in the morning she fixed breakfast, packed my lunch, and had dinner ready when I came home. But she had no appetite.

The next day I went to a Rotary meeting. When Chuck and I returned we found Carmelita in tears. "I just feel awful," she said. "What am I going to do?"

"The time has come," I said, "to get you to a real specialist." Dr. Anson Clark had left the Mayo Clinic and was living in Dallas, Texas. He had married a woman who owned some oil wells. He had given up his practice to look after the oil company. I called him.

Dr. Clark was emphatic in his orders. "Call Gersh Thompson at the Mayo Clinic. Tell him you're a friend of mine. Gershom is head of the urology section. Tell him you need help."

I got the call through at once. Dr. Thompson said, "I'll meet you in front of the Methodist Hospital at ten o'clock tomorrow morning. There will be a room reserved in the hospital for your wife."

Chuck and Gladys drove us to Rochester. They tried to be cheerful and Carmelita perked up with some of her old pungency. Dr. Thompson was pacing the sidewalk outside the hospital when we arrived.

The next morning Dr. Thompson phoned me. "We found the opening. Apparently the bowel has attached itself to the bladder wall and somehow worn an opening. We have her scheduled for surgery tomorrow morning at eight o'clock. Dr. John Waugh will do the surgery. Mrs. Hearst asked me to call you and give you the information."

I had a load to shoulder, but at last I knew what had made Carmelita so ill. She had diagnosed her illness correctly. This consoled me, to know finally what the trouble was. But who would look after me? I could not depend on Harald, who came and went at odd hours. I did not dare try to live by myself. Irene Davis was out of town. But somehow, somewhere, someone heard me calling.

A graduate student stopped to see me that afternoon about doing some individual study during the summer. I asked, "Arnie, would you and your wife look after me for a few weeks until Mrs. Hearst comes home?" I explained the circumstances.

Arnold Grummer nodded. "Sure, why not? Mabel will be glad to help out. Sure, we'll come. We haven't settled anywhere yet so we'll bring our bags right over."

The Grummers moved in. The next day Chuck and Gladys took me to Rochester. Carmelita was in her room coming out of the anesthetic.

The resident doctor said, "Come with me. I want you to go upstairs to the laboratory."

I felt an alarm go off in my mind. But still I was not prepared when the laboratory technician brought out a tumor as large as my two fists. "A malignant tumor," the resident doctor said. "Dr. Waugh will tell you about it."

Stunned and inarticulate, we went back to the room and waited for Carmelita to regain consciousness.

Cloudburst

THREE WEEKS can seem forever. But time passes. The shock, worry, and pain fade. Only the scar on memory remains. But for three weeks I watched the sun come up and the sun go down, gratified that another day had passed.

We stayed overnight in Rochester, shocked by the revelation of Carmelita's true illness. The next morning the surgeon, Dr. Waugh, met us in one of the hospital lounges. He said, "We had no idea of a malignancy. We only expected to repair the perforation in the bladder wall that Dr. Thompson discovered. The size of the tumor surprised us. It must have grown rapidly. But I think we got it all. We always hope that is true."

"It has to be," I said, my voice thick with apprehension. "She's an important person."

Dr. Waugh smiled a tired smile. "We say five years. If there's no recurrence in five years we assume the malignancy will not again appear."

"How long will Carmelita be here?" Gladys asked.

"About three weeks, barring unforeseen complications. She'll be pretty sick for a few days, most uncomfortable. But we'll give her as much relief as we can."

We came back to Carmelita's room. She seemed pleased we were there. I grieved, she looked so small and white and weak. The intravenous jar overhead and the drainage tubes over the side of the bed made her look even more helpless and imprisoned. "Get me help," she whispered to me. "I need special nurses."

Outside, in the hall, we met the Catholic chaplain and the chaplain from the Presbyterian church. The Father said jovially, "I thought she ought to have some Protestant help too."

Carmelita's request disturbed me. Special nurses? Where would I find special nurses and how would I pay for them? I struggled with the problem.

Then Sarah, Uncle George's widow, stepped forward. "I'll dig out my old uniforms and stay with Carmelita. I can stay with Carmelita a week or so. The children can manage."

More showers of blessings. Marilyn Moss, whom Carmelita had

encouraged to study nursing and who had just graduated, called me. "I owe Carmelita something for what she did for me. I would never have had the courage to oppose my parents if she hadn't supported me. I'll go and stay with her."

Then Gladys said, "I'm not a nurse but I can sit with Carmelita while Sarah and Marilyn rest."

The three women rented a small apartment near the hospital and set up a three-person shift to take care of Carmelita.

I can never repay those three women for the care they gave Carmelita and the relief they afforded me. I lived now on a plateau of hope. I was glad for the company of the Grummers. They kept my spirits from sinking with their cheerful attention. Mabel was an excellent housewife. She cleaned the house, made the beds, washed our clothes, fed Arnie and me well-flavored, balanced meals. Arnie studied, read, and played golf during the day. But one of them always accompanied me to the car in the morning and met me when I returned from the farm at night.

Each night I called the hospital to see how Carmelita had spent the day. On Sunday Chuck and I drove to Rochester.

I looked at Carmelita anxiously. "You look better," I said. As I stood up I leaned over and kissed her. "A bit pale and you need a shampoo but otherwise pretty good."

"How did you get up here? It's not visiting hours," asked Carmelita with more vigor in her voice than I expected. I was delighted.

I said, "Did you think that all my years in a hospital taught me nothing? We just took the elevator the nurses and doctors take. And who would stop us?"

Chuck patted her hands. Carmelita said, "Chuck, you have real farmer's hands. I wish mine were half as strong."

Chuck smiled at her. "They know how to work."

Gladys came home with us. "I think Marilyn and Sarah can leave soon. Carmie can go on general duty. Now we must start thinking about a housekeeper. It'll be a long time before Carmie can take over."

Again an alarm sounded in my mind. How would I find a housekeeper? There weren't housekeepers anymore.

"Of course we'll have a few weeks. Carmie won't be coming home for a while. Can the Grummers stay?"

"As long as I need them, they said. We get along fine, at least I do. We have diverting conversations."

"Like what?" Chuck asked.

"Well, let's see. For one thing Arnie's father is a Lutheran minister and strict and orthodox on church dogma. But in his social life he's liberal—smokes cigars, drinks wine, plays cards, doesn't object to dancing. On the other hand, Mabel's folks are Methodists and open-minded as far as dogma goes, but closed up on social issues—no drinking, dancing, or card playing. We have some fine arguments."

"I can see," Chuck said. "But where do you come in?"

"I don't. As a backslid Congregationalist, I don't take sides. I just keep the discussion going."

A few days later Gladys called. "I think we have a housekeeper, a Mrs. Mae Idso. She took care of Monica Wild in her last illness. She's a very nice person. You and Carmie will enjoy having her with you."

The next day when I returned from the farm I said, "Arnie, probably you and Mabel should sign up for an apartment one of these days. If things go well, Carmelita should be home in two more weeks. We have a housekeeper lined up. How will I ever repay you two for what you've done for us? I was just desperate and then you happened along".

Arnold Grummer propped up his golf clubs and said, "Why nothing to it. Mabe and I got free room and board. I play golf every afternoon. Mabe has time to read and do some sewing. It's the life of Riley for us."

I shed a few tears. My emotions were close to the surface these days. "Okay, Arnie, when you sign up for my class this fall, I'm going to ask you why you frittered away the summer playing golf when you might have been working on your degree. And you can punch me right on the nose."

The attempt at humor fell flat, but Arnie smiled.

Sarah and Marilyn came home. I tried to tell them how indebted we were to them.

"Save it," Sarah said. "You have a very sick wife on your hands. You can worry about us later."

Three weeks later Carmelita came home.

Mrs. Idso appeared with her suitcases, ready to take charge of the house. She was a tall, middle-aged woman with a pleasant face and soft voice. Her warm, compassionate treatment of Carmelita endeared her to us both. She became the good friend so often searched for, so seldom found. She wore dresses with cheerful colors, cooked food to suit our tastes, and helped me in and out of the car. Afternoons, while Carmelita rested, she visited friends. Her son and his family lived in town and she spent time with them. Sometimes she shopped for things for the house.

Mrs. Idso did not drive a car, but Gladys or Betty Reninger would act as her chauffeur. And Hart Madsen, our grocer and friend, would deliver groceries. Mrs. Idso said, "Imagine in this day and age a grocer who delivers." But Hart never failed us, even if it was only a pound of butter.

Carmelita moved from bed to bathroom to dining room to davenport. One day, leaning on Mae's arm, she ventured out into the backyard. She tired easily and often went to bed right after supper. I fluttered around and tried to wait on her by bringing a glass of water, a box of Kleenex, or a book. I even tried to make the farm affairs interesting. But she hid in the cocoon of her illness, as if to escape from the signs of shock and pain.

I found myself impatient with her. Why didn't she get well faster?

At first I could not do enough to show my joy at having her home again. But her continued retreat into her wounded body and spirit irritated me—all the medicine, the long nights, the repetition day after day of going to lie down, her indifference to the house, her lack of interest in my work.

I tried each morning to be cheerful, to lift her spirits with words of encouragement. But every time I pulled her out of the well she slipped back. Or so I thought. I did not know how it bruised her spirit and mind to know she had had a cancer and perhaps would have it again. No wonder people with medical training are poor patients. They know only too well the hard roads of illness, that what appears as solid ground is really a hidden swamp.

I told Carl Hundley, when he boosted me on the tractor, "I feel better out here in the open air doing some work. The house is like a hospital. It even smells sick."

I might have disparaged any notion about the healing effect of working with the earth, watching crops grow, cultivating plants. But I affirmed over and over by act and concern my dependence on the farm for a renewal of my own spirit. I liked working with Floyd Bunnell and Carl, discussing problems with Chuck, being out in the fields. I liked to be alone disking, plowing or harrowing, watching the edge of my machine cut a new swath, just lapping the moist earth worked over on the round before.

Sometimes at the far end of the field I would stop and shut off the motor. After the steady blast of the exhaust in my ears, the silence seemed a big bubble of quiet which enveloped me. Gradually I could hear a meadowlark, a crow, a dog bark, the rustle of grass and weeds in the wind, and, if I was near the road, the humming electric lines. If the sun shone and warmed the air, I opened my coveralls and leaned back against my heavy straps and took a deep breath. For the moment I would forget illness, anxiety, guilt for my irritation, even my own handicap as I absorbed the atmosphere of the place.

I became more than an onlooker. I became a part of the country where gophers sat up if I whistled and killdeer ran down the rows with a feigned broken wing to lead me and my iron horse from their nests. I shared an existence dimly remembered, as if I had once lived like a wild fox or pheasant.

After one of these moments of devotion it seemed a sacrilege to press the starter button and fill the air with the belch of a machine and its stinking breath. True, farm work wore me out. But it was a good kind of tiredness—I ate well and slept well. I could not say the same for the fatigue I felt from teaching a three-hour class.

I wished Carmelita would break out of her shell. When she did, it came as a surprise. I drove into the garage one night and gave the customary beep of the horn. Instead of Mrs. Idso, out came Carmelita. She wore a dress, not a bathrobe, and her hair was neatly combed.

"I came to help you," she said. "Come in. We have company."

I held her hand against my face. "Gosh, you look nice. Talk about my heart leaped up when I beheld. . . . Mine just about leaped from its socket. Who's here?"

"Reningers, Corley Conlon, Peg Fullerton. I wanted to see people. We're having a drink. Mae fixed some cheese and crackers. Hurry."

I had to go through the living room to reach the bathroom and I gave everybody a big smile. My Carmelita had come back to me. I was dazed by the surprise. And there was more. Carmelita followed me into the bathroom and said, "Stand up and I'll help you pull off your coveralls." After I cleaned up I went into the bedroom for a fresh shirt, and behold! The bedside table by Carmelita's bed held nary a pill box or medicine bottle. How pleasant and orderly the room seemed. "It can't last," I thought as I went to join the others.

It didn't but the relapse was short. A few mornings later Carmelita got up and ate breakfast with Mae and me. She made sandwiches for my lunch. "I'm on the mend," she said. "Two weeks from today I go back to the clinic for a checkup. I can fly. I can go alone. Cheer up, Jim. I must make these trips every three months. Just a precaution."

It wasn't long after this that I received another pleasant surprise. Carmelita or Mrs. Idso always put my mail on my desk. This time I found an opened letter addressed to Carmelita from Mosby and Company. I pulled out the letter and a check fell out. I glanced at it and then looked hard. It was stamped $2,500. The accompanying sheet said, "We are enclosing a check for one-half the royalties on the book, *Orthopedic Nursing* by Funston and Calderwood."

Carmelita stepped up behind me. "I feel guilty for all the expense of surgery and hospital bills. Now I can pay back a little."

I was flabbergasted. "My god, one-half the royalty? You struck oil or something?"

"I told you this company was one of the two largest publishers of medical textbooks. It must be selling well. But I would expect Mosby to have contacts with a number of medical schools."

"All three editions of *Country Men* didn't do this well."

"Of course not." Carmelita became impatient with me. "It's not the same thing. Do you expect to make money writing poems? You know better than that. Isn't it enough that John Frederick in his column in the *Chicago Daily News* wrote how unusual it was for a book of poems to sell out three editions? You can't even buy a copy of *Country Men* now unless you pay a premium."

I backed down. "I know you can't measure poetry in dollar's worth, but gee, twenty-five hundred bucks . . . that ain't hay!"

Carmelita ignored me. "He also said that at your best you wrote the finest poetry of our day. That from John T. Frederick!"

Now the worst was past. Carmelita gained in strength and energy day by day. She drove the car and did some shopping. But I asked Mae Idso to stay a few more weeks.

When the holidays came we decided to throw a big New Year's

party to celebrate Carmelita's return to health. Mrs. Idso had gone. Gladys and Carmelita set her up in an apartment on College Street. They helped her furnish it and helped her move. Mae Idso was our friend for life. She was a lovely person and she came like a gift from heaven when we needed help.

"I want Meryl Norton to come to the party," Carmelita said. "She's very important to me. We roomed together in nursing school and went to Europe together. We both became administrators and teachers in nursing schools. Besides, she's my best friend."

We brought in the New Year with toasts and songs. Bun Newman brought his guitar. He and Oz Thorson and Chuck and I sang until our throats were sore.

Meryl Norton remained with us a few days and it cheered Carmelita to talk with her. I stayed home to help wash dishes and clean up the house. Then I said plaintively, "I can't face another glass of punch or plate of canapes or casserole of oysters, scalloped. The inner man protests. I want to get back to plain and simple living."

Two years passed like covered wagons going west. Every time Carmelita flew to Rochester for a checkup, the wagons formed a circle to fight off the Indians. But the Indians did not show and Carmelita was home free.

I groaned over income tax reports, gas tax reports, crop reports, livestock markets. I met my Monday night classes and told Dr. Reninger, "Bill, I now know the secret of teaching. You put a pin on the end of a stick and continually jab the students saying, 'Write, write, write.'"

On the stormy days I stayed at home and wrote poems. I wrote a few short stories, but never felt comfortable with the technique. I published a few poems in *Poetry, Virginia Quarterly,* and *Commonweal.* I gave a few talks too. I talked to the three service clubs—Rotary, Lions, Y's Men. I gave a talk to the students and faculty in the big auditorium on the relation of art to reality.

"Don't forget," I said, "that they are only distant cousins. Art is a made-up thing, an imagined world, not real life at all. It must seem like reality though it is an artificial image. Yet the resemblance must make you believe in it. Life is seldom as neat and orderly as art expressions. Reality sometimes seems only a bunch of dangling participles. The function of art, at least of writing, is to show some insight, revelation, intuition to make our lives more meaningful. We must have some kind of order and meaning in our lives. And most of us need a sense of purpose to explain why we are here."

I told my students, "There is no golden key to unlock the door to success. You learn to write by the hard dedicated application of your talent to purpose and discipline in the cause of original expression. You cannot learn to play the piano by reading a book of instructions."

I often used this story as an illustration. "A man wished to attend a concert at Carnegie Hall in New York. He thought he would walk to the hall from his hotel. But not being familiar with the city, he lost his way. He met a young man with a violin case under his arm and thought, he can give me direction. He stopped the young man and asked, 'Can you tell me how to get to Carnegie Hall?' The young man answered, 'Yes, sir, you practice and practice and practice.' ''

"And that," I said, "is how you learn to write."

The college built its own radio station and I read my poems for the first broadcast. With a grasp on the arms of Chuck on one side and Bill Reninger on the other I climbed the stairs to the third floor of the auditorium building. I said to Chuck, "Think of me climbing all those damn stairs and a few years ago I couldn't even brush my own teeth."

On cold days out on the tractor I chilled, on hot days I cooked. At temperatures above ninety I stopped sweating and my own temperature would rise. I wore calluses on my hands from fighting the steering wheel. I banged my legs straddling the transmission housing. But I could hold the cornpicker on the row hour after hour and I could steer the tractor with one hand and with the other reach back to crank the sickle bar of the combine up or down. And I no longer clipped fences when I turned at the end with a six-section harrow.

I had grown strong, tough, and weather resistant. I had to be lifted on and off the tractors but I could drive any of the four we had and they all had different gear shifts. I did admit that after a day on the Trac-Tractor, which had handles for steering, the cords in my wrists were stretched about a mile long.

Moments of frustration burned me at times. The sight of a bloated steer made me want to grab a lasso, snug down the animal, and puncture its side with a trocar to let out the gas. I had done it more than once. Chuck and Floyd and Carl always took so much time. I was sure I could do it more quickly.

I learned to appraise the weight of an animal by sight. Livestock buyers had more experience but I was pretty good at it and would set my estimate against that of a buyer. Once in a while I had to eat crow, but not often.

Poems that refused to come right would frustrate me too, and sometimes I would gladly have thrown my typewriter through the window just to hear the glass break.

It galled me to make mistakes, but I made them. There were so many things I couldn't do that I tried to be nearly perfect in what I did. It is human to err, but I acted as if it didn't apply to me. But I wasn't too dumb to learn from the experience of others.

Right after the end of the war, George Gates from the English department would come out and help with the fall plowing. He paid in labor for hay for his horses. We were glad to have him. He didn't need to be shown how to do the work. He plowed with our old Caterpillar tractor. George was stingy with headlands and sometimes when he made a sharp turn the crank on the tractor would tear out a few cross sections of the woven wire fence. When I saw this, I learned from

George to leave plenty of room at the headlands for turning.

We had to buy about twenty thousand bushels of corn each year in addition to what we raised. The little curly-haired, white-faced calves grew into big appetites. It surprised me that Texas calves would not eat corn at first. We had to teach them to eat it by grinding it and sprinkling it with cottonseed or linseed meal.

Chuck said, "The little buggers have never seen corn before." But once they learned to eat it they were off and running. I enjoyed watching five hundred heads bobbing up and down at the feed bunks. It gave me a twinge when the time came to ship them to Chicago. Even as a boy I disliked the idea of violence to animals.

We tried to lead a cheerful life and keep up our hopes that there would be no recurrence of the malignancy. One Sunday morning after breakfast, Harald Holst rose from the table. He caught a whatnot hanging on the wall with his shoulder, raised it off its two hooks, and precipitated the whole works to the floor. The shelves held a collection of liqueur glasses of various shapes and colors. The crash of glass made an abrupt end to the conversation. "A lovely sound, Harald," I said, "that of breaking glass."

Jane Birkhead wailed, "Oh, Harald, you're so clumsy."

"Only glasses, Harald," Carmelita said. "Forget it." Then we all laughed and it was a joke between us for months afterward. But Harald did not forget. On every trip out of town to music conventions or on vacation he sent back a liqueur glass, unique in color and shape. They were beautiful little glasses—fragile, winking their colors when the sun struck them. Carmelita begged him to stop when the shelves were full.

I remembered this as a kind of golden time when we were all friends. We bathed in contentment and shut out misery, pain, and worry.

Periodically, Carmelita visited the Mayo Clinic. Each time she came back with a clean report. Almost three years had passed since her surgery and I began to breathe more easily. But I did not reckon on the hidden malignancy of cancer cells.

Carmelita began to have pains in her shoulders and neck. They came intermittently and she explained these pains as muscle strain from lifting or gardening or driving the car. She told her doctor at the clinic but he assured her that the pains came from nerves, anxiety, or fatigue.

My spirits sagged and I had premonitions of disaster. Still, the Mayo Clinic said she was all right and I believed they ought to know. But the pains increased in frequency and intensity. In February I met the plane as she returned from her examination. She saw me in the car and ran toward me, her feet twinkling in the snow. She stepped off the platform of the air terminal and fell into a drift of snow. But she jumped up and ran smiling, shaking the snow from her sleeves.

"Will you believe it? They say I'm all right, Darling. A good report all the way." She could never say that again.

On the way back to town we noticed cars drawn off the side of the pavement. I pulled off wondering if there was an accident ahead. Then Carmelita said, "Look."

Over in a field of unhusked corn a herd of deer were grazing. They took no notice of the people in the cars watching them. Carmelita began to count. She reached eighty and was still not finished. "Where did they come from, all those beautiful creatures?"

I said, "There are deer along the river in the woods. I had no idea there were so many. That farmer won't need to bother about husking his corn." No wonder the fellows who farmed along the river knocked off a deer now and then. A herd that size could be destructive.

She sighed and caught my arm. "How free and easy their life seems. No past, no future, just now. Enough food, shelter among the trees, sex at mating time. What an uncluttered way to live. They drift across the field unaware of tomorrow."

A fishbone feeling stuck in my throat and I could not say, "I wish there was no tomorrow." I squeezed her arm against my side. We drove on toward town. This was one of the special moments that come too infrequently to a man and woman deeply in love and full of concern for the future.

Either the pain diminished or Carmelita pretended to ignore it. She slept well, took naps, her appetite was capricious, but she had always been touchy about food. She did her housework and acted cheerful. I thought she did not look well but told myself, "Perhaps I'm imagining things."

Carmelita scorned bridge playing. "I should waste my afternoons over a silly deck of cards." Her eyes flashed, her feet well apart, a favorite stance when roused. She visited with her many friends.

"How about that mystery story that cries for revision?" I asked her.

"Not yet. With my last royalty check, Mosby's asked me to start revising the book. They want to publish a new edition next year. It'll be a big job. A lot of new things to consider, new drugs, new procedures. . . ."

The Hearst family exhibited a conservative attitude in politics by supporting the Republican party. Most branches of the family floated on the Republican current, never questioning their direction or destination. My father had ridden a horse in the Bull Moose parade, bearing a flaming torch when Theodore Roosevelt split the party and campaigned against Taft in 1912.

But Chuck and I kicked over the traces and cast our lot with the Democrats. For the life of me I could not see where a high tariff gave any advantage to farmers. The long farm depression of the twenties and the spirit-breaking Depression of the early thirties only reinforced my convictions. No doubt I was influenced by the losing battle for parity prices in which Father fought so bravely. Chuck and I reasoned that farmers sold on world markets at world prices and the tariff raised the prices on the things farmers had to buy.

I fired my first shot in the Hoover-Roosevelt campaign. At my own expense I had printed a small booklet labeled "Hoover's Farm Policy" and inside were blank pages. I mailed one to every farmer in Cedar Falls Township. For the first time in its history, the township cast a majority of its votes for the Democrats.

A neighbor, Art Larsen, said, "My mother doesn't believe you can be a good man and be a Democrat. But that little booklet opened my eyes. I wonder who got it out?"

I kept still, but it was heady stuff. I now attended precinct caucuses, became a member of the county committee, and a delegate to the state convention. I shook hands with labor leaders in Waterloo, with black leaders, and with the rank and file. I discovered that politics consisted of organized sources of power and of welding into a chain all its scattered parts. I also learned that seasoned leaders, even at the precinct level, hang onto their positions and shove off the efforts of newcomers. "Old bulls and young bulls," I thought.

Henry A. Wallace and his third party posed a problem for me. I liked H. A. well enough and had worked for his farm paper. But a third party did not rouse my enthusiasm. I remembered what a shock ran through the Iowa Democrats when Roosevelt dumped Wallace in favor of Harry Truman for his vice president. Wallace, sensitive and sure he was president-bound, reacted with his third party.

I knew that one of H.A.'s friends, an initiate in the occult, had prophesied that Henry would become president. This man, a real mystic and Tibetan scholar, assured Wallace that his star was rising. Imagine how Wallace must have felt when Roosevelt died and Truman took office. Henry had just missed the presidency by a few years.

I believed that Wallace organized a third party, not because of resentment or anger, but because he thought the angels' arms were around him and, like Gideon's army, he would triumph.

What infuriated me were the smears brushed across all the Wallace campaign. Cries of "communists" thrown like dung against his good name. When Wallace came to Iowa he was denied the opportunity to speak to students at his alma mater, Iowa State College, where a Republican candidate, Harold Stassen, had been permitted to speak. The University of Iowa at Iowa City also said no to Wallace. And of course the Iowa State Teachers College fell into line. This roused me to break into print.

I called a reporter on the *Waterloo Courier* and gave an interview. I did the same thing with the *Cedar Falls Record*. I really let fly. It incensed me, this refusal to let students hear the ideas of a man who was one of the state's prominent citizens.

"This man is a noted scientist, the third generation of editors of the state's most important farm paper, a former vice president of the United States. His uncle, John Wallace, has served on the Board of Regents and yet our universities and colleges are too timid to expose their students to the ideas of a man of intelligence and probity. Our college might as well be a trade school."

This is what I said and what the papers published. Carmelita said the phone rang all day. After dinner that evening she answered the phone and called me and said, "The dean of the trade school wants to speak to you."

My burst of anger and the forthrightness of my words had bothered me as I worked in the field that day. I wondered if I had gone too far. I disliked exposing my ideas in public. I even disliked reading reviews of my books. But tonight I looked at Carmelita and grinned. It was all right. The phone call must be from Martin Nelson, dean of the faculty. I thought that if Martin could be humorous about the interview I could relax. I picked up the receiver and asked, "Martin, are you mad at me?"

I never understood why "communist" was such a dirty word. But I lost interest in politics as Carmelita's pain increased. Her suffering could neither be hidden nor her frailty disguised. I knew as surely as the world turns that we were in for it. A weight of doom settled on us both. Where once hope bloomed was now a small dried stem. Carmelita took the first step away from me. I could only watch her go.

On her last trip to Rochester I called her every night at her hotel. The evening came when the desk clerk said, "Mrs. Hearst moved out today."

Moved out? Where would she move to? I remembered the name of the doctor who looked after Carmelita, who coordinated the data from the various sections. I asked the operator at Rochester to find this man. In a short time the doctor answered. I identified myself. "Where is my wife?" I demanded.

"She's in Mercy Hospital. We found a metastasis to the spine. With this virulent type of cancer, it is type IV, there is little we can do but try to keep her comfortable. I'm afraid she found the news a shock."

"What kind of a sadist are you," I asked, "telling her month after month not to be alarmed, that the pain would go away? And why the hell didn't you call me when you sent her to the hospital?"

The doctor said, "I've really nothing more to say."

The next day Chuck, Gladys, and I drove to Rochester and brought Carmelita home to die.

I said savagely to Dr. Henderson, "If Entz had found that opening into the bladder wall when he should have, we might have stopped the cancer before it spread. I ought to sue the son of a bitch."

Jim Henderson shook his head. "It wouldn't help Carmelita and I'm sure Dr. Entz did the best he could. Sometimes a fistula is hard to find."

Then I began to have strange behavior with my heart. Finally

Chuck took me to the hospital, right out of the hayfield during an attack. I had an electrocardiograph made. The graph showed fibrillations but no heart damage. "Nervousness mostly," Dr. Henderson said. "It'll quiet down."

One night when Jim Henderson was out of town I called Dr. Barnett because Carmelita needed some attention. After Dr. Barnett had seen Carmelita he came out to the living room where I was. I asked him, "Stanley, how long do we have?"

Dr. Barnett eyed a spot on the ceiling, puffed out his cheeks. "It's awfully hard to tell. A lesion in the spine, type IV, I would guess a few months." Then he added softly, "I'll tell you, Jim. The day will come when you will pray for her to die."

You must be crazy, I thought, as I let him out. I'm going to keep her right here at home where she is comfortable and I can be with her all the time.

For a few weeks Carmelita fixed our meals, directed the cleaning woman, even did some shopping. I tried to believe it would last. "We're getting along fine," I boasted. I dared not look in the corner where the dark future sat waiting.

When Carmelita could no longer manage the house, my sister Louise came from Bremerton, Washington. Her husband was still in the navy, a lieutenant commander in the shipyards. Gladys and Betty came every day to visit and run errands. Louise, a cheerful, practical person, reported that Carmelita showed some of her old fire by declaring, "It's my home and I'm still the boss." We all applauded.

Sometimes the girls would fix supper on trays and leave so Carmelita and I could be alone. "I'm curious, Jim," Carmelita asked, "why you got upset some Sunday mornings when I went to church."

"If you want to know the simple truth," I answered, "it was because Sunday was the one morning I could stay in bed and I wanted company. I got over it, didn't I?"

Carmelita touched my hand. "Is that all? My goodness, I imagined all sorts of crazy reasons. We had plenty of time for lovemaking."

The way back was a dead-end road. Our next door neighbor, Norma Priest, came over each morning and gave Carmelita a morphine injection. A friend of Carmelita's from the New York office came out and stayed a week. Both she and Norma Priest were registered nurses.

In spite of my assertion that I would keep Carmelita at home, the day came when she needed hospital care. Even she recognized this. When she was wheeled out of our bedroom on a stretcher toward the ambulance, my eyes filled with tears. I knew she would not come back. The knowledge devastated me. But Carmelita refused to be sad and joked and smiled gently. The owner of the ambulance, Mr. Nelson, an old friend of mine, had come himself. After Carmelita was taken from the room he came back and laid a hand on my shoulder as if to say, "This is not the end."

Louise and Gladys cleaned up the bedroom, threw out the bottles of medicine, removed cotton pads, the thermometer, and made the empty bed.

I stood up at the medicine cupboard and removed the remaining tablets of morphine and codeine and put them in an envelope and hid them in a corner of my desk. "There's enough here," I said grimly.

I drove to the farm mornings and worked until noon. In spite of myself, the tears would roll down my cheeks as I maneuvered the machines in the hay field. Afternoons I went to the hospital to be with Carmelita. She asked me to read the Psalms aloud and each afternoon in the quiet room I read to her.

The tumor grew and pressed on her spine and she became partially paralyzed. She begged me for special nurses. "Mortgage the farm," she whispered.

Once more Sarah put on her old uniforms and took her turn at night duty. Wonder of wonders, Meryl Norton took a leave of absence from her duties as educational director of the nursing school at the Moline Public Hospital.

"My best and oldest friend," Carmelita told me. She seemed relaxed and content with Meryl there. Then Ruth Wardin, a friend whose children had grown, put on her nurse's uniform and offered to help. Louise and Gladys visited with her mornings.

Dr. Henderson alerted me. "I don't know how long the morphine will control the pain. I'm giving her some curare now."

I said, "If I could get a hypodermic needle into one of her veins and shoot in a bubble of air, I would."

Dr. Henderson looked horrified. "You mustn't think that." Suddenly I remembered that Dr. Barnett had said, "The day will come. . . ."

But Carmelita was not quite finished with this world. President Maucker from the college brought in his wife, who was suffering from paralysis and convulsions. He said to Carmelita, "The doctor says it might be polio."

Carmelita said, "Bill, describe Helga's symptoms."

When he did she said, "It isn't polio. You get her to Iowa City to the hospital as quickly as you can. It sounds like encephalitis to me." It was.

She began to descend rapidly into herself and her darkness. She retreated from this world. She knew me and pressed my hand but she had gone on a journey far away from me. Once she begged, "Take me home, Jim." But only once.

Her last afternoon she lay quietly, eyes closed. Once she fretted feebly and the nurse administered a hypodermic injection. She seemed to sleep. I stood up and leaned over and kissed her cheek. It was the last time. She moved slightly. I asked, "Do you want to be turned over?"

I could barely hear her say, "Yes."

House of Sorrow

SOMEONE TOLD ME after Carmelita's funeral that never had the Catholic church held so many Protestants. But St. Patrick's Church did not seem disturbed nor did Monsignor Mauer, who conducted the Mass for the Dead. The Monsignor was dying from a cancer of the prostate and he knew it. I admired him for his courage and wrote a note to him to tell him so. He had been a staff of oak for Carmelita during her illness.

The day of the funeral was a beautiful October day. The sunlight filtered through colored leaves. Those already fallen rustled underfoot. In a distant part of the cemetery a cardinal whistled. No wind and the air warm—a conspiracy on the part of nature to express her harmony and ignore the sad occasion.

Years later I wrote a poem about it called "Scatter the Petals" and my friend, composer William P. Latham, set it to music. I did not write any more poems for two years.

Following an old custom, people came to the house after the funeral. Gladys and Betty served coffee and cookies. No doubt the neighbors sent in food. I hid in a cloud of grief and withdrew into the isolation of my own feelings. Yet I was aware of a sharp anxiety that kept asking me what I would do now. How would I care for myself and my home? Mae Idso had married an old friend and moved to Wisconsin. I knew of no one to call on.

In the confusing way that things happen, the Internal Revenue Service men brought back the farm books that afternoon. Several weeks before they had picked them up for an audit. When I had said that I must leave to go to the hospital to see my wife they politely expressed the hope that she would soon be better. When I had said she would not get better, they shrugged and were silent. They were always the hounds of government, sniffing for some trail of fraud and deceit. I told them to leave their figures and findings and I would attend to them later. My sharp tone left them no choice and they surrendered reluctantly.

Then a ray of sunlight pierced the gloom. Lois Sherman, superintendent of Sartori Hospital, phoned me. One of her practical nurses wanted to leave and take a housekeeping position. Lois Sherman had been one of Carmelita's students in the nursing school at Iowa City and she took an interest in my welfare. The next day Vy Rickert came to live with me.

I think Gladys took for granted that she and Chuck would make a home for me. But I knew this would never solve my problems. I had lived too independent a life for that. Mrs. Rickert and I found each other congenial and passed the days without friction. I warned her that it would be a sad and silent house and hoped she had friends who would offer her a change and recreation.

Chuck and Gladys, from the kindness of their hearts, decided I needed to get away from the house and all the aftermath of death. My close friend and attorney, Roland Merner, said he would attend to all the legal details connected with Carmelita's death. He was amused by my innocence in assuming that Carmelita would be buried in our family plot in Fairview Cemetery.

"Didn't you know a Catholic cannot be buried in a Protestant cemetery without special permission?"

I shook my head in surprise.

"My boy," Roland said, "Father Mauer had to do some tall explaining to the Archdiocese in Dubuque to get permission to lay her in unhallowed ground."

I took a deep breath. "I never suspected that. But Roland, permission or no permission, Carmelita stays with our family. Just before she went to the hospital she said to me, 'Jim, you're all the family I've got. Please look after me. God, I could have bawled. That appeal just broke me up. Of course I would look after her. Christ, I was her husband."

Chuck, Gladys, and I took my car and drove to New Orleans. There we did all the tourist routines—drank coffee at Morning Call, went down to the levee to watch the ships unload. I saw enough bananas come off a ship on an endless belt to last this country ten years, or so it seemed.

We had dinner at Antoine's and decided it had become a tourist trap. We hired a taxi and the driver showed us the sights—the cemeteries with the tombs all above ground because of the high water level. "Talk about cities of the dead," I said. "Some of the mausoleums are regular marble houses."

We drove through the French Quarter and admired the intricate ironwork on the balconies. The driver, with a leer, suggested that we visit the Quarter at night but I was in no mood for frivolities. I gazed incredulously at the great spreading live oak trees with their dripping moss and balls of mistletoe.

I was amused by the southern talk of a mechanic when we pulled into a garage in Vicksburg. The car lights had been going off and on. The mechanic traced the wiring and said, "What do you-all know, that little old wheelchair in the trunk got a wire in its teeth and bit it plumb in two." He even made me smile.

As we headed toward home we swung through the Arcadian bayou country where the people speak a French patois and scarcely any English. The land of Longfellow's "Evangeline" seemed like a foreign country. We stopped a few days in Austin, Texas, to visit some of Gladys's friends. Frank and Mrs. Dobie asked us to their house one afternoon and Frank showed us his books and regaled us with stories.

"He's a great guy," Chuck said. "Always fighting the authority of the university, but they keep him on the payroll."

We came home by way of Norman, Oklahoma, where we had dinner at the country club with a man who had been an officer in the WAVES when they were in Cedar Falls. He was almost a stranger without his uniform. It was warm in Oklahoma and we found our winter clothes a little heavy. But we struck snow and ice in Omaha and were back in a midwestern winter.

I had sent Vy postcards along the way. I was a bit surprised at the warmth of her greeting. "I've been awfully lonesome," she confessed.

Vy adjusted her work to fit my schedule. She was a middle-aged woman with grown children. Her husband had divorced her and left her to make her own way. She worked in hospitals and in homes. "I wasn't trained for anything," she told me. "I had to take what work I could find."

Carmelita had warned me, "Jim, don't you dare give up your classes. You need the contact with young people looking for answers, the give-and-take discussions with staff members."

She was right. She knew I could not sit moping and feeling sorry for myself when there were poems, stories, and essays to read, criticize, and discuss. But I dwelt in a house of sorrow and each night when I stood up to turn down the thermostat I said to myself, "Thank god another day of my life has passed."

I know it sounds melodramatic but at the time I meant it. It exhausted me to carry on my daily work. I lived in a state of continual fatigue.

Friends meant to be kind and they often stopped to see me. But each one of them had problems, duties, and responsibilities. They had spoken their words of consolation. I could not thrust my woe on them. Besides what could they do? I needed someone to fill the terribly vacant space I carried in myself. I felt abandoned, left on the doorstep of my fate, with no one to take me in. It was love and the close affection of a loved one that would assuage my hunger.

At the moment I had no desire for sexual satisfaction. My need went deeper than that. I wanted a woman who would bind me to her by her care and approval. I was sure that never again would a woman find me worth her surrender. There were days when I despised myself and my crippled body.

On the surface Vy and I managed very well. She prepared an early supper on class nights and set out the chairs. There was enough space in the living room for the students. She emptied the ashtrays and straightened the house when the students left. She was a good cook

THE GRAIL

The snow falls like flakes of light —
Wherefore we come, Lord, bearing our promises.

Let the wind-lash curl the drifts and smother
The world in flying ice.

Frost knits the road into a carpet of iron
And locks the pond against the sun's finger.

We alone move through Death's false harmony
Saying:

If a tree drains its body of life,
Shall the root perish?
Who holds safely now the small seed?

Let it not vanish, Lord, let it seek haven
And if in the spring there remains one spark of
    growth,
Only enough for one pale blossom,

We shall come forward singing,
Our hands curved to the plow handles
Our eyes raised to the light.

What greater praise canst thou have
Than that we seek the grail,
Not in the heavens, Lord, among the stars' cold
    radiance,

But in the furrow, the plowed field, the meadow,
The places where it blooms for man in his short life.

— JAMES HEARST

and tried to give me the food I liked. But it all had the same taste. I was sunk in a morose mood, silent and remote.

Each morning I called Gladys in an effort to make contact with the family, with someone who would care that I still existed. Then I began to go out to the farm and work again. In spite of the assurances of my friends that to keep "busy" was a saving grace, such therapy did not work for me.

My despondency filled the house and Vy Rickert must have found it a lonely place in which to live. While I spent the day at the farm she visited friends, shopped for groceries, or attended the movies. She looked after me in a motherly way but she had her own psychic wounds. My aloofness, my darkness did nothing to lift the heavy atmosphere of the house.

One day she told me she would like to go back to the hospital and work. "It's hard work," she said. "But I'm with people and we women go places together." Then she added half to herself, "It would be better for me. It's so lonely here."

I understood but could not promise any change in the way I lived. I did my work, ate my meals, and went to bed. I took a sleeping pill each night which made me dopey and slow to rouse in the mornings. I took a morbid satisfaction in knowing I had an envelope of morphine and codeine tablets hidden in my desk.

But this was playacting and I knew it. My greatest virtue was my endurance, my resistance to defeat. I had inherited from my parents a combination of Scotch-Irish and German tenacity for living and a disdain and contempt for the ones who gave up.

When Vy said she wanted to leave, her words shocked me out of my isolation. My move now was to find a woman to replace her. Sharp as a knife point, the old fear jabbed me—the fear of being left alone and unable to cope with an empty house. I knew I must have someone. For instance, if I fell, I could not get up alone and it might be days before anyone found me.

One of the faculty men said his mother-in-law would be willing to keep house for me during the three summer months. She taught in a school for delinquent children during the school year. I relaxed and Vy promised to stay until Mrs. Crissman arrived.

She turned out to be a doughty warrior of the old school. She expected schedules to run on time and order maintained. She repeated that in her next life she would be the clinging-vine type and not the one who gives orders. I wished that I had waited until her next incarnation.

I searched my acquaintances for someone I could talk to and who would listen with a sympathetic ear. I knew a divorced woman who had two adopted children. I invited them to have Sunday breakfast with me. Mrs. Crissman spent Sundays with her daughter. I liked the rampaging little kids, the stir and bustle. Suddenly the house became livelier and some of the grayness melted away.

To my surprise, Mrs. Crissman set a stern mouth to such "goings on." She said, with a policeman's tone, "It hasn't been a year yet."

This irritated me, but I could pass it off. What I couldn't pass off was the sharp irrational anger on the part of Chuck and Gladys. They resented this friendship and made no bones about it. I did not try to answer their attacks. I was still too lonely, too deep in my unhappiness to reply. Chuck would not have cared but Gladys picked at him with her indignation and he joined in just to keep peace.

To this day, I still do not understand their deportment. But I was in for a bigger shock. Louise came barging out from Seattle and took up arms against me. I could not believe it. Louise and I had always trusted each other. Louise had confided in me, told me problems she did not repeat to anyone else. I remembered the time when she had irregular bleeding after her period. She came to me because she said, "I can't go to Uncle George."

Now she came, loaded for bear, angry and upset. "What in the hell is the matter with you?" I asked her. "I haven't robbed a bank or seduced my neighbor's wife. Why are you so vindictive?"

"That awful woman," Louise said, "and those awful kids."

"What do you know about it? You haven't even seen them."

"I don't need to. I've heard all I need to know."

I was clearly puzzled. "About what? All you need to know about what?"

Louise flared back, "I have an interest in the farm and I'm not going to risk it."

"Risk it for what? I don't know what you're talking about."

Louise looked ugly. "Tomorrow you and I are going out to the farm and talk with Gladys and Chuck. Chuck is going to have Roland Merner there to tell us how to dissolve the farm partnership you and Chuck have."

I could not take it in. All these years since Father died Chuck and I had run the farm together. We had paid off the debts Father owed his brothers and sisters, built new buildings, fenced the entire farm with hog-tight fences, installed bathrooms and hot water heaters in the houses occupied by the hired men, and paid for new machinery. We set out a new orchard, installed a complete drainage system, filled in gullies, and grassed the waterways. We were on good terms with our hired men. Now Chuck and Louise wanted to wash me out. I refused to fight back. This thrust was too ugly to counter.

Years later, when this was just a bad memory, I thought I should have shaken them both until their teeth rattled and told them to shape up and behave themselves. But I sat listlessly while the lawyer explained the legal process of dissolving a partnership.

Roland Merner did not like it. He phoned me the next day. "You can't stop them but don't worry, my boy, those crows will come home to roost."

He was right. They did come home to roost. But when they did I would have had it otherwise. I was too much of a family man and I loved my brother.

Louise, in triumph, flew back to Seattle. James McAlvin, our cousin, was there on a business trip and Louise asked him to dinner. Jim put it to her when he heard about it. "What business is it of yours? Why do you stick your nose in Jim's affairs? Why can't he have a woman friend if he wants to? You act as if he had married her and I wish he had."

Jim told me about it later. The two of us had been raised together and were as close as brothers. We were the same age and Jim had worked on the farm summers. He lived in Chicago but had often spent a weekend with Carmelita and me. "What's this all about?" he asked.

I shook my head. "I don't really know. I didn't know this gal very well but she's had a hard time and so have I and we sort of gravitated together. Sometimes I think it was because Louise and Gladys don't have children and it infuriated them to think I might end up with a couple."

"Why don't you?"

I shook my head. "This brouhaha scared her and I quit seeing her. It's more restful this way and I don't want any more trouble."

Jim said, "Gladys was the worst, wasn't she. Chuck hasn't the guts of a louse when she gets on him. Why don't they have children?"

"Their secret. Let's forget it. And thanks for your offer of money, Jim. But I'll make it all right."

I stopped to see Carl Hundley, one of our hired men. I said, "Carl, Chuck and I are dissolving our partnership. I think he ought to keep the home farm where he lives. I'll take this one. Would you like to rent it?"

He nodded and said, "Yes, I would."

"Chuck and I will divide the machinery and you can buy it from me. You'll have two tractors, a plow, disk, and harrow. We'll probably share the bailer and combine. You and I will have to buy a corn planter."

Carl asked, "How do you want me to buy the machinery?"

"You can give me a note for it until you can pay for it. I'll have Roland draw up a lease. It'll be a livestock lease. I aim to keep on raising hogs and feeding cattle. And if Norma wants to go into the chicken business we could fix up those two new brooder houses for laying houses."

Carl wasn't so sure. "They'd make good places to farrow sows in."

I shrugged. "Have it out with your wife. We can make pens for the sows in the old horse barn."

"Do you want to help?" Carl asked.

I nodded. "Yes, I want to keep doing field work as long as I can. I need to get away from town and my classes."

As I drove home I thought, "Well, that's settled. Carl and I will get along together all right and we ought to make some money."

Later in the summer Dr. Craig Ellyson of Waterloo stopped for a visit. Ever since he had come to see me in the hospital at Iowa City, Craig and I had seen something of each other. He had a fine voice and once he came out to the farm and sang a concert for me. I appreciated our friendship.

As he stood up to leave he asked, "Anything I can do for you?"

Half joking I said, "Yes, find me a housekeeper. Mrs. Crissman leaves at the end of August."

"Maybe I can," he said.

"You mean it?"

"It's like this. Johanna's elder sister came over from Germany a couple of years ago. She's a nurse, an R.N. But she doesn't want to work in a hospital. She's been babysitting and caring for some of my older patients. But she'd like a home and a chance to be useful."

"Tell her she's found it, though I don't need a nurse. Can she *"sprechen sie"* English?"

"Oh, yes, no problem there. But she'd want to come and see Johanna on weekends. Could you manage?"

"I could try. How much should I pay her."

"Whatever you're paying now. But, Jim, remember Annamarie has been through the bombing. She looked after an elderly couple in Berlin. When the sirens sounded she would have to get them up, dressed, and taken to a bomb shelter. Sometimes she would have to do this two or three times a night. She's nervous, sensitive, and you'll need to be careful with her."

"Why not bring her over to see me and the house? Then she can decide if she wants to look after me."

Annamarie Wilkens came to keep house for me. She was tall, thin, blue-eyed, and wore her light blond reddish hair in a coil on top of her head. My god, she was neat and a good cook. I said to her, "Don't be so deferential, Annamarie."

"What's that, Jim?" She worked hard at improving her use of the American language.

"Don't try to anticipate my wishes. You just go ahead and do things the way you want to. And speak German if you can't think of the English word. My mother was German. I knew the German alphabet before I did the English one."

She's the best thing that has happened to me, I thought. I began to feel like myself again. With Carl in charge of the farm and Annamarie of the house, I stood on solid ground and the clouds of depression started to blow away.

Annamarie liked to play classical records and she liked to walk. "Doesn't anybody in this country walk? Every time I go for a walk some automobile stops and wishes me to ride."

She amused me too. One morning after a warm rain, when night crawlers wiggled onto the cement sidewalk and could not wiggle off again, Annamarie swept the front steps. She came back and stood in my study door, hands on hips, a frown of amazement on her face. "Jim," she said explosively, "this country not only has the tallest buildings, the longest roads, greatest rivers, but it has the biggest angleworms.''

In spite of my determination to take care of myself, weekends bothered me. Annamarie would fix my Saturday night dinner and then leave on a bus for Johanna in Waterloo.

I used the utmost care in going to bed and getting up. I dried my hands before I grasped a towel rack or doorknob. I planted my feet squarely in front of the lavatory and kept the wheelchair close behind me. I was alone in the house.

I had asked Harald to leave when Carmelita was ill at home and I needed the bedrooms for her friends who came and stayed a few days. I knew that if I fell I might have to wait until Sunday night when Annamarie returned.

I made my own breakfast as I had many times. I swore at the kitchen for its awkward arrangement. I was up and down, up and down—to the refrigerator then to the stove, to the bread box, toaster, sink. When I had finished washing dishes I felt as tired as if I had done a day's work.

I remembered how an old acquaintance had tried to soft-soap me with, ''As long as your mind is all right, it doesn't matter about your body.''

I thought, ''The hell it doesn't.''

What did matter was to keep up my endurance, to fight back, not to give in to the inexorable demands made on me by circumstances. This called for day after day resistance to fear, anxiety, the unexpected, the possible accident.

Jessie Loomis often stopped to see me. The Loomises had been our friends for years. Frederick, a doctor, had less time but not less affection for Carmelita and me. Jessie was a painter. The Midwest knew her as one of its most gifted artists. Her shows drew crowds of admiring people and her pictures sold readily.

She had helped persuade Annamarie to come to my house. Now she had another idea. ''Jim,'' she asked, ''do you know about Patty Johnson?''

''The famous columnist for the *Waterloo Courier?''*

''She hasn't worked for weeks. She goes to Des Moines twice a week to see a psychiatrist. You know her, don't you?''

''Sure, since she was a little girl. We do all our banking business at the First National Bank where her papa is the president.''

''You don't like him?''

''Yes, but I like her mother better. He can be a bastard when he wants to be tough about a loan.''

''Patty needs help just as you need help. I think it would be good for both of you if she would come over on Sunday afternoons and cook your dinner.''

''Can she cook?''

"Probably not. But she could try and so can you. Annamarie spoils you. It won't hurt you to eat a meal slightly scorched or underdone."

So I called Patty and persuaded her to come over the next Sunday afternoon. She looked frail and fatigued and spoke in a little girl's voice.

"What the hell is the matter with you, Patty?" I asked.

She stared at me and tears came into her eyes. "I can't talk about it."

But she came every Sunday afternoon and cooked my dinner. I helped with the dishes afterward. At first she had no confidence in herself and, as I told Jessie, "We ate some pretty awful dinners."

But soon she got used to the house and to me and the way to fix food. Once in awhile her mother came with her and then we had a feast.

I admired her mother. She was the salt of the earth. She was the solid pillar around which her family revolved. Bernice Johnson was what the Bible would call "a good woman."

The support and friendship shown me by H. W. Reninger were beyond words of appreciation. Bill said to me, "Count on me to do the things for you that Chuck used to do. I'll carry you up and down stairs, take you places, see that your car and house have the care they need."

Such generosity overwhelmed me. I scarcely knew how to reply. "But Bill, you can't do that. You have your own family to look after and your job at school would kill the ordinary man. English, speech, foreign language, religion, philosophy, and drama—all in one department. I should think you would go nuts."

But Bill just smiled. "Then I'm not an ordinary man. Don't worry, we'll make it."

Reninger came from Detroit, a Ph.D. from the University of Michigan at Ann Arbor. A big-city man, he took to rural Iowa like a duck to water. He was the friend, advisor, and father confessor to students from farms and small towns. No student or staff member ever left his office empty spirited.

He used to walk out to our farm for Sunday morning breakfasts. He and my mother would argue the respective merits of Iowa and Michigan apples. His wife Betty had been in almost daily attendance on Carmelita when she was ill. Their children, John and Catharine, had learned to fend for themselves.

"I'm going to give you another class. Can you swing it? That'll double your salary."

"Yes, Bill, and thank you. Carl runs the farm. I just help out when I need exercise and he needs another hand. I've worried a little about money. I'll be all right when Carl and I finish our first year."

I had another offer of financial help. On one of the many times he stopped by, my friend James S. (Bun) Newman asked, "Do you want a job? I'm buying a warehouse business in Waterloo. I don't want a partner but I'll put you in charge of the office. We can build a ramp for your wheelchair and one of the men can be on hand to help you in and out of your car."

A few weeks later Dr. Anson Clark drove up from Dallas in his chauffeur-driven Cadillac. He stayed overnight. "I'm on my way to the Mayo Clinic for a checkup. Let's have a drink and go out for dinner. Victor can help you."

The next morning Anson said, "You don't have to take any guff from Chuck and his wife. Let them stew in their own stink. I have a job for you with the oil company. It pays twenty-five thousand a year and you can live with me."

Gratitude, mixed with caution, flowed through my mind. I said, "Anson, you're a great guy and my good friend too. You'd create a job for me out of the goodness of your heart. But if I'm going to make it, I've got to make it on my own. I must stand on my own feet."

Maybe I imagined it, but I thought Anson looked relieved. I told him, "I have the farm and Carl is a good man. And I have my teaching. That's all the work I can handle."

Anson asked, "What about your writing? You have that too."

"No," I answered. "That is over with. I've run out of poems. I don't know how to prime the pump."

A year later Patty went back to work. This meant the end of Sunday night suppers. Aunt Sarah asked, "Why don't you and Patty get married?"

"Other people have asked me that. But I'm not ready to live with anyone yet. I couldn't be a good husband. Besides Patty must be fifteen or twenty years younger than I am."

Sarah snorted. "Phooey! When did that ever stop a man."

Annamarie made me comfortable. She was extremely sensitive and seemed wound up like a spring ready to jump at any suggestion I made. She lived on exclamation points. I had hoped she would relax after we learned each other's ways but she did not. I was sure her experience in the war was partly responsible for her being so tightly strung.

I felt continual tension in the house. Annamarie tended to my every want but she lived for her weekends in Waterloo with the Ellysons. I knew she yearned to visit Germany too. There were nights when she returned from Waterloo clucking and fussing about the children. She was not used to children. And they absorbed the attention that Annamarie also needed.

One day out at the farm, while I was disking a field, I thought of Gloria Braddock. When she and Dick were divorced he stayed on the staff of the English department but she and her baby moved away. I asked Priscilla Fox about her.

"I hear from Gloria," Pris said. "She works in the office at Bucknell University. I'll give you her address."

Carmelita and I had entertained the Braddocks. However, our acquaintance was brief. But she knew me and she might be interested in keeping house for me, or so I hoped.

I wrote to her. Her little boy was three years old now. He would liven up the house.

She wrote back. She would indeed like to come and keep house for me. Could I give her more details of what I expected of her? The tone of her letter was warm, friendly, as if she wanted a home.

Before things went any farther I phoned Dick Braddock and asked him to stop by. When he came I asked, "Dick, would you mind if Gloria came here and kept house for me?"

Dick gave me a hard look. "You're damn right I would. It would embarrass me."

Then, trying to be wily, I said, "But Dick, I need Gloria. I can't live without a dependable housekeeper. She wouldn't ever be in your crowd. I'd see to that. Come on. Give a little, for my sake."

Dick glowered. "What about the woman you have?"

"She's restless and besides she isn't here weekends and it makes me nervous to be alone that long."

"All right, Jim. But keep her out of my sight. Of course you need help and I'll say this for her, Gloria is an excellent housekeeper. So go ahead if you want to."

My next job was to explain the change to Annamarie. "When you first came here, Annamarie, you didn't want to work in a hospital. Have you changed your mind now that you know the language and customs better?" I felt like a high-level diplomat.

Her face lit up. "Oh, yes, I would. I like to care for old people who are sick. Do you want me to leave?"

I knew this was the moment of truth. "I think you'd be happier and you'd certainly make more money in a hospital position. You are a registered nurse. And frankly, I would like someone who stayed here weekends. I'm a little anxious about being alone that long."

"Where would I go?"

I called Lois Sherman, superintendent of Sartori Hopsital. "Lois, would you want another nurse, an R.N. from Germany? A sister-in-law of Dr. Ellyson?"

Miss Sherman said calmly, "I never have too many R.N.'s. Ask her to come for an interview."

Annamarie came back elated. "I have a room to myself, a corner room in the nurses' home. Thank you, Jim."

A few weeks later, with a trunk and a suitcase, Gloria Braddock and son Michael came to live with me.

Changes

I PUSHED MY HEALTH PROBLEMS into the background to attend more immediate and pressing ones. I made no demands on my housekeeper for help with my personal needs. I could thank my strenuous, muscle-training days in the physiotherapy department for my limited independence. I now took for granted my ability to take care of myself, drive to the farm, and walk in from the garage. I centered attention on my classes and my responsibility for the house and farm. Carl and Norma kept the books so I was freed from that.

But it seemed to me that I lived one step removed from the actual experiences of the day. I did not live in a dream or sleepwalk my way from desk to farm to bed. But I rode in a dimension half a step beyond, or outside, the facts of my concern. Yet I functioned well, wrote checks for the bills, paid my housekeeper promptly, jotted down brief comments on my students' work.

I put on my work clothes and worked in the fields with Carl. My neighbor, Leo Priest, watched out for me and came over to tighten a towel rack, level a square of sidewalk, or repair the platform in the garage where I bumped it.

But it was time to stop floating in a space filled with a jumble of thoughts and anchor myself in the present. The pending arrival of Gloria and Michael brought me closer to earth and my thoughts into focus. I regarded the change as a move toward security. Gloria was well known at the college and could meet most of my friends as old acquaintances. And with Michael to care for, I hoped we would be a family. I craved someone to care for as much as I needed someone to care for me.

One night I drove home from the farm in a daze. I dragged myself from the car. My muscles ached. The sight of food made me nauseated. I woke in the night hot and thirsty and called Annamarie for a glass of water. I did not get up the next morning and slept heavily. When I woke up, Sarah was in the room. She said, "Annamarie is gone. She called me and said you were sick. Dr. Henderson is out of town so I called Dr. Nielsen."

I muttered, "What about Gloria and Michael? They were to come today."

"They're staying with the Reningers until you get over the flu."

The next day Chuck stopped in. I heard him ask Dr. Nielsen, "Is he really sick?"

Good old Chuck, I thought. Suspicious to the last. Does he think I've lost my nerve and taken to bed as a way out? I was pleased to hear Dr. Nielsen say, "A temperature of 104° is sick enough for me. I imagine it is for Jim. He'll be in bed for a few days. Why?"

Chuck stammered and mumbled his words. "Well, Gladys thought . . . well, maybe."

I told Sarah and she laughed. "Oh yes, Gladys told me, 'That Florida cracker just came to marry Jim.' Though I don't know what difference it makes to her."

I sighed. I would have to explain to Gloria that Gladys would not be friendly. She had not been friendly with any of my housekeepers. I told Sarah, "She's possessive. She wanted me to live with them."

This amused Sarah. "You couldn't live with Gladys. She'd make you miserable. She just can't bear to think you can make it on your own."

A week later Gloria and Michael moved in. I could just barely get up and go to the bathroom. I was weak, my god, I was weak. The least exertion made me sweat. But the first morning after they settled in I rolled out to the kitchen to say good morning. Michael screamed at the sight of me. Gloria shushed him. She fixed breakfast and said, "I'm going to lie down. I don't feel well. Can you get along?"

I called Dr. Henderson. "Jim, will you come and look at my new housekeeper? She's under the weather. Maybe I gave her the flu."

But when Dr. Henderson came downstairs he said, "She has a gallbladder upset. I think the strain of moving and the nervous excitement probably caused it. She'll be all right."

The next day went better. Gloria said, "We hardly know each other and Michael is not used to a man in the house. Things will settle down, Jim, if we're patient."

Michael got used to me, and he and I became good friends. If Gloria wanted to spend an evening with one of her many friends, I would babysit Michael. The three-year old would climb up on my lap and I told him stories. I said to Gloria, "I've remembered more 'Mother Goose' than I thought I knew."

When I stayed at home to work on student papers, Gloria often went to the basement to wash our clothes. I kept an eye on Michael. I had no idea how quickly a small boy could disappear. One minute Michael would be playing quietly in my study, the next minute he would be gone. I would call Gloria and she would find him in the back yard or running down the street.

Once Gloria came to me, her voice tearful and pleading. "Michael is having a tantrum and I can't stop him."

What I knew about bringing up children would hardly lick a postage stamp, but I never lacked for good intentions. I took myself into the spare bedroom where Michael, face to the wall, kicked the base-board and screamed. I brought my wheelchair up beside Michael, beat on the wall with my fists and screamed.

Michael stopped, regarded me with astonishment, and said grave-ly, "Jim, you go back in the study and work." That ended the tan-trums.

Sometimes Gloria and I would be invited together to a party or we would go to a play or concert. I enjoyed having a woman companion, especially one as sensitive and appreciative as Gloria. This introduced me to the problem of babysitters.

"Gosh," I said to Gloria. "People with young children have a prob-lem going places. I never thought of it before."

Confidence and humor began to seep back into my talk and action. Bill Reninger told me how much better I seemed. And I knew it. I no longer needed to go to the farm every day. When Carl was short of help, I responded. But with an additional class to prepare for, I spent more time in my study. On pleasant afternoons I drove to the cemetery and sat by Carmelita's grave for a few hours. I did not feel morbid. It eased me to just sit there and be quiet or read for an hour or two.

I thought of brother Bob and my mother and father. All the mark-ers were in a row in front of the large headstone with "Hearst" carved on it. Here lay part of the family I belonged to, a big family where the trouble of one was the trouble of all. It helped erase some of the anger and sorrow that the vindictive action of Louise and Chuck aroused in me. It stunned me to have them unite against me just at the time when I was least able to defend myself. But here in the quiet cemetery, with thoughts of Carmelita so close to me, a great deal of bitterness washed away.

I missed not working with Chuck. Until Gladys broke into the fam-ily, Chuck and I worked together, went places together, even got drunk together. We were a good team. I still shuddered to recall the night when cousin Bill Hearst, Al Earhart, Chuck, and I drank fresh cider spiked with alcohol. It would be an understatement to say that we were under the weather for a day or two afterward. But this was all past. My hurt faded slowly. Gloria and Michael were my family now.

Late in May I was out at the farm helping Carl when we saw a storm coming. Carl helped me off the tractor into the car and I drove into the machine shed for cover. Wicked-looking clouds rolled up, riding a strong wind. Hail fell with the rain. Hail on the galvanized iron roof of the machine shed roared like artillery fire. But in a few minutes the storm drifted past.

Just before I reached home I pulled into the gas station to fill the car's tank. Roy Wickert, the manager, looked at me in amazement. "You better get along home." Then I noticed his big plate glass win-dow was shattered.

Alarmed now, I hurried home. Gloria came to meet me. "We had a terrible storm. All the south windows are broken. The roof leaks. The rain is coming in all over."

I looked at the south rooms. Broken windows, water on the floors, water filling the lampshade that hung from the ceiling and spilling over on the floor. I said, "Come on, Michael, we're going out to the farm and get Carl."

"Yes, take him," Gloria said. "He's so frightened. But what can Carl do?"

By the time I brought Carl back, Leo Priest had come over to see what he could do. I said, "The storm windows are in the basement, let's put them on the south windows."

Leo nodded. "That's what I did at my house. When we get through here, Carl, we must go over and board up Mrs. Hammer's windows. She's out of town." There never were such good neighbors as the Priests.

The storm windows held out the wind and rain. Gloria had not exaggerated. It was a terrible hail storm. All the south windows in town were broken and most of the roofs battered. The stained glass windows in the churches looked as if someone had thrown baseballs through them. Thousands of roofs had to be reshingled.

The south side of the house was badly pitted where the wind drove the hail against the siding. "Funny, we didn't have much of a storm at the farm only three miles away," I told Gloria.

"It was awful. See, the window shades all cut to pieces. I was so frightened but I didn't dare let on because Michael needed me to reassure him."

"He clung to me all the way out to the farm. I wasn't sure I could steer the car. I hope we get telephone service pretty soon."

Insurance companies even brought in carpenters from the small towns close to Cedar Falls. My insurance company had a man at the house the next day. In spite of sanding and painting, the south side of the house always bore faint scars of the storm.

I swung slowly from the orbit of the farm to the orbit of the college. I spent many hours going over students' papers. I wrote short critiques of their work. Years later I heard from former students who still treasured those yellow sheets. I taught a summer session of twelve weeks. Dr. Reninger tried to keep my classes small. But a few extra students argued their way into every class.

"Why all the urge to enroll in a creative writing course?" I asked.

"Students have something they want to say. Colleges didn't offer an opportunity like this until lately. The classes were composition courses or something called 'rhetoric,' where the teacher assigned the topic. Jim, you've written and published three books of poetry. This gives you status. Students know you can tell them how it's done."

I whistled. "As if I could . . . as if anyone could . . . as if anyone knows. . . ."

"Well, they think you can and that's good enough. And Jim, don't let Paul Kelso impose on you by sending you all his problem children."

"No, but Bill, some of his problem children write good things once they muster the courage to write out their problems. I know as head of the counseling service he gets some odd numbers. But the ones he sends me often turn out to be my best writers."

"That's your business but don't let him impose on you. Remember, I'll back you up when you say 'no.'"

"A bolt out of the blue." The cliché was never more appropriate than when I answered the phone one morning and heard President Maucker say, "I've received an anonymous letter accusing certain members of the faculty of various crimes and you're one of the accused."

"You kidding?" I asked while I floundered in my mind to think of any misdeeds I had committed.

"No, I am not kidding. I would throw it in the wastebasket but all the members of the legislature received a copy and they demand that the Board of Regents investigate."

"What've I done?" I asked, subdued by the sober tone in President Maucker's voice.

"You're supposed to be living in sin with your housekeeper. That's just about the way the accusation is worded. I wanted you to know so that if you're called to testify you'll know why."

I hesitated but at last I told Gloria. I tried to make a joke of it but she was not amused.

"A divorced woman is always a suspect. Her private life always a subject for public discussion. She's suspected of being a tramp."

I had a friend on the Board of Regents, V. B. Hamilton, from Hampton. He had been the secretary of the Iowa Farm Bureau when my father was president. Our family knew him well. I called him by phone and asked to see him before the Board of Regents met. "Come for breakfast," I urged.

Mr. Hamilton came and settled for a cup of coffee. I at once introduced Gloria and Michael. "I want you to know my partner in crime," I said.

"Ham" smiled and shook hands with Gloria. She went on with her housework. He said to me, "I don't give a damn about your domestic arrangements, except to hope you are well looked after. But Jim, I want to know this, are there any communists in your department as the letter states? Here is where the legislature would take fright. We have to go to them for appropriations, you know. Tell me honestly, are there?"

I leaned forward and spoke earnestly. "I know all the staff well.

There are simply no communists. I see that Joe Fox is named in the letter. Well, Joe is outspoken, critical, and tough but no more a communist than I am. He has defended his right to teach some communist material—the Lenin-Engels work and Marx—on the argument that students should be able to recognize the communist line when they hear it. I absolutely agree. It's a force to be reckoned with."

Mr. Hamilton rose to go. He patted me on the shoulder. "That's all I wanted to know. The personal crap in the letter doesn't interest me. Anonymous letters ought to be flushed down the toilet. But we have a problem here with the legislature. Don't worry, your sin won't interest us."

I thanked him and said, "My mother once told me never to become involved with people who work for you. You have an advantage because their job depends on you. I've never forgotten it."

The fire lit by the anonymous letter burned for some time on the campus of the Iowa State Teachers College. The Iowa Bureau of Investigation was called in and its operatives sniffed and snooped through the ashes. The nastiest trick the bureau operatives used was to promise that all information given them was confidential. Then they went to the folks under discussion and told them what had been said about them.

As in any institution, among our faculty there were angers, resentments, threats of revenge which the investigators exploited deliberately and dishonestly. Most of what they heard was gossip and cheap shots taken at administrators for lack of promotions, salary raises, or just recognition. Years passed before some of the hard feelings softened. I was sure that some of the betrayals would never be forgiven.

Gloria and I lived together without friction. We sustained a friendly attitude toward each other and I regarded Michael with affection. But still I was not satisfied. Gloria took excellent care of the house and helped me in every way she could. But I wanted someone I could share my life with, who lived with me because there was love and not pay between us. There was an emptiness, a vacancy in my emotional life, and I wanted a woman to fill it.

Jessie Loomis kept me under her wing and dropped in frequently to see me. We would get in my car and drive out in the country where we could talk privately. Jessie proposed a plan to me. She and Fred were building a new house and why not add an apartment for me? She could keep an eye on me. I could share their meals. Fred would look after me if I was ill. She had talked to Fred about it and he agreed.

It was a tempting offer but it had a fairy tale quality about it. "Oh, Jessie," I said. "I'd love living with you and Fred. You're the most generous people I know. But I couldn't accept this proposal. It's too much."

"You're crazy," Jessie said. "It would be an ideal solution for you."

I put my arm around her. "Listen, Sweetie. Right now we're good solid friends. I'm as close to you and Fred as to anyone. Let's keep it that way. How long would it be before I would be asking to go to bed with you. No, I'll not mess up your life."

"Oh dear," Jessie said. "It seemed like such a good idea."

That summer I went to Iowa City for two weeks to work out in the physiotherapy department. My tendons and muscles had contracted since I stopped doing so much farm work and I had trouble standing up straight. Then, too, I wanted to get away from home for awhile and think about my life.

Dr. Steindler had retired from the state hospital but Mercy Hospital had built on an orthopedic wing just for him. I followed him to Mercy.

It was a pleasure to renew my acquaintance with Dr. Steindler. We had a long visit before he prescribed my treatment. I asked the sisters for a low bed so I could be independent of help from the nurses. Twice a day I took the elevator down to the physiotherapy rooms, where one of the therapists wrapped my legs in hot woolen cloths until the legs were thoroughly heated.

"Isn't this part of the Kenny treatment for polio?" I asked.

"Right, the same procedure."

Then the therapist stretched my leg muscles and tendons while I lay on the treatment table. After that I walked in the parallel bars and rode the exercise bicycle. Then I rode back upstairs and dressed. The days were hot and the hot cloths added to my temperature. So I often went out on a balcony at the end of the hall and sat in the shade until supper time.

One evening Marjorie Gould, from the state hospital, came to see me. She and Dr. Larsen were revising the Funston-Calderwood book, *Orthopedic Nursing.* Dr. Funston had died soon after Carmelita. She brought the galley proofs for me to read.

Marjorie Gould was superintendent of nurses at the state orthopedic hospital where Dr. Carroll Larsen was chief of staff. He had been appointed to the position when Dr. Steindler retired under the university's mandatory retirement plan at age sixty-five.

I discovered that Mary Engle was in the hospital having corrective work done on her feet. Dr. Steindler told her I was there. We were friends of long standing and pretended that some day we would run away together and buy a motel. When Paul, her husband, came to see her he stopped to visit with me. Paul Engle, poet and director of the famous Iowa University Writers Workshop, was probably my oldest friend.

Paul asked me to come to Stone City on Sunday for lunch. "Can you find someone to bring you, Jim? I hate to make the round trip. It's about twenty miles."

"I think I can," I said. The next evening when Marjorie Gould came to see me I asked her if she would like to take me to Stone City and have lunch with the Engles.

"I'd love it," she said. "I've heard a lot about Stone City where Grant Wood had his art colony but I've never been there."

Sunday turned out to be a warm sunny day. Miss Gould and I left Iowa City about eleven o'clock. By that time the day was hot. At the Engle's I sat out-of-doors in the shade with a wet towel around my neck. "If I get too warm I stop sweating and my temperature pops up. Bad habit."

There were no other guests and we ate a cold lunch sitting on the wide stone steps of the mansion. We visited and Paul told Marjorie the story of Stone City. He explained how a penniless Irishman named Green came to Iowa and ran the limestone business into millions of dollars. He built the great house on whose steps we were sitting. It had a fireplace with an imported Italian mantel in every room downstairs. He built a hotel for his guests, a private chapel where the Mass was read every Sunday, and a barn for his racehorses.

I looked at my watch. "It's getting on toward four o'clock. We better start back to the hospital so I can check in by five. Paul, wheel me down to the big oak tree. I should take a leak before we start back."

Paul wheeled me down to the tree and I stood up with one arm on the tree to steady myself. I looked off across the valley. "Nice view," I said as I emptied my bladder.

"You're pretty handy getting around," Paul said.

I nodded. "I hate to admit it but the exercise, the everlasting plugging away at muscle training pays off. Oh, how I hate exercise. It was invented by the devil. I spent three winters in that damn tank, in that damn physiotherapy department walking up the damn stairs, and crawling on the damn floor. But I can take care of myself so it was worth it. At what a price!"

"You don't get any sympathy out of me," Paul said. "If you want to sit on your ass the rest of your life and wither away, go ahead. I work hard too."

I sat down. "Work isn't work if you like what you're doing. Exercise is dull, monotonous, grinding, takes every ounce of willpower. For weeks you see no improvement and then suddenly you can."

"I'll take your word for it," Paul said and wheeled me back to where the women were.

The next summer I received an invitation that pleased and troubled me. Amy and Norman Stageberg invited me to spend a few weeks vacation with them on the North Shore of Lake Superior. "Go on and go," Gloria urged. "Michael and I will take a vacation too. I'll pack your bag."

"Listen, Stag," I said. "Have you any idea what you and Amy are letting yourselves in for? Taking a person like me on a vacation? I have an unruly bladder. I can't dress and undress myself unless the bed is the right height. I have to be pulled up and down stairs in a wheelchair unless the hand railings are where I can reach them. You and Amy wouldn't have any fun on that vacation."

"We know all that," Stag said. "When I was in Indonesia with the air force during the war I saw guys worse off than you and they got around. If you turn out to be too much trouble we'll just throw you in the lake." He dusted his hands.

So I went with them and they lifted me out of my doldrums. The cabin where we stayed had only one step at the door. The largest room inside held three beds. Stag hung up a curtain to give us all privacy in dressing and undressing. The bathroom was long and narrow. I could brace my arms against the walls and walk to the stool, back to the lavatory, back to the door, and turn around to sit down in my wheelchair.

I stood up and fried the eggs and bacon for breakfast, Stag set the table and toasted the bread, Amy made coffee and the beds in that order. It was friendly, warm, familylike.

"Gemütlichkeit," Amy said.

The days were sunny and warm, the nights cool. We slept under blankets. The big lake lay outside the door and sparkled in the sunlight, shone pale at night. We could see the ships on the horizon hauling grain and ore from Duluth. The air smelled like a pine forest and a family of ducks gabbled along the shore.

Amy's sister and her family had a cabin not far from ours and we often had potluck dinners together. To explore the country, Stag and I drove north to Hungry Jack's Lodge near the Canadian border. We ate lunch there. I was amazed by the depth of the forest. The road, a single trail, wound in among the trees mile after mile. I saw ravens for the first time, birds like crows but much larger. We crossed log bridges over swiftly flowing streams, rode in a perpetual twilight. I understood what was meant by the silence and mystery of the forest.

I was happy with the Stagebergs. Stag was the linguistic expert in the English department and the author of several books. But here in a wilderness surrounding a great lake we were as carefree as if we had never heard of a classroom. We laughed and sang, had drinks before dinner, watched the changing light as the sun moved over the trees. On our way home we bought some little smoked fishes and ate our lunch in a state park.

When we reached home I knew I was healed. My days of being one of the poor in spirit had passed. I sensed a new vigor and firmness in my attitude. It had been the right kind of a vacation. I would be forever grateful to the Stagebergs.

A new light shone in my eye when I looked at women. The sickness of my fatigue after Carmelita's death was replaced by a strong desire to face each morning as a fresh start. Someone suggested how nice it would be if I married Gloria and helped raise Michael, but my relationship with Gloria did not lead to marriage. We both knew this was not our destiny.

My affection for Gloria was the kind a man might have for an elder daughter. And Gloria showed no signs of wanting to marry me. She did say one day when we were both talking of the days ahead, "Michael and I will stay with you the rest of your life if you want us to."

In a rare display of affection I put my arm around her. "I'm grateful for the offer. But let's wait before we make any commitment. Who knows what the future holds? You're young, warmhearted, sensitive, and with good taste and besides you're a good homemaker. You should have a husband your age who could share with you a more exciting life than we live here."

"What about you?" Gloria asked.

"I'll manage with housekeepers. At the moment I don't see how or why any woman would want to share my life."

Gloria mocked me. "Don't be a fool. I know plenty of women who would like to be Mrs. James Hearst and crawl in bed with you."

We had probed far enough into each other's privacy and we broke up our seriousness with laughter. I smiled. "I like you when you're funny."

But the ear of the future must sometimes hear the bold assertions we make and set up ways to make us eat our words. One day I received a phone call from Meryl Norton. "Why, Meryl," I said. "What a pleasant surprise. Are you coming to see me?"

I had known Meryl almost as long as I had known Carmelita. I knew she had left her position at the Moline Public Hospital and moved to Bremerton, Washington, with her mother. She had studied at the University of Minnesota and the University of Washington for a degree in public health nursing. She now worked in the Public Health Department in Bremerton. She had relatives and friends in Algona, Iowa, where she had been born and raised.

After her father died, Meryl left Moline and helped her mother dismantle and sell the family home in Algona. They had moved to Bremerton where Meryl's two married sisters lived. She and her mother built a home high on a rocky point surrounded by giant pine trees.

She arrived by taxi with her suitcase and wearing a smart little hat. I literally pounced on her. "I'm pleased as a kitten with two tails to see you." I put my arm around her. "Can you stay awhile?"

Meryl answered, "I can stay overnight if you'll put me up."

I introduced her to Gloria and Michael and then Meryl and I talked. We were still talking when bedtime came. Gloria made up a bed in the spare bedroom.

In the morning after breakfast Meryl said, "I must go now. I take the Rock Island to Minneapolis and fly from there to Seattle. My brother-in-law will meet me at the airport. It's a good hour's drive to the ferry dock where we cross the sound to get to Bremerton."

I hated to have her leave. I put my arm around her and kissed her. "Gosh, it's been good to see you. I wish you could stay for a few days."

Meryl smiled. "Saturday's child must work for a living. You look well, Jim. Please take care of yourself. I'll be back someday. My brother Ellwood lives near Sioux City and when I come to visit him I'll come to see you."

The house wore a blank face when she left. Gloria and Michael shrank in size, like people at the wrong end of a telescope. I couldn't bring them back into focus again. A blanket of alienation wrapped me as if to hide me from anyone who was not a stranger.

I drove out to the farm, a place that always comforted me. It was a place of growing crops and thriving animals. Here I could use both muscle and brains. Here I was at home. I liked the work and what it stood for.

Norma and I started a chicken business. In the spring we drove to Independence to pick up a thousand baby chicks from the hatchery there.

I asked Leo Priest, "Did you ever drive an hour and a half with a thousand baby chicks yipping in the back seat? It drives you crazy."

"Back home in Missouri we hatched the eggs under hens, none of this hatchery business," Leo replied.

"So did we when I was a boy, and in incubators. But now you go to the hatchery."

We bought "sexed" chicks, Leghorn pullets for layers and a couple hundred cockerels of a heavy breed for meat. I did not ask if they were Rhode Island Reds or Plymouth Rocks. I just knew they were a heavy breed and cheap.

Norma fattened them, dressed them, and sold them. She and I delivered them. I enjoyed driving around with Norma. She had a lively sense of humor and a keen interest in her work. I teased her. "Too bad you're married to Carl. Then I might have a chance."

She gave me an odd look. "Why don't you find someone to marry, Jim? Not Gloria, but someone who'd share your interests and look after you."

"Any candidates?" I asked. Then I added, "I'm thinking about it."

Sunday was my day to write letters. Like a nervous horse backing and filling at the starting gate, I wrote a letter to Meryl. It didn't suit me when I finished it but I did not know how to rewrite it. In effect I said, "I wish you would come and take care of me and my house."

I sweated it out waiting for the mail. After a week a reply came. It was a warm, friendly letter. But Meryl said that, much as she would like to look after me, she had her mother to care for and, of course, I would understand.

The letter woke me up like a dash of cold water. How could I be so stupid! I rubbed my eyes. I had left out the most important part of the letter.

I grabbed my typewriter, rolled in a sheet of paper, and began. "Hell, Meryl, I'm just clumsy. I don't need a caretaker, I want to marry you. Come out here and be my wife."

This started a courtship by mail. No Victorian novelist ever used the letter technique with greater earnestness than Meryl and I did. Our letters crossed in the mail and I answered questions before Meryl had asked them. The correspondence picked up speed and intensity.

Finally I persuaded her to resign from the health department and join me. Then came the question of setting a date. She wanted to give the department time enough to find a replacement for her. I needed to break the news to Gloria. At last Meryl wrote that she would arrive in Cedar Falls on the first of December. She planned to drive so she would have her car.

This upset me and made me anxious as an old hen. Cross the mountains in winter weather? She must be out of her mind. Chuck and I had driven to Seattle in August and there was snow in some of the passes then. I did not intend to have an avalanche prevent my marriage. I refused to believe that the marriage would not take place, that my luck had run out.

I had been born a yea-sayer. But my accident, Carmelita's death, Bob's death, the death of Uncle George and my parents, and the squeezing me out of the farm partnership eroded my faith in my future. I thought some malignant design must haunt me, some dark portent, and this kept me forever apprehensive. I knew my prayers had been heard when Meryl wrote that she would come by train.

When Meryl's mother phoned me to welcome me into the family I was convinced that our proposed marriage was no illusion. I dared fate to rob me again. I had the nerve.

I told Jessie Loomis and she hugged me and began to plan the wedding. "It'll be at our house," she said. "Just a few of your friends to welcome Meryl. What about Gladys and Chuck?"

"Let'em sit," I said. "They've shown damn little interest in my welfare. Be sure to ask the Priests and the Hundleys. They've helped me at every turn."

I told Betty and Bill Reninger and asked Bill to stand up with me and for them to be witnesses.

Gloria discovered what was in the wind before I had a chance to tell her. Either Betty Reninger jumped the gun and told her or Gloria read some of Meryl's letters while I was at the farm.

She began to draw away—to speak in distant tones, to stand aloof from daily problems and decisions. When I explained to her that Meryl and I planned to be married she commenced to cry. "I can't afford to move," she said, and sobbed bitterly.

"I wanted to be sure Meryl and I would be married before I told you. Now quit weeping and listen. I'll give you a month's extra pay and also pay your transportation to your parents' home in Florida. You know how often you've talked of going home."

Gloria didn't wait. She packed her things. She resented Michael's affection for me and kept him out of my way. One day she announced that she was ready to leave.

"But I can't stay alone. I expected you to stay until Meryl came."

"Some of your fine friends will look after you. I'm not wanted here and I'm leaving."

If that is the way you feel, I thought, the sooner the better. I called Mrs. Van Sant, who had just made two soft, warm wool shirts for me. "Do you suppose your mother would be willing to stay with me for a few days?" I explained my problem.

Mrs. Van Sant assured me that her mother would be happy to help me out. Her mother liked to earn money. She had stayed with me before and I was indebted to her for her friendly ways and careful attention.

She came. Gloria left with baggage and Michael. I waited for Meryl to come.

Another Start

PLANS FOR THE WEDDING gained momentum. Sarah wrote me from Phoenix, Arizona, where she had gone to escape the north wind. She offered to fly back and open her house for the wedding. Bless her, Sarah had always been right at my elbow when I needed help.

But Jessie had the reins in her hands and was driving the horses. She told me, "I'll tend to everything. You furnish the bride and the minister."

I wrote to Meryl that I knew a priest, a rabbi, and a minister. Who did she want to perform the ceremony? She asked for the Congregational minister. I knew the Reverend Mr. Hughes and he accepted my invitation.

"Now listen, Jessie," I said. "Meryl wants a quiet wedding so restrain yourself."

"I'll just have a few of your friends here and perhaps a little supper after the ceremony."

So I left the planning to Jessie, too busy with my own affairs to remember her predilection for making an affair like a wedding into an occasion. I did want to be married away from my house and I was thankful to the Loomises for offering theirs. They had supported me, too, during my years of trial.

Jessie and Fred had made me their guest many times. Fred would come and get me and take me home. Except for Sarah, the Loomises were closer to me than my family. Even the Loomis children took me for granted as an ever-present guest.

The main problem for me was to see that Meryl arrived. Bill Reninger went to the courthouse in Waterloo and secured the marriage license. Dr. Henderson said it would take about three days to get a report on the blood test. The wedding day was set for December fifth.

Problems find solutions, scattered pieces of a puzzle fall in place, things do work out. Meryl's brother Ellwood proved the man of the hour. He drove from Sioux City to Omaha and gathered Meryl off the Union Pacific. He drove back to Lawton, and he and his wife Mildred brought her to Cedar Falls. By the time they reached my house Ellwood had already driven over five hundred miles. But he delivered the bride, spoke a few friendly words to me, drank a cup of coffee, and he and Mildred drove home another two hundred miles. I told him that this was above and beyond the call of duty.

Meryl was here, in my house! The vast cloud of loneliness drifted away like fog before a fresh wind. There were a few anxious hours when the blood test reports were delayed, but they showed up in the nick of time.

Jessie called and said firmly, "I've invited Chuck and Gladys. They've just got to be here. And Meryl's brother and his wife will make part of your family for each of you. Then Betty and Bill will be here and Fred and me and the children. I asked the Reverend Mr. Hughes to come at five-thirty, he and Mrs. Hughes . . . the other guests at six."

Rain, rain, and more rain poured through the icy ruts and gurgled in the storm sewers. It melted drifts of snow and splashed windshields and beat on windowpanes. But it did not dampen the spirits of the people in my house.

Meryl looked beautiful in a purple velvet gown. I wore a shirt and tie and a jacket made by my tailor for the occasion.

The Reverend Mr. and Mrs. Hughes were at the Loomises when the bridal party arrived. "Let's have the ceremony now," Meryl said, "before anyone comes."

She sat in a chair beside me. The Reverend Mr. Hughes read the service and offered the prayer. Bill Reninger produced the ring. The Loomis children sat in a corner, round-eyed.

Gladys and Chuck were so friendly and seemed so pleased to be there that I was ashamed to think I had not expected them to be invited. It made a nice balance of family, Meryl's brother and his wife and my brother and his wife. Jessie looked triumphant. Fred kissed the bride.

Then in walked the guests bearing food and gifts. A few? Jessie had asked at least forty of my friends, who surrounded us and filled the house with smiles and chatter. Champagne corks popped, toasts were drunk, an elaborate supper appeared. Maxine Thorson had baked an enormous cake.

When it was over we drove home through the rain. I sat in a kind of stupor. The celebration had been more than I bargained for. Inside me a glow reminded me of the many friends who wished me well. No doubt Meryl must have been shocked to face so many strangers who kissed her and hugged her and shook her hand. But she will live through it, I told myself.

Before we went to bed, blushing and timid, I confessed, "I haven't been with a woman for a long time. I may not be any good anymore."

Meryl put a gentle arm around me and said, "Don't worry."

I did not need to worry. I rose to the occasion.

To the end of my life I would remember how gentle, how kind and compassionate Meryl was with people. She was often defeated by machines, by *things,* but with people she had an inner sense of their needs and her quiet assurance restored their confidence.

How quickly we settled into a domestic routine. Meryl loved to go to the farm with me. We took our lunches and sat in the car and ate them together. Or, if she had household chores, she would walk a mile or two into the country to meet me when I came home. When I glimpsed her coming along the side of the road, "my heart leaped up . . ." and we rode home together.

She liked cornhusking. She rode in the wagon beside the corn-picker which I pulled with the tractor. On warm October days she would see wild ducks and geese migrating, rabbits and pheasants running down the corn rows. When I needed help she was my mechanic. Once she took a hammer from the tool box and broke a stone that had become lodged in the elevator. I had stopped the tractor and called back, "How long since the corn has been coming into the wagon?"

She, with her face turned toward the innocent October sky, answered, "Oh, it's been coming right along."

"The hell it has," I said. The snapping of the safety clutch on the elevator had stopped me and the corn had backed up until the whole picker was packed. But she broke up the stone and away we went. If a chain came off she trudged back along the row until she found it. Then she walked to the corncrib and called Carl to come and put it on.

"Since I can't get off the tractor," I said, "I make Meryl my assistant."

One afternoon a storm blew in from the northwest with heavy rain-bearing clouds. I surveyed the sky and said, "I believe we have time for one more round."

We almost made it but the rain caught us forty rods from the end. The drive wheels on the tractor began to slip and cut in, husks and leaves wound around the snapping rolls, the side draft from the loaded wagon pulled the picker off the rows and soon we were stuck. We huddled like drenched chickens until Carl drove down in the car and rescued us. Cold, wet, soggy, we started for home with the car heater going full blast.

To my surprise I began to write poetry again. After two years of silence it gave me a queer but good feeling to face the open sheet of paper again. But the work must have lacked my former signature. The editors sent it all back.

"Shit!" I said, angry and frustrated. "Either the editors don't know a good poem when they see it or I've lost my edge."

Two years of steady practice passed before I placed my poems again. "No wonder Faulkner said, 'I write when the spirit moves me and it moves me every day.'"

I accepted the discipline. Some part of each day I sat at my desk and wrote. Most of what I wrote I threw in the wastebasket. But gradually I regained confidence in being able to say what I had to say in the way I wanted to.

"I'll never learn all I should know about writing but, by god, I'll give it a whirl. I've told my students often enough that you don't learn to play the piano by reading a book about it."

So I dug in and worked. Writing for me was never easy. More than once I told myself, "No one but a stupid fool would sit day after day trying to arrange words in original patterns." But I did just that.

We lived the social life of the campus. We attended concerts, lectures, met visiting poets and writers, and went to parties for artists after their performances.

Bill Reninger proved to be a rock to count on. He took Chuck's place in helping me up and down stairs, in and out of the campus buildings. Scarcely one entrance had a grade-level entry. This was before the new buildings were built with ramps and elevators. I knew I could never repay Bill for this consideration but I gladly accepted his help.

Years before Meryl and I were married, Bill Reninger, Paul Diamond, Ferner Nuhn, Chuck, and I formed a discussion club. Half the members came from the college, half from the town. Each month we met for dinner and one of the members spoke. One rule was that no word went beyond the walls of the meeting room. After his talk, the speaker defended himself against criticism by the other members. We made a roster of speakers so we would all know in which month we were to perform. The last speaker was the chairman for the next meeting. We had no officers, no minutes, no dues. My mother nicknamed it the "Deep Thought Club."

As I write this in 1980, the club still flourishes and LeRoy Redfern sends out the notices of the meetings to all the members and periodically we contribute to his postage bill.

We held the dinner meetings at the airport. In order to have a private dining room we often had to go upstairs or down to the basement. Bill literally carried me up and down those stairs. It was too much. We both recognized the strain on Bill. The club found another meeting place.

One day I said to Meryl, "Do you suppose we could take a trip together?" I added, "I could drive part way. What do you think?"

"Let's try it. We can go to Lawton and visit Ellwood and Mildred and stay in a motel."

The journey worked out well. The motel caused no problems. We decided to drive to the West Coast. Two of Meryl's sisters lived in

Bremerton, Washington, and my sister Louise lived on Puget Sound. On this journey we faced, for the first time, the fact that bathroom doors in most motels are too narrow to admit a wheelchair.

In some towns we drove from motel to motel where Meryl and the manager, yardstick in hand, would measure the bathroom doors. Sometimes just removing the door made enough space. Wherever we found a convenient motel, Meryl wrote down the name and place. It is true I could get up from the wheelchair by myself and walk into the bathroom and often I had to do it that way. But it was safer if I could keep the wheelchair behind me as I stood at lavatory or stool.

We reached Bremerton after five days of driving. We stayed with one of Meryl's sisters, Cleora Loss, and her husband Ralph. The motels were full. We spent one day up on the Strait of Juan de Fuca with Louise. "A hell of a long way to come for a one-day visit," her husband, Johnny Speer, said. But I thought, "Nuts to them." I still smarted from the hurt Louise gave me at the dissolution of the farm partnership.

We had discovered we could travel by ourselves. We made several trips to the West Coast in the next few years after I finished teaching summer school. We stopped in Lander, Wyoming, to see Meryl's brother, Dr. Edmond Norton, and his wife Ginger. Ed was a veterinarian and I enjoyed his stories of the trips he made to some of the ranches.

We spent three summer vacations on the North Shore of Lake Superior where the Stagebergs had taken me. There we slept late, ate fish, picked wild raspberries, and spent pleasant hours with two of my old friends, Grace Gaarder and her sister Alva Lodwick. Meryl met them by chance in a grocery store and we visited back and forth from their cabin to ours. We even went to the garbage pits at Tofte to watch the wild black bears come in and snuffle through the waste.

Our success on these trips gave us the confidence to attempt our next adventure.

My methods of class procedure, or the lack of them, disturbed me. I surmised that there must be other and better ways of conducting a creative writing class. It seemed to me that I ran the class the way the early aviators flew their planes, by the "seat of my pants." I had not taken any education courses when I was in college and all I knew about teaching I learned from watching Bill Reninger and George Gates when they helped me with my first classes.

"I'd like to go somewhere to school," I told Meryl, "and learn how an experienced teacher handles a class in creative writing."

"How about Iowa City?" she asked. "The Writers Workshop there is one of the best in the country."

But I dissented. "No, I know most of those guys and Paul Engle is a friend of mine. It might be too cozy."

The next time I met Paul I asked for suggestions. He gave me strange advice. "Try Mexico," he said.

It had never occurred to me to even think of Mexico. "But," I protested, "I don't know any Spanish."

"You could learn. Other folk have," Paul reminded me. "There's a branch of the University of Guanajuato at a small town called San Miguel de Allende, mainly an art school, all the classes taught in English. The creative writing man used to be editor of *Colliers.*"

I found the address and wrote a letter of inquiry. It impressed me that the school was recognized by the North Central Association and classes could be taken for credit. The director of the school, Sterling Dickinson, wrote that other people who used wheelchairs had attended the school but that there were steps and steep paths from building to building.

"We would be taking an awful chance," I said to Meryl. "But I'd like to try it."

Paul told me, "Things will be different down there."

I filled out a formal request to Dr. Reninger for a leave of absence. It was granted. "Finish the first semester which ends January twenty-sixth. You can have the second semester for your trip. When does the term begin in Mexico?"

"January twenty-eighth but I think we can be a few days late." I did not know then how true that was.

Meryl and I plunged into the study of the Spanish language. Hazel Strayer told us that one of her former students, now head of the drama department at Iowa State College at Ames, Frank Brandt, had taught school in San Miguel. Meryl and I drove to Ames to visit the Brandts. We learned how to drive in Mexico, what roads to take to San Miguel, what clothes to pack, the procedure at customs at the border.

"But," as I said afterwards, "you can't really tell anyone what it's like."

It took us five days to make the trip. When we left home the thermometer read a minus twenty degrees. By the time we reached Laredo, Texas, we were sweating in our heavy winter clothes. "We took enough clothes to go around the world," I said. "Just packed the old Packard full."

I listened to the girl in the AAA office in Laredo as she phoned for our reservations in Monterey, Mexico. It encouraged me to learn that I could understand some of her Spanish. She said the señor used a *silla con ruedas*, a chair with wheels.

Customs at the border proved to be something of an ordeal. I stayed in the car and Meryl ran back and forth with papers for me to sign. Since the car was registered in my name, that meant additional signing. The customs officials regarded the car with suspicion. Apparently too many folk from the States had driven cars into Mexico and sold them for inflated prices. Meryl and I had to promise, in writing, to come back in the same car we took into the country.

Finally everything was in order and we started for Monterey. It was two o'clock in the afternoon and I was nervous for fear we might not reach the city before dark. One hundred kilometers down the road was a checkpoint where guards with guns stopped us and checked our papers. "They act as if we're escaped criminals," Meryl protested.

The highway was wide, smooth, equal to the best in the States. We drove the longest straight stretch of highway to be found on the North American continent, or so the sign said. We pulled into the motel about five o'clock and the manager, a pleasant English-speaking person, answered our questions. We ate in the motel restaurant where I ordered our dinners in Spanish and we got what I ordered.

We found the road signs fairly easy to follow, though we worried a little about finding our way out of Monterey—the Pittsburgh of Mexico. We climbed to the top of the plateau that runs like a spine the length of Mexico.

Meryl was nervous but she drove. I did not drive at all in Mexico. I sat, like a tightly wound spring, peering at the road signs. *Cuidado el ganado* (watch out for livestock) appeared often and so did *Puento angosto* (narrow bridge).

Mexico is different. It is not like Europe. It is dark, Indian, strange.

We met no difficulties except our own apprehension. We filled the gas tank at each town we passed through, for we had learned that the government owned all the gasoline stations. There was one station at each edge of town. It was 168 kilometers from Saltillo to Matehuala and the needle edged toward empty on the gas gauge before we got there. It gave us great relief when the town came into view. The low octane gas did not burn well in the car.

I had a startling experience that was repeated several times. On a lonely stretch of road, desert country stretching away on both sides, I asked Meryl to stop the car so I could relieve myself. She handed me the bottle and stepped out to get some exercise. About half done with my chore, I looked up and there were four or five Mexicans peering in the car windows. Nothing can "stop the flow" more than an unexpected audience. I had no idea where these people came from. The country looked bare and empty when we stopped. I jumped like a hunted rabbit and ever afterward watched carefully when we stopped for my relief.

We reached San Miguel de Allende on a Sunday afternoon. We pitched down a steep hill paved with cobblestones. A crowded bus struggled to climb the hill, pushed by a yelling band of men and boys. Burros everywhere were loaded with great, wide loads. A parade with a band marched down the street. The engine stalled. Meryl turned into the curb to stop the car. She got the engine started and we crept down the hill.

"If that's the only way out of this town we're never going to leave," Meryl declared. She was frightened and exhausted.

We couldn't find the hotel but we found a policeman. I greeted him in my best Spanish. To our great relief the cop said, in perfect English, "Good afternoon, sir."

We discovered this was all the English he knew. With my bad Spanish and his gestures, we found our way to the Instituto Hotel.

The room on the first floor was large with a large bathroom. Red tiles were on the floor. Tall French windows opened on to a courtyard. There were two ample beds, a closet, two chairs, and a dresser. There was a candle on the dresser and, overhead, an electric light. A pitcher of water and two glasses stood on the dresser beside a sign which said, in English, "This water came from our own well."

The dining room opened at eight for supper. We were assigned a table and a waitress. I decided that my Spanish was better than the girl's English as I ordered from the menu. Most of the people in the dining room were not Mexican, many of them middle-aged and older. I said aloud, "Supper at eight o'clock?"

A man sitting alone by the window said, "You may as well get used to it—dinner from one-thirty to three, supper from eight to ten. Mexicans eat late and then go to bed. The heavy meal is at midday."

The next morning Meryl hurried to the registrar's office to enroll me in the creative writing course and to sign herself up for a course in ceramics. We also wanted to take courses in the Spanish language and in Mexican history. To Meryl's surprise the classes were not yet in session. "When do classes start?" she asked.

The dark girl at the desk said, "When the professors and the students get here." After a few more days of waiting apparently "they" got there and classes began.

The hotel and college buildings were surrounded by a high stone wall with broken glass and steel spikes embedded in the top. A guard was on duty at the entrance day and night. The grounds and buildings had once been the home of a count. Now the owner was the former governor of Guanajuato whom we knew as Don Enrique. The school leased the grounds from him.

We met Sterling Dickinson, the director, a man from Chicago who had been the prime mover in organizing the art school. He had important connections in the States and with Don Enrique. The school flourished.

Meryl found the building where the creative writing class was held. There were steps. The manager of the hotel said, "Take Pasqual with you."

Pasqual was the *mozo* (hired help, bell boy) at the hotel. He told me that once he spoke a little English but gave it up because it was too difficult. He was short, broad, swarthy, with high cheekbones and straight black hair.

Meryl drove the car the half block to the classroom. Then Pasqual picked me up in his arms and carried me up the stairs where Meryl waited with my wheelchair. He handled me with ease. My weight didn't even make him breathe hard.

"Call me when you wish to return," Pasqual said to me. Then to Meryl, *"¿Ahora ceramica?"* and off they went.

I was both pleased and disappointed with my class. James Norman Schmidt, editor and writer, conducted the class. He used the same techniques that I used—encourage the students to write, read their work in class, discuss it, and make suggestions. This pleased me. What disappointed me was the lack of a fresh approach, new methods of class procedure. This teacher was a professional. I wanted him to bring more solid answers to the students' questions and needs than I could. The class was small and the members varied in age from twenty to sixty. No great talent showed.

Meryl found rather primitive equipment in her ceramics course. Kick wheels and a horse trough to wash in. But she bought a smock, a sponge, and went to work.

We found a few friends. We were both sick. The Mexican doctor told me to quit drinking tequila and go easy on the fresh fruit. The wide bowl of mixed fresh fruit on the hotel table was always a temptation.

The weather enthralled us with the bluest blue sky we had ever seen and a warm midday sun. Day after day the sun shone, not a cloud in the sky. Nights were cool, sometimes so very cool we went to bed to get warm. We did have a small electric heater, but its warmth was not adequate for our large room.

A scarlet flycatcher perched on a dead branch just outside our window each morning and the pink stone cathedral across the town reflected the morning light. The cathedral bells woke us each day. The little bells turned over rapidly and filled the air with their clanging while the bass bell rocked slowly back and forth with a solemn boom, boom. Burros honked and brayed and behind the walls, in a small park, a company of militia with its band drilled twice a week early in the morning.

Meryl walked the few blocks to town every day. Sometimes she drove the car so I could go. A wheelchair does not roll well over cobblestones. We began to enjoy our experience. I said, "I was scared as hell at first but I don't know what I was scared of."

A young girl from the registrar's office, Carmen Ramirez y Magana, took us under her protection and saw to it that we arrived at the right classes at the right place at the right time. Our class in Spanish usually met out-of-doors on the steps where several sidewalks crossed. We found a friend in Carmen and the next year she came to live with us in Cedar Falls and attended the city high school. She stayed that year and came back several years later to work in the local hospital and learn something of hospital administration. We loved her as if she was our own daughter. She named her son after me. We were heartbroken when she died.

By the end of March we decided to go home. I felt I had absorbed all the information I wanted from my class. I had written stories and poems and kept regular hours at the typewriter. We did not leave behind many special friends. The *norteamericanos* who lived in San Miguel formed a small colony and kept to themselves. "All screwy," I said. "Expatriate bums."

It took us three days to drive from San Miguel de Allende to San Antonio. From there it was a two-day drive home. At the border the American customs officials turned our car inside out. They even unscrewed the bumper knobs on my wheelchair. I growled, "What's this all about? Can't you see we're just two Iowa farmers?"

The official smiled a tired smile. "We have a tip that a drug shipment is coming through. It could be fastened to your car without your knowledge. When you stopped for gas, as everyone does when they come across, someone would take it off."

The next day in a San Antonio motel we read in the paper that the customs officials had confiscated a quarter of a million dollars worth of heroin. Apparently they knew what they were talking about.

Home seemed good to us. We had had enough of Mexico for the time being. I had a summer school session to prepare for. I typed out the notes I had made in the class at San Miguel. Then I started work on a new manuscript of poems, trying to get enough together for another book.

I found I could write again. The happiness of having Meryl with me released the bonds that had held me prisoner since Carmelita died.

Two years later we went back to San Miguel de Allende for the winter term. I was asked to teach the creative writing course. I declined. I said, "This is my vacation, to sit on the other side of the desk. If I wanted to teach I would've stayed at home."

This time we made the trip with no apprehension. We both spoke Spanish easily now, knew the roads and motels, and had the Ramirez family for our friends. Carmen's father was a *ranchero* and farmed about twelve hundred acres of ground. He used two Caterpillar diesels for pumping water for irrigation and a John Deere tractor for plowing. It was an odd picture to see a tractor plowing on one side of the road and a yoke of oxen plowing on the other. This was but one example of the many contrasts which showed a country raising itself from its past into modern times.

The one thing that depressed us in Mexico was the poverty. We have rural slums in Iowa and ghettos in our cities, but I had never seen anything like the impoverished conditions of the Mexican poor. Hogs on our farm lived in better houses.

We came home on St. Patrick's Day after a heavy snowstorm. Carl and Leo Priest had to shovel out our driveway before we could get in the house.

I sorted out my poems, many of which had been published in magazines, and sent a manuscript to Carroll Coleman at the Prairie Press. Coleman accepted the manuscript and the next year published a book called *Limited View* in hard cover. Again it was chosen as one of the fifty most beautifully printed books of the year by the American Institute of Graphic Arts. All of Coleman's books show the touch of an artist.

The edition quickly sold out and the Alan Swallow Press issued a paperback edition. On the cover, Swallow used the copy of one of Grant Wood's lithographs, a lithograph that Grant Wood had given to the Hearst family.

For a long time I had used the sun porch as a place to hold my classes. We moved into the living room when the weather turned cold. With a class list of ten students, and not more than fifteen present, Meryl could find chairs plus the davenport to seat them all. The growing pressure to take in more students concerned us both. The basement contained a large recreation room and I tried to think of some way I could get down the stairs. There was a grade entrance but to use it I would have to wheel around the yard outside the house and this would be hard to do in winter snow.

We spoke of the problem to the Maxwells, good friends of ours. James Maxwell, an engineer, worked for the Waterloo Construction Machinery Corporation. One evening he dropped in, as he said, to "case the joint." He came several evenings and sat on the back stairs to plan an elevator. He thought and measured and measured and thought.

A week later he arrived after supper with the foreman of the company and two long channel iron rails. These they fastened to the walls. "Lucky you have a straight shot here and no turns to complicate things," Jim said.

He explained. "The tricky part is getting these channel iron rails absolutely parallel, otherwise the platform will bind."

They installed a platform wide enough to take the wheelchair. It ran on nylon rollers. An electric motor was hidden in back of the stairs. An endless roller chain was fastened to the front and rear of the platform with switches at the top and bottom of the rails to provide automatic stops. They placed a long rod along the wall which would permit the rider on the elevator to stop the motor at any place in the ascent or descent.

"You're now in business, Bard," Jimmy Maxwell said.

Now the classes met in the recreation room in the basement. Meryl bought and hung a burlap curtain to close off one end of the room where I had my exercise bars and sandbags. It left a large room with a fireplace at one end. Meryl hung a number of pictures on the walls and put down a carpet.

I approached Dr. Reninger. "Bill," I said, "I'm a bit weary of teaching creative writing courses. You have young people on the staff right out of the Writers Workshop with a Master of Fine Arts degree. They're closer in age to the students than I am. Let them work with the students who want to write poems and stories and plays."

"Could you handle a larger class?" Dr. Reninger asked.

"If I had the chairs I could take care of forty-five or even fifty students."

"You can have all the chairs you need. Call the maintenance people."

At the beginning of the fall semester I took on a class called "Introduction to Literature." It met on Monday evenings at seven o'clock and lasted three hours. At the first meeting of the class I discovered that a number of the students were teachers of English from the towns surrounding Cedar Falls.

One of them said, "We need a refresher course. We can come to an evening class."

I always called my students by their first names, at least I did before I was confronted with forty-eight students, some of them almost middle-aged. It helped break down the formality between student and instructor, which was especially important in the creative writing courses. Now I puzzled over this name problem. Should I return to a more formal address in this class with older men and women in it?

I asked one of the older women about it and she said, "Please treat us as you do your younger students. It makes me feel like a young student again to be called by my first name."

At first Meryl and I trembled a little when forty-five or more students came crowding in the side door on a Monday evening to tramp down the basement stairs. The first night of class Meryl stood under the outside lights to flag down any wandering student who could not see the house number. Our house number is 304 Seerley Boulevard. There is a building on campus called the Seerley Building. One young woman who arrived a half-hour late convulsed the class when she declared indignantly, "Nobody told me this class was held in a private home. I went to 304 Seerley Building and opened the door and walked into a broom closet."

I said, "We'll try to make this room more interesting."

The students told Meryl that they liked coming to a home. It was a change from a classroom and reminded them of their own homes. They liked Meryl and smiled and spoke to her when they met her on campus. When the young women in class decided to have a party at Christmas time, Meryl helped with the hot chocolate and cookies.

A small bathroom in the basement contained a stool and lavatory. Meryl kept paper towels and Kleenex there too. I gave the students a ten-minute break after the first hour and a half. They could smoke if they wanted to during the break. Three hours is a long time to sit still. I tried to finish the classwork after two hours and a half. Few of us have a three-hour attention span, especially in the evening after a day's work.

There were times when I came up on the elevator after class thoroughly exhausted. I told Meryl, "I feel like a mother dog that's been sucked dry by her pups."

I wrote a poem about it and called it "Dogma." The *Virginia Quarterly Review* published it. Apparently the editors were not put off by the awful pun.

I was given a graduate class in "Frost, Eliot, and Yeats." Bill told me, "You can be tough with graduates. They'll take it and hand it back." It was a different experience to speak out critically without fear of hurting someone's feelings.

I was given an afternoon class in "Contemporary British and American Poets." I liked this class. I received first-rate papers from some of the students. And with these subject-matter courses I became aware of what it meant to read and comment on forty-five papers a week. But I always found some papers that were exciting to read.

The years passed on academic feet. The college organized an honors program and I found myself teaching an honors class. I then worked with students in an individual study program. I became the chairman of several thesis committees and was a member of the staff graduate committee. The college now gave a master's degree.

"I wonder if the administration knows what it's doing, giving responsibilities like this to me," I said to Meryl. "I don't have a degree of any kind."

With irony in her voice Meryl answered, "Maybe the administration just overlooks that."

The next class given me was titled "Romantic Poets of England." The class was open to seniors and graduates. I opened the course with a study of the poetry of William Blake.

"My god, I never understood Blake myself and here I am teaching him to these poor unsuspecting students."

The college went through the upheavals of the sixties. Marches, parades, sit-ins, draft card burnings. A Minority House was set up but black students occupied the president's house for twenty-four hours. President Maucker took it in his stride. He did not retreat because of a handful of rebellious students. He had supported his faculty and their right to speak freely all through the McCarthy witch hunts. The *Des Moines Register,* in a lead editorial, praised him for his courage.

The time came for Dr. Reninger to retire. But first, as chairman of the Planning and Organizing Committee, he helped the college gain university status. It was now the University of Northern Iowa.

Keith McKean came out from New York to succeed Dr. Reninger as head of the Department of English Language and Literature. The first thing Professor McKean did for me was to lop the "visiting" from my title and make me a full professor. I appreciated that.

At the spring commencement, Bill Reninger and I were given the cherished Distinguished Alumni Awards.

I said to President Maucker, "Bill, I'm sixty-five. Should I retire?"

"You keep on teaching as long as you're asked to teach. I hope that'll be for some years yet."

A curious thing happened to us in the spring of 1963. I received a telegram from the Aspen School of Contemporary Art, Aspen, Colorado. I was invited to give a lecture to the school. No remuneration, but my expenses would be paid.

Meryl and I puzzled over this. I did not know anyone in Aspen or in the art school there. Meryl said, "Why don't we go? It'll give us a vacation and a chance to see the mountains."

So I wired back that I would give the lecture on the date named.

I asked Meryl, "What will I say? I don't know enough about the plastic arts to wad a shotgun."

"Talk about art as expression and use writing as an example."

We traded the Packard for a Checker cab. The Checker had no hump in the floor of the back seat and Meryl could easily slide the wheelchair in and out. There was almost enough room between the front and back seats to set up a card table. Jack Hearst, who was six feet four, could stretch out his legs in the back seat.

On a warm June day Meryl and I packed our suitcases and started for Aspen, Colorado. We might not have gone if we had known what this beginning would mean to us.

More Work—Less Play

WE STARTED EARLY IN THE MORNING and drove to Kearney, Nebraska, the first day. The next day we reached Denver and almost fell apart driving the long thoroughfare through the city. At the west edge of Denver we stayed overnight. We had taken turns at the wheel but now I left the mountain driving to Meryl.

"I am prairie raised," I said. "I want to see where I'm going. These curving roads and hairpin turns aren't for me."

Meryl had driven many mountain roads in Washington on public health work and they posed no hazard for her. She told me about driving back into the forests on corduroy roads and over log bridges to find a family who had hidden away because they had a child with cerebral palsy, which made them feel guilty, as if God had punished them for sin and their child was proof of their guilt. How we humans punish ourselves in our ignorance of the true facts. Once Meryl got the child in school, once the parents learned that other people also had children with birth defects, a great relief like a saving grace came to them.

On the advice of the AAA in Denver we drove the long way into Aspen by way of Glenwood Springs and Carbondale. Independence Pass had not yet been paved. We had reservations at the Hotel Jerome and pulled up beside it about three in the afternoon.

The Jerome showed the same quaint character as the town. We heard that the furniture had been carried over the mountains in ox-drawn wagons. Legend said it came from Marshall Field & Co. in Chicago. Heavy, dark, Victorian, so ugly and monstrous it fascinated us. The funny little elevator had one door that opened onto the lobby and one on its other side that opened onto the floors upstairs. An old man in a wrinkled uniform operated it.

The bulky furniture occupied so much room in the bedroom I could scarcely move in my wheelchair. I looked in dismay at the high bed. "You'll have to help me in and out of that thing," I said. "My god, what a place."

"These old Victorian pieces are so awful that they are kind of attractive," Meryl said. She pushed and pulled and finally cleared a path so I could get to the bathroom.

We washed our faces and hung up our clothes. The phone rang and I answered it. A voice said, "This is Robert Van Dahl. I direct the writing workshop here. Miss Price sent me to welcome you. Come down when you're ready and we'll have a drink.''

He met us in the lobby and took us out to a patio beside the hotel. We sat at an iron table with spidery legs under a huge umbrella. He ordered cocktails and a plate of canapes. He was a pleasant but rather formal young man. I said afterward, "I'll bet no one calls him Bob."

Van Dahl said, "One of the New York painters is having a show tonight. There's always a party at the opening of a show. I want you to be my guests. It will be at the Gallery, eight o'clock. By the way, have either of you been in Aspen before? Do you know where to go?"

I said, "Yes, I was here in 1948. We stayed at the Prospector Lodge, ate at the Red Onion, and went to a night spot called the Golden Horn."

Van Dahl spread his hands. "All three still going strong. But you'll find a lot of changes in twenty years time. We would like to have you make your talk at the Gallery tomorrow night. Geraldine Price is the director of the Aspen School of Contemporary Art. She will introduce you. You can meet at the show tonight."

"Let's try the Red Onion for dinner," I said. "No steps, easy to get into."

The crowded restaurant, the smell of food, and fatigue from the trip upset my stomach. "That drink did not set well with me," I said. I would learn that it took me a while to become used to the altitude. Halfway through dinner I pushed back from the table. "I'm half sick. Let's go back to the hotel and lie down."

We rested until almost eight o'clock. Then we got up and found our way to the Gallery. Van Dahl met us and introduced us to Geraldine Price. She was an unusual person and at once attracted my attention. There was a hard sparkle in her eyes but she was soft of speech and most friendly. She knew how to turn on the charm. She was a good-sized woman with signs of energy suppressed behind a mobile face. She had dark hair partially covered by a scarf and wore long silver earrings. She introduced me to some of the faculty. Their names and reputations impressed me. "How come," I said, "finding such artists in a dinky little town in Colorado."

Miss Price gave me an amused smile. "You don't know Aspen. The Music School is run by the Juilliard administration from New York. The Humanities Institute has such famous speakers as Albert Schweitzer, Felix Adler, Norman Cousins. You'll find waiters in dress suits in some of the restaurants."

"I beg your pardon," I said.

"You must hear a program by the symphony orchestra. Men from the Boston Symphony, New York Philharmonic, Minneapolis Orchestra fill the first chairs. They teach the students both individually and in master classes. They make expenses and it's a nice vacation for them and their families."

I moved back and forth and examined the pictures. Most of them were what I called "abstract art." I stopped in front of one of the large pictures and puzzled out loud. "What is this all about?"

A bearded man just behind me said, "Tell me what you see."

"Well. . . ." I hesitated, then plunged ahead. "I see a large canvas covered with black paint. The paint runs over the edges as if it were blanking out everything. . . ."

"And what else?"

"I see a blue square down in one corner. Blue is the symbol for hope, the Virgin. . . ."

"Anything more?"

"A red dot in the center of the blue square. It might stand for fire, passion, creative energy. . . ."

"You saw something, didn't you," and the man walked away.

A young girl stood beside me wearing a paint-stained smock. I asked her, "Do you know who the man is who just talked to me?"

"He's the painter. It's his show."

The next evening Van Dahl and I sat at a table in the Gallery. Students flowed along the walls and sat on the floor. Geraldine Price made a few announcements. Van Dahl introduced me. I talked about art as expression and its resemblance to reality. After my talk Van Dahl and I answered questions the students asked. The students pushed me pretty hard but I held my ground.

"Bright kids," I said to Meryl. "They knew I didn't know much about painting or sculpture."

Late that fall, when Meryl and I had almost forgotten our Aspen journey, a telegram arrived. "Would you consider directing a poetry workshop in Aspen for eight weeks next summer. Wire reply." It was signed by Geraldine Price.

"Now what!" I exclaimed. "I gave up teaching summer school here so we could have our summers free."

"But a workshop isn't like regular classes," Meryl said. "It might be a nice vacation." Meryl liked mountains a lot better than I did.

"It's a New York address. I suppose she's lining up her faculty for next summer. I wonder why Van Dahl quit?"

"I wonder too," said Meryl.

"Sure, we could try it. But what about a place to stay? The hotel is too expensive and too crowded. We need more room."

"I'll write to Miss Price," Meryl said. "Perhaps she can suggest something. She knows you use a wheelchair."

After Christmas we received a letter from Geraldine Price. She suggested that we write to a Mr. Hasty at the Pines Motel. He had apartments to rent. Darius Milhaud, the French composer, rented a house on the grounds.

Mr. Hasty had an apartment on the ground floor which he would rent for one hundred dollars a week. "Jaysus," I said. "Eight hundred dollars for the summer. I'll bet I won't be paid much more than that."

At the end of the school year we packed our suitcases and put the wheelchair in the car and started for Aspen. In my haste to get ready, as I stood in the bathroom to shave, I fell against the wall. It hurt my shoulder. It did not seem much of an injury. I did not fall, just bumped the wall. But the farther we drove, the more the shoulder ached.

"Let me drive a while," I said. "Maybe using my arm will loosen up the shoulder."

It did not help. The shoulder hurt more than ever. Meryl felt we should get to Aspen as soon as possible and decided to drive over Independence Pass. The pass had little paving, the road was like a washboard and shook the car and my shoulder. At the three narrow places where cars scarcely have room to pass, Meryl set her jaw and drove on.

We found the Pines. Mr. Hasty had built a ramp to help us over the curb. The motel had buildings on both sides of the street and we were across the street from the office. It looked attractive. A large lawn with trees was surrounded by flower beds. Our apartment opened on a patio beside the swimming pool.

An old garage had been made over into an apartment. It had a living room, bedroom, and bath. The kitchen took up one side of the bedroom and the bath was built in a narrow closet. Mr. Hasty removed the bathroom door so I could angle part way into it.

The floor of the bedroom sloped toward the wall and when I turned over in bed I found myself wedged against the wall and could not move. My shoulder ached so badly I could not sleep and when Meryl tried to make me more comfortable I muttered, "Why did I ever come to this goddamned place!"

As soon as morning came, Meryl, worried and anxious, telephoned Mrs. Hasty for the name of an orthopedic doctor. We forgot we had crossed a time line and Meryl had roused the good lady from a sound sleep. But Mrs. Hasty called the doctor, the hospital, and woke her husband to help me get in the car. My arm was so useless I could not even pull up my zipper.

Dr. Robert Oden met us at the hospital. It was early, before breakfast. He noted my paralysis and asked where I had been for treatment. I mentioned the names of some of the men at the Steindler Clinic and he knew them all. I told him my first wife had written a textbook and I named Funston-Calderwood and *Orthopedic Nursing*. He dove into his office and came back with a copy of the book. "It's my bible," he said.

He put a strong hand on either side of my head and lifted. "Pain diminish any?" he asked.

I nodded, "It almost disappeared."

"You have a pinched nerve. I'll put you in traction for a few days and that should take care of it."

For three days and nights I lay in a hospital bed with a halter around my chin fastened to a rope over a pulley and a ten-pound weight on the end of the rope. The pain went away. Geraldine Price and several of her staff came to see me. They all were kind and sympathetic.

It was a pleasant, well-managed hospital. I believe the Mennonites administered it. The nurses were all R.N.'s and gave me all the attention I asked for.

When I returned to the Pines I viewed our quarters with an objective eye.

"Can we make it do?" I asked Meryl.

"I think so. My bed is a bunk built against the wall, hard as a rock, impossible to make. But we'll manage. At least we're here."

We managed. The living room floor was flat and I could wheel out the door beside the pool. I learned to stand at the bathroom door and walk inside. "It's so narrow I doubt if I could fall down if I wanted to." Mr. and Mrs. Hasty and their son, Bud, made us feel at home and helped in every way they could. We enjoyed the wide yard and the flowers and often held class out on the lawn.

The students surprised and pleased me. They came from colleges and universities all over the United States. I found their schedules confusing, but I had never conducted a workshop before. Some students signed up only for two weeks, some for four, some for the full eight weeks. New students appeared in the middle of the summer and some for the last few weeks.

I met each student for a private conference once each week. On Friday the whole group met as a class to read and discuss their work. Meryl set up an appointment sheet with the name of each student and the hour of conference. She posted this outside the front door.

The system worked. Some of the students admitted that they came just for a vacation, some came because their parents wanted them out of the way during the summer, some came because they had an innate desire to write. Saturday and Sunday were free days and the young folk fished, hiked up the mountains, attended concerts, played games. We saw our first games of rugby and lacrosse.

Aspen shone with the glitter of the indolent and the well-to-do. It was a mecca toward which tourists flocked to worship at the altar of pleasure. The town bulged with wealthy divorced women and the fake gurus who battened on them. I was told that there were more millionaires per square foot in Aspen than in any other town in the country.

In the early days the parks teemed with hippies—dirty, insolent, and lazy. I thought of the town as the facade for a movie, all front and no depth. It took me several years to learn that there were native Aspenites, people who worked and suffered, prospered and failed, just as people did in Cedar Falls.

We lived next door to the famous French composer and his wife, the Darius Milhauds. One day Madame Milhaud invited us for tea. The composer used a wheelchair too. His dark, heavy face lit up with a small boy's enthusiasm when I mentioned my favorite French poet, François Jammes. "I doubt if you would know him," I said. "He's a rural poet."

"But he is my friend," crowed the composer. "I have set some of his poems to music." Months later I received from the Milhauds a biography of François Jammes, written in French.

The afternoon passed pleasantly until I grew restless, and then we went across the lawn to our own apartment.

"We are too different to become friends without a long acquaintance. We come from such different cultures," I told Meryl, when we discussed our visit.

We saw the Milhauds nearly every Sunday at the concerts. We bowed and waved and exchanged a few words. We both had permission to drive our cars to the front of the tent because we both used wheelchairs. We always attended when one of Milhaud's compositions was being performed. The composer himself directed, sitting in a chair facing the orchestra.

I met an old friend at a faculty meeting. Years before Meryl and I were married, Harriet and Thomas Larkin taught in the art department at the Iowa State Teachers College. Then Tom joined the staff of the art department at the University of Michigan. The Larkins moved to Ann Arbor. But here they were in Aspen with Tom as a staff member of the art school.

The Larkins asked us to a Sunday night supper and there we met a well-known young potter and a young composer from the Juilliard School of Music. We enjoyed the evening, pleased to be with friends in this curious town.

Late in July, Geraldine Price stopped in one morning for a cup of coffee. She asked me, "Will you come back next year and conduct the workshop?" She hesitated and then said, "The students like you and I like Meryl and you. Think about it."

I spoke to Tom Larkin about the offer. He advised me, "I've been here several summers. Geraldine is a good director, runs a first-rate school. But don't get tangled up in her affairs. Don't take sides as she may want you to do when she goes into battle. She's fun to work for if you keep your distance."

Meryl said, "If we come back next year, we are not going to live at the Pines. We need more room and a better kitchen and bathroom. I'm going to look for a more convenient place."

She spent days with real estate agents looking at houses, condominiums, apartments. Several times she took me to see one of her discoveries. But always the bathroom door was too narrow or the turn from the hall too sharp for the wheelchair. Neither Meryl nor I liked condominiums. They are too closed in, with no elbow room.

Meryl described carefully to the real estate agents what kind of housing we needed. But either they did not quite understand our problems or they showed her only what they had available. She walked her legs off, visiting place after place and coming home discouraged.

One evening when she came home she said, "I met a strange real estate man today. His office is at the west end of Main Street. He speaks with a foreign accent but he's very friendly. He's coming to see us tomorrow morning."

Sure enough, the next morning as I left the bathroom for the breakfast table, I spied a tall, thin, black-haired man sitting on the sofa in the living room. He jumped up, shook hands, and bowed. With what I thought was European courtesy, he begged me to finish my breakfast and he would wait.

That was how we met Hans Gramiger, known on his letterhead as "Hans of Aspen." He became our friend and advisor. I explained our problem and Meryl's lack of success in finding a solution. "I'll show you something," Hans said. "I'll drive your car."

We drove toward the east edge of town, swung up on Waters Street to a circle drive at the end of the street. "Calderwood Circle," Hans said. "Restricted neighborhood." He chuckled, "You can't hang out your washing."

He showed us a pent-a-bolt duplex. He said, "The Timroth brothers, contractors, built it for themselves. One lives on one side and one on the other. I show you."

He knocked on the door and asked Mrs. Timroth if he could show the house. I went in with Meryl. It had a large living room with a corner fireplace, a kitchen large enough for a breakfast table, two good-sized bedrooms with a fairly large bathroom between them, and a utility room off the kitchen. In back of the house a small grove of aspen trees grew, and an irrigation ditch burbled softly through them. It felt like home. "You can live on one side and rent the other," Hans said.

"But we're only here in the summer."

"I can rent it for nine months, no problem. This is a quiet, secluded place in a fine neighborhood."

"If we had a ramp for the two steps in front and a grab bar over the stool in the bathroom, . . ." I said, half to myself.

"I build them," Hans said. "I can fix anything."

"Let us think about it," I said. "This is the best place we've seen."

"I can show you other houses," Hans offered.

"Not today. I have students coming in a few minutes."

"You come here to work?" Hans opened his eyes in surprise.

I canceled my afternoon appointments and Meryl and I drove to the Bank of Aspen where we carried an account. I asked to see Mr. Bailee, the president. I asked him, "How about Hans Gramiger, can we depend on him? He's eager and accommodating but he is different."

Bailee laughed. "Hans is a character all right. He is always fighting the city or the planning commission. But he is absolutely honest. And if I had a house to sell I'd call him because I know he'd work at it."

I told Hans, "Wait until we get home and think it over. We almost bought a house in Mexico once but changed our minds after we got home. Don't wait on us if you have a chance to sell it."

In September we made Hans an offer. It wasn't high enough to meet Timroths' price. But we stood pat and after several letters Hans wrote, "If you will add a hundred dollars the house is yours."

It was face saving—but Hans's or Timroths'? I never found out.

I borrowed the money and paid Timroths in cash. "It's easier for me to borrow the money here," I wrote to Hans, "than to try to mortgage the property in Aspen. Now we have a clear title and if you will manage the property and collect the rents, we can pay off our loan at the bank."

I wrote to Geraldine Price and accepted the workshop position for the next summer. I told her about the house.

She wrote in answer, "I've been out to see the house. The aspen grove will make an ideal place to hold your weekly meetings. I have some benches from the old symphony tent, and if we arrange them on the slope it will be a wonderful little amphitheater."

I held the workshop post for eight years. I came in contact for the first time with the hard-nosed, sophisticated, intellectual students from the Ivy League schools. And I discovered drug addiction. One of the young men at a public program was so high on marijuana that he leaped on top of the table and shouted his poems. I dragged him down by his shirttail.

One of the girls from Oberlin had such bad LSD trips that she would come to her appointment hung over, bedraggled, and in pain. She had talent too.

I tried to be sympathetic but firm. I knew some of the students carried a heavy load of isolation and depression. Some of the young people had parents who were too rich to look after their children, or were divorced, or were alcoholics.

Once the workshop put on a program of poems read in different languages and then translated into English. Madame Milhaud read the French poems, a girl from Wellesley the Greek, the harpsichordist the Spanish, and a young friend from the British school at Carbondale the Latin. The program drew a large audience.

We soon became acquainted with a few people. The Larkins built a house just around the corner from us. Beth Chalmers, a stately white-haired widow, became our good friend. We had a speaking acquaintance with Gordon Hardy, head of the music school, and with a few musicians. We had dinner with Roland Hayes, the famous black tenor (now eighty years old), and his wife. I had met Hayes years before when he gave a concert at Cedar Falls. My brother and I procured some seed corn for his Georgia farm.

The Aspen climate agreed with me, though it took a week or ten days each summer before I rested easy in the altitude. But the low humidity, warm days, cool nights, flocks of hummingbirds, and an occasional Stellar's jay gave me a good feeling and I ate well and slept well.

Some of the students became my friends, friendships that have lasted many years. I bore, with patience and cheerfulness, the crises caused by Geraldine Price's life-style.

Once a young man rode up to our front door on a bicycle and introduced himself as George Madsen, managing editor of the *Aspen Times*. The newspaper owned a radio station. George asked me to do some broadcasts, interviews, and conversations on the noon program he conducted. I accepted the invitation. George was a good interviewer and conversationalist. He asked the right questions.

From this start a friendship developed between the Madsens and the Hearsts. We met Martha and the four Madsen children and we enjoyed the dinners we had together.

Meryl insisted that we should know a doctor to call on if we needed medical help. I thumbed through the yellow pages of the telephone directory and noticed the name of Jack Crandall. I said to Meryl, "Years ago I met a Dr. Crandall from Marshalltown at one of Paul Engle's cocktail parties. We spent some time together, got a little drunk. I can't believe the long arm of coincidence would reach this far."

I dialed the number and asked to speak with Dr. Crandall. When the doctor came on the line I introduced myself.

Dr. Crandall said, "Hello, Jim. What're you doing out here?" We had our doctor.

We liked Jack Crandall very much and his wife Gisina and small daughter Christina. Dr. Crandall said he lost his first wife when she became enamored of an architect. He moved to Aspen to lick his wounds and met Gisina on the ski slopes.

Hans Gramiger hovered over us like a good spirit. He attended to our needs or found the right person to help us. He treated us as if we were part of his own family. He sent a check regularly to the bank to pay on our loan, was careful of who rented the duplex, and maintained it well.

But in spite of friends, climate, music, and lectures I looked forward to the end of summer and our return home. Aspen lulled me into a state of fantasy, a play world somehow detached from the world of actual events. The *Aspen Times* fostered this feeling, with its pages filled with the diversions of fishing, hiking, jeep rides, kayaking, skiing on the glacier, music programs, lectures at the Humanities Institute, and lists of restaurants and night spots. On the back page were printed a few paragraphs of national news.

"It's an entertainment town," Bette Gallagher said to me. "It's an expensive fun place, often full of sorrow and gnashing of teeth. Notice that we have no hamburger joints, no urban sprawl, everything on a high level of quality if you can afford it." Bette ran a real estate business and was given to moments of frankness.

My wheelchair caused no problems for me in Aspen. No one paid any attention to it. I enjoyed this escape from the eyes of the curious.

When we drove up to the Chart House for dinner, Herbie Balderson's waiters met us in the street to carry me up the steps. At Toklot, fourteen miles into the mountains, where one ate venison sausage and sourdough pancakes with wild honey, a phone call would open the gate so we could drive up to the back door. "I get spoiled in Aspen," I said.

My students listened to me with friendly attention. One afternoon, during a group session, I said, "I was romantic when I was your age. On a date I treated my girl with the same courtesy I did my mother and sister. I wasn't all over her in the back seat. I must seem like an anachronism to you, a throwback to the age of chivalry."

The students were just leaving the aspen grove when one slim gal turned back, put her arm around me, kissed me and said, "Mr. Hearst, we're romantic too." I was touched.

Ever since those winters in Iowa City in the physiotherapy department, where I nearly killed myself trying to reeducate my muscles and regain control of them, I could handle my personal needs. I got in and out of bed alone, dressed and undressed myself, went to the bathroom unaided, stood up when I wanted to, drove the car, walked up steps. I was proud and cherished my independence. But now something happened to upset my physical well-being. I began to have back spasms. My back muscles would contract and relax in uncontrollable rhythms.

Sometimes they would disappear for weeks at a time. But during the seventh year in Aspen, they settled in and stayed. They came when I stood up or lay down. They were so severe that the whole bed would shake. I fought them when I stood up at the lavatory or stool or just to tuck in my shirttail. Dr. Crandall tried one remedy after another but nothing relieved the symptoms.

One morning Dr. Crandall bounced over in his jeep to share a breakfast cup of coffee. He often did this. He said, "I called Clark Millikan at the Mayo Clinic about you. He's head of the neurology section. He read your history and it interested him. He's coming to Aspen for his vacation. He loves to fish for trout. I'll bring him over to see you."

On a Sunday afternoon a few weeks later, Dr. Crandall brought Dr. Millikan to see me. He wore his waders and an old hat with flies and lures stuck in the band. He sat down and said to me, "Tell me about it."

When I had finished Dr. Millikan said, "We don't know why these spasms come now after all these years. Somewhere in your body changes are taking place and you can no longer control these involuntary muscle movements."

I asked impatiently, "Can't you just cut the string?"

Janet Millikan, who had come with her husband, laughed at my simple solution. But her husband frowned. "Surgery is out. We don't know enough to stop these irrational impulses. Any surgery that would stop the spasms might make all your muscles weak. You could neither stand nor grip with your hands."

"What do I do?" I asked.

"There's a muscle relaxant that will help you. It's also used as a tranquilizer and it will make you sleepy. I'll give Jack a prescription for you. Come and see me at the Mayo Clinic this fall."

That was the beginning of a slow deterioration in my physical health. The drug relieved the spasms enough so I could live with them. It made me drowsy and I woke up with a dopey sensation in the morning. I could still move around as usual but I no longer enjoyed a drink before dinner. Liquor made me faintly nauseated.

I did not know enough about my condition to be discouraged. If I stopped the drug for a day or two the spasms came back. I fought them, swore at them, but the more I struggled the more severe they became. Once in a while they landed me on the floor. When they did I sat up, pulled my feet back, Meryl stooped over behind me, locked her arms under mine, and hoisted me to my feet. I wondered at her strength, but Meryl knew how to lift and once partway up I could raise myself.

This creeping helplessness angered me. I did not blame God (or the devil) but blamed my body for allowing itself to forget the long, hard hours of exercise that had made it useful again. I swore at my back and at my legs . . . sometimes I just swore.

I was now seventy years of age, five years past the mandatory retirement age. President Maucker had said, "As long as the head of your department asks you to teach, keep on teaching."

Dr. Reninger had retired and now spent his winters in Florida. He came back for one year to act as vice president when J. W. Maucker resigned and John Kamerick succeeded him.

Keith McKean, now head of the Department of English Language and Literature, asked me to continue with my classes. Dr. McKean tried to rouse the department to action. He urged each member of the staff to attempt some project beyond class work. He offered to act as a literary agent for anyone who had a manuscript to publish. I found him an inspiring and enthusiastic literary man.

I liked my class in the English romantic poets, though I still eyed the poems of Blake with suspicion. I knew Blake wrote more meaning in them than I could understand, but I liked the poems. "It's a little like teaching Yeats—all hints and references to another world which may mystify you, but they enthrall you." I told my classes just that, adding that I was not a competent Blake scholar.

The department moved to Baker Hall. Keith saw to it that I had an office on the first floor. Meryl cleaned it, hung pictures on the wall, taped up the Sandburg statement that Marilyn Skow had lettered for me in old English script, and saw to it that I had a desk and typewriter.

The office was a place where I met other members of the staff and visited with students. I worked there too, spending many afternoons working on an account of early boyhood recollections of the farm. I wrote prose at the office and poetry at home. The satisfaction of knowing I had an office with a key to lock the door welled up out of a need for privacy most of us recognize.

Was I becoming a venerable institution at the university? I shut my ears to any reference to my years of service. Yet I knew what the younger men said. My spirit refused to grow old. I enjoyed the affection of women friends and talked as if I still had an unlimited number of tomorrows. But the mirror showed an aged face. I drove out to the farm several times a week to rest my soul and talk with Carl.

A student, a young woman, asked me if I ever was sorry I gave up the farm for the classroom. I did not know how to answer her. If my partnership with Chuck had been sustained at Maplehearst Farm, what would I have gained or lost? Every farmer at the end of the year, if only in his mind, casts a balance sheet. But I could never decide what to put in the credit and debit columns. There was no use looking back now. The road I took had been decided for me.

It pleased and amused me when Stageberg, now retired, and I played poker once a month with the younger men of the faculty and town. It helped me bolster the illusion that, like a tree, the rings on my trunk did not keep me from growing. I corresponded with a number of my students, argued with them, gave them advice. I had published a dozen short stories and eight books of poems, all of which had sold out. I took a perverse pleasure in knowing my early books of poems brought premium prices.

Until lately Meryl flew out to Bremerton once a year to see her sisters and their families. One of my former students would always come and look after me for a week. It renewed my youth to believe for a week that I was the same age as they were.

These days Meryl helped me in and out of the car. I could no longer stand up in the kitchen and scramble the eggs for breakfast. I swallowed three, sometimes four, different drugs to control my back spasms. And here lay my difficulty: if I took enough drugs to relax the back muscles, I was too weak to stand; if I diminished the dosage I was in trouble again. Damned if I do, damned if I don't.

I mailed Geraldine Price my resignation from the Aspen School of Contemporary Art. No more summer workshops for me.

The workshop had been a stimulating experience. I met people who painted, carved sculptures, wrote poems and stories. It was great to know Ken Lash from the San Francisco Art Institute who conducted the prose workshop. Later Ken came to our university to join the art department as head. And I worked closely with Wayne Lanter, who took over the prose workshop when Ken gave it up. Wayne had been a big league baseball player who decided to swap his catcher's mitt for a desk teaching English. We were all friends and both Ken and Wayne came generously to my aid when I felt too miserable to see my students.

But since we owned a house in Aspen, Meryl and I decided to spend some part of our summers there. We visited our friends, attended concerts, ate at fine restaurants, drove to Toklot where Stuart Mace and his wife still fed us sourdough pancakes. We liked the low humidity and we escaped Iowa's sultry summer days.

I would get up at the crack of dawn to attend a seven-thirty Rotary Club breakfast at Buttermilk Mountain two miles out of town. Either Tom Sardi or George Madsen would help me up the terrace to the restaurant. One morning three of us visited after the meeting had adjourned. Boasting a little I said, "I'm a full professor at the University of Northern Iowa without a degree."

John McCollum, the former Metropolitan tenor, said, "I'm a full professor at the University of Michigan with a B.A. degree."

Phil Farkis was the best French horn player in the United States, according to my trombone teacher and French horn player, Dave Kennedy. Phil had the last word. He said, "I'm a full professor at the University of Indiana on a high school certificate."

It was this kind of banter and tossing words back and forth that made the Rotary meetings such pleasant occasions. Often the guests, like me, outnumbered the members. But the men all made me feel welcome.

For us the glitter of Aspen began to show a little tarnish. One of my friends, a silversmith, had died. Toklot no longer received guests and Stuart Mace had sold his beautiful teams of huskies, the same teams we so often saw in the movies. A condominium of three hundred and fifty units had been built just behind our aspen grove and a fourplex beside us. Beth Chalmers had moved to Santa Fe. Sally Dale committed suicide. We still visited the Crandalls and the Madsens. We went back and forth with the Larkins, who lived almost next door. Hans Gramiger took us on trips around town to look at property we could not afford to buy.

All things in their time, I thought. Very soon the summer will come when Meryl and I will find it more comfortable to stay at home than make the journey to Aspen.

After All These Years

To STAY AT HOME, to be free from classes, to do nothing but the tasks I assigned myself—this dream of luxury haunted me. "I doubt if I teach much longer," I told Leo Priest, my neighbor. "I'm getting ready to sit and appreciate. Remember when your son Bob worked out on our farm and when we'd get impatient, Bob would say, 'sometimes we ought to just sit and appreciate.' "

"Let's not go to Aspen this summer," I suggested to Meryl. "All the packing and unpacking, the trip out and back, makes me tired to think about it."

"It wasn't so bad last year," Meryl said. "Carl and Norma drove the car to Denver and we flew."

"But when we get there we have to unpack the dishes, the bedding, et cetera, et cetera. . . ."

"You sound like the King of Siam in the musical comedy. You'll miss your friends, the concerts, the Rotary Club breakfasts, won't you?"

"I'm tired and you have to help me with so many things these days. I'm more comfortable right here. It was fine when I could do everything for myself, not so good now."

Fate stuck a large finger in my pie. For several years Meryl had suffered discomfort after meals, lately an acute pain.

Dr. David Hansen said, "Sometimes bad things happen." He ordered her to go to the hospital. After a week in the hospital he said surgery was indicated and Meryl underwent a serious abdominal operation. Dr. Williams did the surgery but Dave looked after Meryl with an ever abiding care and I am still grateful to him.

But again I found myself out on that limb of desperation where I must have help immediately. At the last minute I was able to draw on my account of good fortune. Nancy Thompson, the writer, came to stay with me. Nancy left a husband and three children until I found more permanent help, someone who would stay during Meryl's convalescence.

The laboratory report showed no malignancy. We had more to be thankful for.

"I couldn't have stood it," I cried to my destiny. "First Carmelita,

223

then Meryl. I could not have stood it." But I knew I would stand what I had to stand. That is what I had always done.

Miss Gleasner came and looked after us. She kept our ship afloat until Meryl recovered her strength and could take over the care of the house and me. By Thanksgiving we were alone and Meryl was well enough to do the things she needed to do. We had a lot to be thankful for.

At the university, Keith McKean resigned as head of the department and Dan Cahill took his place. Dan was a literary man and a writer. He had just published a critical biography of Harriet Monroe, the woman who created *Poetry, A Magazine of Verse* and was its first editor. I asked him, "Do you want me to stay on?"

"I wish you would for one more year."

"I'll be seventy-five. I think I've earned a rest."

"If you stay on you can make up your own course for the last semester."

This was a big, fat and juicy carrot in front of the donkey's nose. But I was always able, without much strain, to give in to temptation. It really isn't hard once you have learned the knack.

For years I had imagined a graduate seminar where the students could read whatever they wanted and come to class to discuss it. What discoveries would they make? All my classes as a student and as a teacher had the textbooks and reference books assigned. Here the students would be on their own and could read anything they wished to read. How I would have loved a class like that when I was a college student.

"Draw up a prospectus for the course," Dr. Cahill said. "I'll present it to the curriculum committee as an experimental course. How are you going to shape it?"

"I've often been curious," I said, "about what students think literature is for, except as a source of grade points. I want the course to bring in some answers to the question: what is the good of literature?"

"Write out a prospectus and summary and I will present it to the committee."

It turned out to be a stimulating experience. Twelve graduate students signed up for the course. They sat around a long table in the classroom and I let them talk. And talk they did. They read a wide variety of books, from how General Electric treats its workers to Yevtushenko's poems. We discussed religion, sex, art, pacifism, family relationships, psychiatry, and education. I acted as a referee and directed the arguments to the subject under discussion.

As soon as the members of the class became acquainted and also decided they could trust me, they let down their hair. They spoke with frankness and, sometimes, brutality. For some it was as though a dam had burst and all their repressions came rushing out. I learned more about the value of literature than most of the students. I suspect the students selected books that expressed and defined their problems and concerns.

I said, "There will be no final examination but I want a paper from each of you describing what the course meant to you and your opinion of its success or failure. I want to know if the course broadened your horizons."

One young woman wrote, "I did not like being put down by other students. I am not a verbal person. I think slowly before I speak. I shall always remember the great freedom I felt in being able to read the books I wanted to. For this privilege I thank you."

Just before the fall semester ended Dr. Reninger asked me, "Is it true this is your last year?"

"I've sent in my letter of resignation. I've waited long enough. I should have quit five years ago."

"Then I'm going to suggest to John Kamerick that we give you an honorary degree. It's time the university thought about giving honorary degrees and you should have the first one."

His words pleased and embarrassed me. I thanked Bill and then forgot the incident.

I had my own troubles to struggle with. I was losing my ability to stand up by myself. I could no longer get in and out of bed without help. I blamed the drugs I took to keep down the muscle spasms. "They relax all the muscles," I complained, "not just the back ones."

I relied more and more on Meryl. I seldom drove the car. I preferred to have Meryl take me to the office or wherever I wanted to go. The security people on campus grew accustomed to seeing our car parked in restricted areas if it was convenient for me. In fact the chief, Rollin Evers, told me to send him the tickets I got for illegal parking. He was gracious about it but I am afraid I tried his patience many times.

My physical weakness angered me but I gave up trying to fight the inevitable. "But I am not humble about it," I warned Meryl. "So don't be surprised at my lousy feelings about it."

I told Ken Lash, head of the art department, "I've quit smoking, drinking, can't chase little girls. I'm surely on the road to sainthood."

Then Meryl lost the sight in one eye. She woke one morning with only peripheral vision in her right eye. Dr. Rao diagnosed it as a torn retina. This meant immediate surgery. Dr. Rao suggested either the Mayo Clinic or the University of Iowa. As an alumnus of the University of Iowa, Meryl chose Iowa City.

Carl Hundley drove her to Iowa City. The men in the eye clinic put her off a week because they said their operating room schedules were full. But a torn retina needs immediate attention so, of course, the surgery failed to restore her vision.

It took Meryl several months to recover from the shock of the surgery and blindness in one eye. She had the courage but not the strength. I realized that she too had celebrated a good many birthdays.

Now we needed help again. A real urgent need this time because of my growing weakness.

The first thing I did was to call the social service agencies—we have a lot of them in Black Hawk County. From each one I received the familiar runaround. Each one disclaimed any responsibility for helping me but gave me another phone number to call. After the sixth call I gave up in anger and frustration.

I called a neighbor and friend, a retired member of the English department. Alden "Bish" Hanson stayed nights. Another good neighbor, Mrs. Mikkelson, looked after meals and the house. Then Caroline Thompson said her niece had done practical nursing and would help us. And so Luisa came to stay with us and her cheerful and constant care carried us through.

One of my friends, who owned a funeral home, called and said, "Any time you need a driver to take your wife to Iowa City, I have one for you."

"Private enterprise to the rescue," I said. No help from all the government agencies. And to think of the tax money the Hearst family had paid into the treasury of Black Hawk County since 1859.

"Goddamn the whole outfit, lazy arrogant women, sitting on their butts in their cozy offices, drawing fat salaries," I declared. I have not forgiven them.

I lacked the tone of authority my former energy gave me. "I don't mind growing old," I told my reflection in the mirror. "But I'm sick as hell of being tired."

My growing impatience became apparent. I would no longer sit through a three-hour play. I expected friends to call first if they wanted to see me. I refused abruptly any invitations to make talks. And at dinner parties I was ready to come home at half past nine. Once I went to parties and got home at sunrise. Not anymore.

I kept my mornings free so I could work at my desk. Meryl protected me by answering the phone and doorbell. I liked the peace and quiet of my home, the evening hours under a reading lamp with a mystery story, or visiting with friends, or playing poker.

I insisted I would not go out to lecture. "I've shot off my mouth enough," I said. I turned down requests from the Universities of Illinois, Indiana, and Alabama. "I would spend two days going and coming for a fifty-minute talk."

When asked to lecture there, I wrote Buena Vista College and suggested Robley Wilson in my place. He is the editor of the *North American Review*. I wrote, "He'll do a better job than I could."

I wrote to Jack Olds of the Iowa Arts Council, "Look, Jack, I've served my time. Meryl and I have traveled all over Iowa making talks to high schools. Get someone else. I'm all lectured out."

I was writing poems that were as good as I had ever written, or so I thought. I placed poems in *Harper's,* the *American Scholar, Yankee, America,* and some of the prestigious reviews. I continued my work on a boy's life on an Iowa farm early in the century. Three of the chapters had been published, two in the Iowa Historical Society's magazine, the *Palimpsest,* and one in the *Kansas Quarterly.* I wanted to put together enough chapters for a book.

The bickering between faculty and administration at the university irritated me. "Like a bunch of spoiled kids," I grumbled.

I told a colleague, "Once I made an honest living by hard work on the farm. You teachers keep complaining about class loads, hours of teaching, committee work. You don't know what it takes in the world 'out there' to earn a living. Did you ever break your butt trying to bale that last load of hay before the rain or fight the dust from a combine in a soybean field or sweat out selling steers on a falling market?"

George Day, the western literature man in the department, agreed. "I ran the family building business a few years after my father died. Seven in the morning until six at night—including Saturdays. And if some contractor is short a few sacks of cement you go down after supper and open up and see that he gets them. University teaching gives you a lot more time to yourself."

I applauded but with inner reservations. I could remember coming from a three-hour class dripping with fatigue and wondering why I ever gave up a pleasant farm life for this nerve-wracking profession.

"I know it isn't as easy as I pretend. But it was harder for me. I came to teaching with no degree, no training, no nothin'. I really suffered. . . . You boys with your doctor's degrees looked down your long academic noses at me. And all the while I wondered if I had anything to offer the students. They came to class and looked at me expectantly and what could I say that was worth their while? I used to listen to myself as I talked to a class and hope that something I said would be important to them."

Once at a party, Lyle Baum asked me, "What's the most fun you've had while you were teaching?" Lyle came from a farm background too and she probably knew some of the dislocations I experienced when I entered the academic field.

I turned to her and said, "I hate to be indebted to you musicians. But one of the best times I had was when Bill Latham and I composed an oratorio or cantata or whatever it was to dedicate the new music building. And I learned more about music while I watched Bill compose music for my words than I ever had before. Oh, I mustn't forget, I learned a lot from Dave Kennedy when he tried to teach me to blow a trombone."

Dr. William P. Latham, composer on the music staff, and I were good friends. Bill and Joan and Meryl and I visited back and forth frequently and we liked the Latham children, Leslie, Peter, and Carol. It was fun to work with Bill. He was patient with me. I couldn't seem to get it through my head that the rhythms of poetry don't always fit into the rhythms of sounds—at least musical sound. We started and backed up several times before we decided on a general theme. We settled on a fairly obvious one: the creative spirit in man. That is what got us under way to come up with "Blind with Rainbows."

Bill Latham left the University of Northern Iowa for the University of North Texas at Denton, Texas. It had the reputation of being one of the best music schools in the country. After he had been there a few years he set five of my poems to music. To celebrate the first performance of the work, he invited Meryl and me to come to hear it and asked me to give a talk to the audience. So we flew to Denton, Texas, in the middle of the winter. Joan and Bill welcomed us with open arms.

There was a good-sized crowd in the auditorium. For a square like me the music sounded a bit far out, but I liked it. All of Bill's compositions haunt the ear after the sounds have died away.

I guess I made a good talk. The audience responded well. But I was a guest of the Lathams and Bill was well liked. I do not enjoy flying but I am glad Meryl and I made the trip.

I must mention another experience that gave me a great deal of pleasure and took a lot of time. Herbert V. Hake was head of radio and television at the university and, at his request, he and I broadcast a weekly radio program called an "Ear to the Ground." It ran for years. At first I prepared a script for each program. When I complained about the amount of time it took, Herb suggested we just choose a subject each time and talk off the cuff.

This is not as easy as it sounds. Herb would open the mike, make the introduction, turn to me, and say, "What are we going to talk about today?" And suddenly my head became a vacuum without a thought in it. Herb might make a suggestion and away we went. We had one corny joke we used every fall. After the first hard frost I would say, "Well, Herb, the frost is on the pumpkin and fodder is in shock."

And Herb would say, "What about mudder?"

I had a lot of fun on that program. Herb was such a joy to work with and always came up with helpful ideas. We had quite a following. A farmer named Robert Buck had a radio in his truck and evidently listened to us when he was doing chores. He wrote us a number of cards of appreciation.

Once I asked, "What's the good of poetry? Why do any of you folk out there read poetry?" And a man who runs a lumberyard in southern Iowa answered, "I read poetry for the same reason that I drink a glass of water—because I need it."

I have not been able to think of a better answer.

The school year bumped and slid toward commencement. I read in the paper one morning that the Board of Regents had approved a suggestion made by President Kamerick that James Hearst be awarded an honorary degree of Doctor of Literature. Well, well. So what Bill Reninger said had come to pass.

"Now you can wear a cap and gown," Meryl said proudly.

"Kind of risky at my age," I said. But I was tremendously pleased. All the years I had taught, in spite of praise by some of the students and recognition by some of the staff, I had moments when I wondered if I was worth what I cost the state. I wondered if I had opened any doors for students, showed them wider fields of knowledge and culture . . . if . . . if. . . . Perhaps this was proof that the university approved of me, academic maverick that I was.

How often I told my classes, "I can't teach you anything. You're too old, too mature. If you decide not to learn there's nothing I can do about it. If I can stimulate you, make you feel the hunger of curiosity, bring you to faith in the value of the humanities, I've done my job."

It reassured me to have the university appreciate what I had tried to do.

In no time at all commencement day arrived. Terry Williams, as the grand marshal, had two stalwart young men carry me in my wheelchair up the stairs to the stage in the auditorium. I stayed in the wings to put on my gown and mortarboard.

Terry said, "That tassel is supposed to be on one side before you get your degree and then slipped over to the other side afterward. But I don't know how the damned thing goes. Ask Bill Reninger."

The stage filled rapidly with selected members of the faculty. Three alumni, who were to be given Distinguished Alumni Awards, sat on the front row. Most of the staff of our department sat down in front, just ahead of the graduating students. The address was given by Judge Blair Wood of the District Court, Waterloo. It was brief and witty.

I remember one thing he said. "You students, on your controversial speaker program, have listened to a communist, a homosexual, a radical lawyer, and you expect me to rehabilitate you in twenty minutes."

When it came time for the honorary degree I was pushed to the front of the platform. The lights shone in my eyes, but I could see Meryl sitting between Mrs. Kamerick and Betty Reninger. Before me, down in the front rows, I could see most of the English staff. Dr. H. Willard Reninger read the charge. He extolled my accomplishments, my teaching, my poetry, my value as a human being. The encomium was beautifully worded.

Then President John Kamerick stepped forward and began, "By the power invested in me . . ." and hung the hood around my neck. Down in front, during the applause, I heard Bob Ward say firmly, "Get up, you guys." Row by row the entire auditorium came to its feet.

It was an emotion-filled moment for me, the whole crowd standing and applauding. I sat there in my wheelchair squinting under the lights. I bowed and smiled, thankful no words were required. Then I moved back from the front of the stage and it was over.

But not over really. That afternoon President and Mrs. Kamerick gave a reception in the Towers Lounge. A crowd of my friends came, people from the town as well as the university. The Gordon Strayers even drove up from Iowa City.

Stageberg whispered in my ear, "Pretty nice to be King of the Mountain, huh?" I just grinned. Stag and I had been friends for a long time.

The degree was lovingly encased in a red folder with the document on one side and Bill Reninger's remarks on the other. Meryl noticed that it had not been dated nor signed. So she marched up to the president's office for John Kamerick's signature and waylaid Bill Reninger the next time she saw him.

"We aren't used to giving honorary degrees," Bill explained. "We haven't learned the ritual."

Meryl said, "No more papers to read, examinations to give, grades to assign. No more staff meetings, no more conferences or committee meetings. Don't you feel liberated?"

"Yes, in a way. I shall be glad not to meet classes or concoct examinations or urge on the lagging scholar. Nor do I feel unemployed as some of my fellow retirees claim that they do. How they bitch about quitting work. Yet ten years ago they bitched about the work and sighed for the day of retirement. The human animal is not easily pleased, especially when he thinks his sky is falling."

I stopped a minute to consider the past few weeks. "One of the pleasant things was the staff party given for Bish Hanson and me. And the picture by John Page that was given me was about the best present they could have chosen."

"You still have your office and no doubt students will come to see you," Meryl said.

She was right. Students did come. But they came with a request, and after the greetings had been exchanged, they asked for a recommendation, a criticism of something they had written, advice.

The next Christmas, Dick Henry called me from Seattle just to wish me a Merry Christmas and hope that I was well.

"What a wonderful surprise," I said to Meryl. "Dick just wanted to give me his greeting. He didn't ask for anything."

Another former student, Larry Ingraham, now a major in the army in Germany, stopped to see me. We spent most of the afternoon visiting. Larry had married one of my favorite students, Alicia Somers. I asked him, "Larry, are you still married?"

He answered, "We're old fashioned at our house. We still love each other after eleven years of marriage."

I said to Meryl after he had gone, "There's hope yet for this world with people like the Ingrahams still building their ship together."

Each morning I sat in front of my typewriter. Sometimes lunchtime came and I had not written a single line worth saving. But I sat there and the poems I did keep often found a place in a magazine, especially if the editor was a poet.

A former student from the Aspen workshop and her husband, the Hendersons, operated a small press in Birmingham, Alabama. It was called The Ragnarok Press. They published a book of my poems called *Dry Leaves*—limited edition, a beautiful book with hand-sewn cover, thick yellow paper, fine type. It sold out in no time.

The next year the Kylix Press at the University of Michigan published *Shaken by Leaf Fall* in both hard and soft covers.

Then the Juniper Press at La Crosse, Wisconsin, operated by John

Judson, brought out a chapbook of my poems called *Proved by Trial*. It sold out and was reprinted.

Kenneth Lash and Robley Wilson, with kindness and generosity, published the James Hearst issue of the *North American Review*. It carried pictures of the farm, of my family, of me at work in the field. It also published a poem by Paul Engle, written for me.

The issue was widely distributed. One of my former students, Vince Caudle, called me up and said, "I was in Phoenix, Arizona, looking at a newsstand and there your smiling face stood out among all the girlie magazines. What in the world are you up to?"

Don Fish, himself once a farmer and now a teacher of literature, had enrolled in several night classes I taught. We had met years ago when he worked for the Extension Service at Iowa State University.

Don said to me, "Time you got out a book of selected poems. I know you're stubborn and won't send out a manuscript unless you're asked. I'm going to work on this."

He did and aroused interest in my work at the Iowa State University Press. I received a letter from Merritt Bailey, director of the press, asking to see a manuscript of selected poems.

I read the letter, passed it to Meryl and asked, "How does one select poems for a book of selected poems?"

"You surely know some of the poems you want to include."

"That's easy, but then what? Do I choose the ones I like or the ones I think are my best work or what?"

Meryl thought about it. One day she said, "Let's type up all the poems we think would qualify and let the editors make the selection."

Mr. Bailey held the manuscript for several months and then sent me a contract and assigned Nancy Bohlen as my editor. "She'll work with you in selecting the poems."

Now I struggled with the business of publishing a book. The advertising people wanted my opinion of the book jacket and flyer. The editor asked for a dedication, a preface, and a title.

I had not thought of a title. I fell back on my farm imagery and suggested a "Field of Furrows." But my editor thought it a little dull. Meryl suggested "Snake in the Strawberries," the title of one of the poems. This pleased everybody.

I wrote, rewrote, and sweat over a one-page preface. "What do you say in a preface? The poems can speak for themselves."

At a dinner party someone asked me about the book and my problem with a preface. This reminded me of a story I heard about a musician who composed a piece for the piano. He played it for a friend and asked his opinion. The friend said that it was very nice but what did it mean. The composer turned back to the piano and played it through again. He said, "That is what it means."

One thing bothered me. "I left out some of my good poems. How could I have overlooked 'The Movers' and 'Landmark'?"

But the next year Don Fish came to the rescue. "Give me the poems that were sent back. I'm going to have them printed myself." And he did. It was a soft-cover book entitled *Landmark and Other Poems.* Good paper, good readable print, well bound, and his daughter Dorothy drew some charming pictures to illustrate the book.

I was shy about personal publicity. I had an aversion to the puffs some writers give themselves. I liked what Keats said—the poet is nothing, the poetry is everything. I fell back on my repeated assertion that I wasn't a poet but a man who writes poetry. It seemed to me there was a difference.

When *Snake in the Strawberries* first appeared, the Coach House book store held an autograph party for me and Don Fish, who had contributed an introduction to the book. I had not been to a shindig like this before. I did not know what to expect. For over two hours I signed my name as fast I could write it. When the store ran out of books I signed book plates that could be pasted in the books.

I swore to myself, "Never again will I go through that, even if I don't sell another book."

The size of the crowd overwhelmed me but I would recover and be ready, pen in hand, for the next signing.

A few interviewers tackled me, but I was not happy with my responses. My mind refuses to leap into the breach when the attack comes and is more likely to curl up and play dead. When the big questions come I go as blank as I did the first time I was in front of a TV camera in Cedar Rapids. With no build-up the interviewer asked me what I thought was the "purpose of life." I was flabbergasted. The purpose of life? How do I know?

Bill Witt, a former student, wrote an article about me for the *Iowan.* It was sprinkled with plenty of pictures because Bill is a commercial photographer as well as a writer. I liked what Bill did. He came over several afternoons with a tape recorder and we just talked. Of course he had to edit the tapes afterward. But he did a darn good job.

I told this to Professor Leslie Whipp when he came over from the University of Nebraska with a television outfit to make a two-hour video tape for the Great Plains Cultural Center. What a day that was, with a regular Iowa blizzard raging. Even the highway patrol had taken its cars off the highways. Yet Les Whipp and his crew and equipment plowed their way through. I thought we Iowa farmers could outfight any kind of winter weather, but that day I gave the laurels to the folk from Nebraska.

"What did you like about the article?" Les Whipp asked.

"Bill and I talked about what started a poem or a painting or a piece of poetry or music composition. I said I didn't believe much in inspiration. Writing for me is hard, concentrated work. But, I admitted, something is given—a feeling, an idea, a rhythm, an image, something that starts the whole process going. Like an archeologist, you take one bone and construct the whole critter."

Then I added, "You must let the poem go its own way too. You mustn't force it. As the French poet Paul Valéry said, 'God gives you the first line, you work out the rest yourself.' "

I began to give off sounds like a professor. "You discipline yourself to arrange words in the patterns we call poetry. It's a long apprenticeship, never easy. You cannot fob off second-class work. Only your best will do and sometimes even that isn't good enough."

I paused a moment as if to reflect. "The work holds you in a kind of spell. Maybe it is a kind of addiction. It takes energy, you must put yourself to it as if you played the game for keeps. You must want to win and you put all your physical, emotional, and spiritual energy into the poem. I know a professional baseball player who gave up baseball to teach literature. I had a graduate student who played professional football and got a degree in English and taught literature. I don't know what the significance is."

I did break my resolve not to give any more talks. Otis Budlong, a farm neighbor and an extensive cattle feeder, belonged to an organization of midwest cattlemen who were all large operators. They formed the organization mostly for the social pleasure of being together. Otis and Bob Buck persuaded me to meet with them. We drove to Des Moines to a dinner meeting and I talked to the group. "I like talking to farmers, even about poetry. We speak the same language."

No doubt, as has been said, it is the exception that proves the rule. Robert Buck persuaded the program committee for the "Iowa 2000" convention to have me on the program. Dr. Willard Boyd, president of the University of Iowa, chaired the program. Loren Soth from the *Des Moines Register*, Governor Ray, and Senator John Culver were some of the other speakers.

I went to Ames and talked to the county delegates of the "Iowa 2000" committees. Mainly I said, "We can have the kind of a state we want in the year 2000 if we are willing to pay the price and I do not mean just in money either."

The platform is not a place where I show to an advantage. I lack the flair to dramatize myself and my words so that the audience responds with glowing faces. It is not the place where I do my best work. The pleasant experiences I have had as a lecturer can be quickly numbered. The pictures in my memory often turn out blurred or dark. But on one occasion they stand out in sharp detail.

When J. W. Maucker resigned the presidency at the University of Northern Iowa, he accepted a position as provost and vice president at the state college in Emporia, Kansas. After a couple of years in residence there he asked the English department to invite me to make a talk and conduct an afternoon workshop on the campus. Meryl and I were delighted to think of seeing Helga and Bill Maucker again. I accepted.

We drove to Kansas City, stayed all night, and drove on the next day to Emporia. The town reminded me a little of Cedar Falls with its quiet streets and arching trees. The campus interested me even more. The college has made a successful effort to adapt itself for use by handicapped students. Everywhere there are ramps and elevators and the center of the campus is closed to automobiles. It impressed me to see the goodwill shown to accommodate students who could not manage the routine of physically able people.

We had a wonderful time. Helga and Bill brought champagne to our motel and we all went out to dinner. The English department gave us a dinner. The workshop and talk seemed to go well. It was one of the most pleasant lecture trips we ever took.

I often visited with my brother Charles. Chuck had sold the home farm and moved to town. His bad heart kept him in touch with the intensive care unit at the hospital. His arthritis limited his mobility.

When I came to visit Chuck would take his canes and slowly move out to the car. On a warm October afternoon, the kind of beautiful autumn day that Iowa shows off when the signs are right, Meryl took me to see my brother. It was the fall after I had retired. We basked in the sunshine, car doors wide open. Our talk drifted from one subject to another, easy as blown dandelion blossoms.

"How much do you keep hidden when you write?" Chuck asked.

I let the answer run around in the cage of my mind like a lively squirrel. I opened the door. "I've loved Meryl for over twenty years. We've settled into a friendly intimacy now. We're both past the burning stage. I don't mention it in my poems except for a hint or two. Remember Kipling said, "They are fools who kiss and tell.""

Chuck shifted his weight to relieve his hip. "You don't sound as lively in your poems as you used to."

"I'm not as lively physically.. Hell, Chuck, I'm damn near helpless without someone to give me a boost. It even tires me to shove the wheelchair. That's what I don't like about growing old."

Chuck yawned. "Yeah, I suppose. Is there anything you do like?"

"Yes. I like being able to say what I please and make no bones about it. And I'll no longer let fools take up my time."

Chuck agreed. "Time becomes important when you don't have much of it left."

We both were silent for a minute. It was such a peaceful day. We had had one hard frost but the grass was still green and the trees were all in bloom. Chuck and Gladys have a beautiful yard, full of oak and maple trees.

Chuck asked, "Anyone ever question you about the kind of life you might have lived if you hadn't had your accident?"

"Once in a while. Not so often now."

"What do you tell them?"

I stretched. I like the fall season when the days are like this—warm, sunny, full of color. "You know, Chuck, I always made fun of commencement speeches and vowed I would never make one. But I did once, to the senior class of our old high school, University High, the Price Lab School. I finished the talk by reading a poem of mine called 'Truth.' It starts out like this, 'How the devil do I know if there are rocks in your field / plow it and find out.' "

Chuck looked at me inquiringly and I went on. "So I said, 'Don't ask me if life is worth living, live it and find out.' "

A cardinal flew into the crabapple tree near the car and began to eat the bright red fruit, apples about as big as my thumbnail. I said softly, "That's what I tell them."

Undertow

The bay of morning shines through
night's thicket, no windpuffs ruffle
the surface, I swim a straight course
from breakfast table to desk and
survey the solitary beach where I work.
The storm dwindles in my mind to a
plassing cloud, all about me lie the
signs of calm, the fresh odor of a
new day rises like a breeze through
pines, the instruments read steady,
direction north, temperature mild.
I settle myself for the day among
the cargo of my thoughts, stamping them
to ship out, when like a shell half
buried in the sand, I find the
handkerchief crumpled by your hands
behind my bookshelf. A sigh sends up
a wave so huge the undertow sucks me
from my mooring and floats me out to sea.

JAMES HEARST is a farmer, teacher, author, and lecturer. He has published his poems in such leading magazines as *Harper's, Saturday Review, North American Review, Good Housekeeping,* and *Wallace's Farmer* and has collected them in ten volumes. James Hearst lives in Cedar Falls, where he is professor emeritus in the English department of the University of Northern Iowa.